Learning to Live Again

A Guide for Recovery from Chemical Dependency

Updated and Revised

Learning to Live Again

A Guide for Recovery from Chemical Dependency

Updated and Revised

By
Merlene Miller,
Terence T. Gorski, David K. Miller

Original illustrations by Jerry Hamlin
(Adapted for the 1992 edition)

Herald House/Independence Press
Independence, Missouri

This book has been developed to be used in conjunction with other books on chemical dependency and recovery. We especially recommend that The Big Book of Alcoholics Anonymous (entitled *Alcoholics Anonymous*) and *The Twelve Steps and Twelve Traditions* be used along with this book.

This book is designed as a recovery manual for recovering people and their families. It is used in treatment centers as a primary resource for patient education programs. Special consulting services are available to assist treatment centers in using this material in patient education programs.

Published by:
Herald House/Independence Press
1001 West Walnut • P.O. Box 390
Independence, MO 64051-0390
1-800-767-8181   (816) 521-3015
ISBN 0-8309-0372-0

Contents

A Word About Words

Terminology is a problem in the addiction field, due largely to the variety of drugs available and what we are learning about them. In the past, people addicted to alcohol have been called alcoholics, and the disease they have has been called alcoholism. People addicted to other drugs have been referred to as drug addicts and their condition called drug addiction. Alcoholics were usually addicted only to alcohol, and treatment was separate from treatment for drug addiction. At the present time, however, it is rare to find a "pure" alcoholic. Many people seeking treatment have used a variety of drugs, and attempting to separate treatment for alcoholics from treatment for other drug addictions is difficult and sometimes counterproductive.

As we have come to learn more about addictions, we have learned that they are similar regardless of what drug a person is addicted to. Alcohol is a drug (though legal and less addictive than some drugs), and recovery from alcoholism is much like recovery from other drug addictions.

We will use a variety of terms to describe addiction to all drugs including alcohol. We will primarily use the term *chemical dependency*, but we will also use *chemical addiction*, *addictive disease*, and *addiction*. When talking about the substance the person is addicted to, we will use the terms *mind-altering chemical*, *mind-altering substance*, *addictive substance*, *addictive chemical*, *addictive drug*, or just *chemical* or *drug*. To describe the person with the addiction we will say *the person who has chemical dependency* or *the person who has addictive disease*, or *the person addicted to mind-altering chemicals*.

We will not use the term *abuse* for two reasons. First, when there is abuse there is an object or victim of the abuse. In child abuse the child is the victim. The term "drug abuse" indicates the drug is the victim.

Second, the word *abuse* indicates a chosen behavior rather than a disease. And because we recognize chemical dependency as a disease, we will not refer to it as abuse just as we would not refer to diabetes as "sugar abuse" or an allergy to milk as "milk abuse." We believe there is choice with addiction, but not in how the body reacts to the chemical. The choice is in what the person chooses to do about the addiction.

Because some things that are true for alcoholism may not be true for other drug addictions, at times we will talk specifically about alcoholism. This does not mean that what we say about alcoholism is not true for other addictions. But it probably means that we don't know yet whether it applies because we don't have the research to support it.

We recognize that people with chemical dependency are both male and female, and no pronoun that we use is intended to indicate otherwise. We will use plural pronouns when we can to be as inclusive as possible. When this is not possible, we will at times use "he" and at other times use "she." This does not indicate anything except the limitation of the English language, which does not have a singular neuter pronoun.

To our students from whom we
have learned so much

I ONLY USE SOCIALLY!

CHAPTER 1

Chemical Dependency Is a Disease

Chemical dependency is a condition in which a person becomes addicted to a mind-altering substance. The substance causes the person to feel good for a little while, but there is a price to be paid in long-term pain and dysfunction. As addiction develops so does obsession, compulsion, and loss of control.

Addiction is characterized by lack of choice. At first, using a mind-altering substance is a choice, but addiction robs a person of choice and dictates the frequency, quantity, and nature of use.

Mind-altering chemicals change brain chemistry and brain function. Once brain function is altered physical, psychological, and behavioral changes result. It is impossible to use mind-altering chemicals without changes in thinking, emotions, personality, behavior, and relationships.[1]

The consequences that result from taking drugs depend on the particular drug used, the person using the drug, and the circumstances in which the drug is used. Certain drugs produce beneficial effects. The changes they produce are useful in combating disease. Other drugs produce damaging effects. The benefits of all drugs should be weighed against the risks. Whether a mind-altering drug is used as medication or for recreation, there is always risk involved.

Some mind-altering chemicals are addictive and some are not. Some are addictive for certain people but not for others. The major addictive drugs can be classified in four groups: downers (depressants), uppers (stimulants), pain-killers (narcotics), and mind distorters (hallucinogens). The drugs usually listed under each of these categories are:

Downers (depressants): alcohol, sedatives, barbiturates, tranquilizers

Uppers (stimulants): amphetamines, cocaine, nicotine (tobacco), caffeine

Pain-killers (narcotics, narcotic derivatives): heroin, methadone, codeine, morphine, Demerol

Mind Distorters (hallucinogens): phencyclidine (PCP), lysergic acid (LSD), mescaline, psilocybin, cannabis (marijuana, hashish)

Addictive drugs create pain. But, because the use of drugs interferes with good judgment, it is difficult to see that the pain is related to drug use. So the drug is used to relieve the pain it creates. Thus, continued use of the chemical leads to continued use of the chemical.

Chemical dependency is a disease. Like other diseases such as heart disease, diabetes, and cancer, chemical dependency has specific symptoms that keep the body from functioning properly. Acceptance of chemical dependency as a disease acknowledges certain things it is not.

Chemical dependency is not a moral weakness. People with chemical dependency are not persons of weak character. They do not use mind-altering chemicals because they lack willpower. They use them because of their disease. People allergic to dust are not considered weak because they cannot control their sneezing. They may be expected to separate themselves from the problem, but they are not considered weak because they have the allergy.

People with chemical dependency cannot control certain factors in their bodies that determine their response to mind-altering chemicals, but that is not a sign of weakness.

Chemical dependency is not a mental illness.[2] The number of people with chemical dependency who have psychiatric problems is no higher than the number of people in general who have psychiatric problems. It is true that as the disease progresses it causes problems that appear to be mental problems. But these problems are a result of the disease, not a cause of the disease nor the disease itself. It is also true that from time to time a person may have both chemical dependency and mental disorders, but they are separate problems, probably resulting from different causes. Chemical dependency is not a mental illness.

Chemical dependency is not just a disease of the homeless, unemployed male. Only 3 to 5 percent of all people with alcoholism are on skid row.[3] Most are employed and have families. Chemical dependency is no respecter of persons. It can affect men, women, young, old, rich, poor, executives, housewives, factory workers, employed, unemployed. Station, status, sex, race, and age have little to do with chemical dependency.[4]

The addictive reaction to the use of mind-altering substances and to abstinence from those substances causes an addiction cycle to develop. An addiction cycle consists of six related symptoms: short-term gratification, long-term pain, addictive thinking, increased tolerance, loss of control over use, and eventual bio-psycho-social damage including severe withdrawal. Let us look at each part of the addiction cycle in more detail.

Short-Term Gratification: First, there is short-term gratification. You feel good now. This strong short-term gain causes you to assume the drug is good for you.

Long-Term Pain: The short-term gratification eventually is followed by long-term pain. This pain, part of which comes from withdrawal, is the direct consequence of using the mind-altering chemical. Long-term pain may develop within hours of use or may be delayed, taking days or even years to build to full intensity.

Addictive Thinking: The long-term pain triggers addictive thinking. *Obsession* is a continuous thinking about the positive effects of using the drug. *Compulsion* is an irrational urge or craving to use the drug to get the positive effect even though you know it will hurt you in the long run. This leads to *denial,* the tendency to ignore the pain caused by the addiction. *Rationalization* is deceiving yourself into believing that the cause of the pain is your job, marriage, divorce, friends— anything to take the blame off the addiction. Rationalizing about the cause of the pain allows development of a distorted picture of yourself as a normal and controlled user. *Delusional thinking* is such strong denial that even concrete evidence that your belief is wrong doesn't change it.

Increased Tolerance: Without being aware of it, more and more of the drug is required to produce the same effect. It may take five drinks to do what two used to do. It may take five joints to do what one used to do. The body adapts to higher levels of the substance and accepts them as normal. When the drug is not present, it feels as though something abnormal is going on.

Bio-Psycho-Social Damage: Injury or destruction prevents normal functioning or behavior. Bio-psycho-social damage means that the health of your body (physical health), your mind (psychological health), and your relationships with other people (social health) are damaged. The sicker you become the more pain and stress you experience. As pain and stress increase, the compulsion to use the addictive drugs for relief from the pain increases. A deadly trap develops. You need the substance to feel good. When you use addictively you damage yourself physically, psychologically, and socially. This damage increases your pain, which increases your need for addictive use.

Loss of Control: The pain, obsession, and compulsion become so strong that you cannot think about anything else. Your feelings and emotions become distorted by the compulsion. You feel stressed and uncomfortable until finally the urge to use becomes so strong that you cannot resist it. Once you use the chemical again the cycle starts all over.

Whenever an addiction cycle develops there is a strong dependence upon the chemical. A person who cannot function normally without something is dependent on it. This dependency may be physical, emotional, or social. In most addictions the dependency is a combination of all three.

Chemical dependency is not a hopeless condition. Like most other chronic diseases, it is treatable. While it is not curable, it can be controlled, just as diabetes can be controlled. Many people with chemical dependency never get treatment because they don't believe there is any way out and because the important people in their lives do not believe there is any hope. Thousands of people with chemical dependency are alive and well and functioning normally; they are free from the pain of their disease because they found the hope that they could recover.

Points to Remember

1. Chemical dependency is a condition in which a person becomes addicted to a mind-altering substance.
2. The mind-altering substance causes a person to feel good for a little while but causes long-term pain.
3. Addiction is characterized by lack of choice.
4. Mind-altering drugs alter brain chemistry and create physical, psychological, behavioral, and social changes.
5. Mind-altering chemicals may be depressants, stimulants, narcotics, or hallucinogens.
6. Addictive drugs create pain, but eventually they are used to relieve the pain they create.
7. Chemical dependency is a disease.
8. Chemical dependency is not a moral weakness.
9. Chemical dependency is not a mental illness.

10. Chemical dependency affects persons of every age, race, sex, station, and status.
11. An addiction cycle consists of six related symptoms: short-term gratification, long-term pain, addictive thinking, increased tolerance, loss of control over use, and eventual bio-psycho-social damage.
12. Chemical dependency is not curable, but it is treatable.

Notes

1. Kenneth Blum and James E. Payne, *Alcohol and the Addictive Brain* (New York: The Free Press: A Division of Macmillan, 1991), chapter 9.
2. James E. Royce, *Alcohol Problems and Alcoholism: A Comprehensive Survey* (New York: The Free Press: A Division of Macmillan, 1989), 5.
3. Ibid.
4. Ibid.

CHAPTER 2

Primary Disease

Chemical dependency is a primary disease, not the result of another disease, but the original disease. If it were caused by another disease, it would be called a secondary disease. Many secondary diseases result from chemical dependency. Cirrhosis of the liver, for example, is a secondary disease that results from the primary disease of alcoholism. Damage to the sinus cavities is a condition that results from addiction to cocaine. You should not confuse the resulting condition with the primary disease.

Sometimes people get treatment for the conditions resulting from chemical dependency and believe they are getting treatment for their primary problem. It does no good to treat secondary conditions until chemical dependency is under control. No effective or lasting healing will take place until mind-altering chemicals are removed from the body.

Chemical dependency damages the nervous system. This means thinking and emotions are impaired. But treatment of these mental and emotional conditions, without first removing the mind-altering chemicals from the body, will fail. Counseling and therapy (before mind-altering chemicals are removed) are ineffective against the destructive power of the chemicals. Abstinence is a necessary first step of treatment.

CRAVING SOMETHING
TO FILL UP THE
EMPTINESS.....

Chemical dependency is a primary physical disease.[1] This means you did not cause it. Like victims of other diseases (heart disease, diabetes, and cancer), certain people have conditions that make them more susceptible to chemical dependency.[2]

The body of a person with chemical dependency does not react to mind-altering chemicals in the same way that the body of the person without chemical dependency does. If you are chemically dependent, you are powerless over the way your body reacts to mind-altering chemicals.

Sometimes it is helpful to compare the disease of chemical dependency to the disease of diabetes. People who have diabetes cannot control the way their bodies react to sugar. They are powerless over that process. Sugar acts as a toxin, or poison, to them. Sugar does not cause their disease, but it triggers a reaction in the body because the person has a disease. People with diabetes cannot change the way their bodies react to sugar. They can only learn to manage their disease. In the same way, people with chemical dependency cannot change how their bodies respond to mind-altering chemicals. They, too, can only learn to manage their disease.

Diabetes is hereditary, passed from parent to child. It has nothing to do with morality or character, mental processes, or choice. Neither does inheriting chemical dependency. Much evidence indicates that the tendency to develop chemical dependency is inherited.[3] You are not responsible for having the disease, only for what you do about it.

Step 1 in the Twelve Steps of Alcoholics Anonymous begins: "We admitted we were powerless over alcohol...."[4] It is difficult for anyone to admit powerlessness. We want to feel that we are in control, that we can handle our own lives. But to be powerless over mind-altering chemicals is not a sign of weakness. Admitting your powerlessness is the first step in gaining the strength to manage the disease.

Let's examine this powerlessness over chemicals. Many people believe chemical dependency is entirely a psychological disorder, that it results from character defects, emotional problems, or immorality. They believe that if these emotional and character disorders are corrected, controlled use is possible.

Other people believe chemical dependency is a reaction of the body to an addicting substance, that problems disappear once the addicting substance is removed and the body has adjusted to the absence of the substance.

Still other people believe chemical dependency is the result of social and environmental factors and that it relates to the circumstances surrounding drinking or other drug use. These people believe that if people learn to drink or use responsibly and do not misuse chemicals, they will not become addicted.

Actually there is some truth in all these beliefs, but only partial truth. Believing that chemical dependency results entirely from any one of these causes can lead to inappropriate reactions to the disease. Chemical dependency is a bio-psycho-social disorder. You cannot separate body, mind, and behavior because they are interconnected.

You are a system. A system is simply a number of parts working together to produce an outcome. Systems are always seeking homeostasis, balance. When a system is out of balance, all its parts adjust in an attempt to reestablish homeostasis. Some people are born with a physical imbalance that puts them in high risk of addiction. They seek to correct this imbalance by altering their bodies, minds, or behavior.

People who inherit a physical imbalance that puts them in high risk do not necessarily become addicted. Their attitudes and beliefs, their behaviors and relationships, their social environment, and the circumstances of their lives influence the development of the disease. However, people who are biologically susceptible to becoming addicted to certain substances are in high risk of addiction if they use those substances, regardless of emotional or environmental factors.

The body of a person susceptible to chemical dependency responds to mind-altering chemicals differently than a person who is not. Although much is unknown about why this is true, research shows that many people with a family history of alcoholism metabolize alcohol (break it down and eliminate it from the body) differently even before there is any indication of problem drinking.[5]

People who have a limited tolerance to mind-altering chemicals are in low risk of becoming addicted. Their bodies cannot tolerate sufficient quantities of a specific substance to adapt to it. Their tolerance generally does not increase over a period of time. It is difficult for these people to consume the quantities of a mind-altering chemical needed to become addicted. Therefore, they are in low risk of developing chemical dependency.

People who are in high risk of becoming addicted can consume large quantities of mind-altering chemicals frequently enough to create addiction. Because of high tolerance, they can mask and ignore physical damage and developing addiction, and they generally don't notice early warning signs of chemical dependency.

They usually reach a control level where they feel better, behave better, and do not appear intoxicated.[6] As their tolerance increases, the body changes and adapts to higher levels of mind-altering chemicals and dependence develops. There is no longer just a tolerance for mind-altering chemicals but a need.

Some substances are more addictive than others. Only a small percentage of people who use alcohol become addicted to it; alcohol is not a highly addicting drug.[7] But heroin, tobacco, and crack cocaine are highly addicting, and most people who use them become addicted.

The extent of the susceptibility will influence how much of a specific drug over what period of time will bring about an addiction. Addiction follows this equation:

Susceptibility + addictiveness of the drug + extent of use = risk of becoming addicted and the severity of addiction.

People with a brain chemistry imbalance are in high risk of becoming addicted.[8] They tend to have less of the brain chemicals that make them feel good and relieve pain. The imbalance may be hereditary or created by malnutrition, stress, or continued use of mind-altering chemicals.

Brain cells send messages to one another by brain chemicals. The chemicals (neurotransmitters) are produced and released by one cell and attach to the receptors of another cell. Receptors also receive body chemicals produced in other parts of the body and "foreign" chemicals such as alcohol, caffeine, nicotine, and other drugs. Chemicals in the brain change in response to stress, pleasure, pain, good feelings, bad feelings.

Some studies indicate that children of chemically dependent parents are in risk of addiction because they have inherited a weakness in their brain cells' ability to produce, release, or receive certain neurotransmitters.

Mark was born with a weakness in the brain cells' ability to produce certain chemicals. As a result, he constantly felt uncomfortable and empty. He had a sense of needing something to feel good. Mark began drinking in his teens along with his friends. As the alcohol was metabolized, it produced chemicals that were received by the brain receptors and created a feeling of euphoria. When the feeling wore off Mark remembered how good it felt and looked for opportunities to feel that way again.

The substance that best corrects the chemical imbalance of the brain is the substance to which the individual is most likely to become addicted. The type of addiction depends on the type of imbalance. Some people are sensation seekers. They need stimulation. They seek substances and activities that will produce excitement and increase energy. Other people are serenity seekers. They feel overly stimulated and seek substances and activities that will quiet the nervous system.[9] Different chemical deficiencies can be medicated by different drugs of choice. People are in risk of becoming addicted to the substance they choose.

When a mind-altering substance is used to correct an imbalance, the substance attaches to the receptors and causes the brain cells to release less of the natural brain chemicals. As use of the mind-altering substance continues, the receptor changes its structure. It becomes less sensitive to the mind-altering substance, and more of that substance is needed for the same effect. This is tolerance. The cell sending the neurotransmitters sends less and less, and the cell receiving creates more receptors.

As Mark continued drinking, certain brain cells sent a message that no more of the natural chemicals were needed. So other cells stopped producing them. Without alcohol in his system, Mark felt worse than before he started drinking.

Over time, more and more brain cells adapt, brain cell systems adapt, and finally other body systems adapt. A new balance is created and feels normal.

As this happened to Mark, the receptors became less sensitive to the alcohol, and it took more alcohol to create the feeling Mark wanted. Now Mark needs the alcohol to feel "normal." He has become dependent on alcohol.

When people are dependent on a mind-altering substance they cannot just stop using without experiencing withdrawal symptoms. Because the cells have adapted, abstinence from the mind-altering substance causes a painful reaction. Since the cells are releasing less of the natural brain chemicals and because there are more receptors, the brain chemistry imbalance is even greater than before the person began using the mind-altering substance.

So the cycle of addiction goes on. They cannot just stop using. Not using creates pain, and the need for pain relief leads to continued use. Withdrawal is bio-psycho-social. As we have just explained, physical addiction occurs because the body develops a need for chemicals. Psychological or social dependence can occur with physical addiction or without it. Nonphysical dependence occurs when there is an emotional or situational need for chemicals. Users who are not physically addicted to chemicals can also have withdrawal symptoms when they abstain. They feel incomplete, anxious, depressed, empty—craving something, anything, to fill the emptiness.

Most people who have problems with alcohol or other drugs have both physical and nonphysical symptoms of chemical dependency. They are physically addicted to mind-altering chemicals and are also psychologically and socially dependent. They progress through predictable symptoms and stages, resulting in death or insanity unless the disease is interrupted by treatment.

People with chemical dependency are not aware of their developing need for chemicals. They usually feel in control, feel good while using, and believe they function better than when sober. People with chemical dependency are powerless to control the response of their bodies to mind-altering chemicals.

While some people, because of genetics, are in higher risk of becoming addicted than other people, an addiction can develop without being inherited. Some people may be in low risk but may damage their bodies by behaviors, lack of proper nutrition, traumatic stress, or long-term abusive use of chemicals.

Once addiction begins it doesn't matter why it began. It is a condition that must be addressed directly. This is much like lung cancer. A person may develop lung cancer because of a combination of heredity, environment, and behavior (smoking). Once the person has lung cancer, it cannot be cured just by figuring out why the person smokes, by changing the environment, or by examining the family history. It must be addressed directly.

If your house is burning, you cannot solve the problem by figuring out why it started. You must first put out the fire. If you have chemical dependency, your body has adapted and cannot go back to "normal" by addressing other issues. You must stop using mind-altering chemicals, and your body must adjust to not having them. In early recovery you must devote full attention to attaining abstinence, rebuilding your health, and establishing a system of care through AA/NA and treatment. You must learn all you can about your disease and how to manage it. You must learn how to live in a healthy way without the need for chemicals. Once your disease is under control, you may need to look at other issues. But you must always remember that you have a *physical* condition that causes you to be powerless over the way your body reacts to mind-altering substances.

Points to Remember

1. Chemical dependency is a primary disease.
2. A primary disease is the original disease, not the result of another disease.
3. Treating the diseases resulting from chemical dependency (the secondary diseases) will not bring about recovery.
4. The body of a person with chemical dependency does not react to mind-altering chemicals in the same way that the body of the person without chemical dependency does.
5. Many people with a family history of alcoholism metabolize alcohol (break it down and eliminate it from the body) differently.
6. People in high risk of becoming addicted usually have a high tolerance for the substance they are in risk of becoming addicted to.
7. Some substances are more addictive than others.
8. Susceptibility + addictiveness of the drug + extent of use = risk of becoming addicted and the severity of the addiction.
9. People with a brain chemistry imbalance are in greatest risk of becoming addicted.
10. A physical need for mind-altering chemicals develops as the body cells adapt to tolerate higher levels of chemicals.
11. Withdrawal symptoms may be physical, psychological, or social; usually all three.

Notes

1. James E. Royce, *Alcohol Problems and Alcoholism: A Comprehensive Survey* (New York: The Free Press, A Division of Macmillan, 1989), 125.
2. Donald W. Goodwin and Julia K. Warnock, "Alcoholism: A Family Disease," *Clinical Textbook of Addictive Disorders* (New York: The Guilford Press, 1991), 486.
3. Kenneth Blum, Ph.D., and Ernest P. Noble, Ph.D., M.D., "Genes, Messengers, and Addictive Behavior," *Addiction & Recovery*, vol. 11, no. 6 (November/December 1991).
4. *Twelve Steps and Twelve Traditions* (New York: Alcoholics Anonymous Services, 1952), 21.
5. Marc A. Schuckit and V. Rayses, "Ethanol Ingestion: Differences in Blood Acetaldehyde Concentrations in Relatives of Alcoholics and Controls," *Science*, vol. 203 (1979): 54.
6. James R. Milam, Ph.D., and Katherine Ketcham, *Under the Influence* (Seattle, Washington: Madrona Publishers, 1981), 52-56.
7. Ibid., 26.
8. Kenneth Blum, Ph.D., and Ernest P. Noble, Ph.D., M.D., "Genes, Messengers, and Addictive Behavior," *Addiction & Recovery*, vol. 11, no. 6 (November/December 1991).
9. Joel C. Robertson, "Preventing Relapse and Transfer of Addiction: A Neurochemical Approach," *EAP Digest* (September/October 1988).

CHAPTER 3

Chronic Progressive Disease

Chemical dependency is a chronic disease. Chronic diseases are those that come on gradually over a period of time. This is different from acute disease. Acute disease comes on rapidly; you may be well one day and ill the next. In acute disease, you rapidly lose your ability to function, and you are very aware that you are ill.

Chronic disease progresses so slowly that there may be a long period between being well and realizing that you are ill. This gives you the opportunity to adjust to the illness; you are able to continue functioning even though you are ill. You may adapt so well that living with the illness becomes a way of life. You develop physical, psychological, and social ways to cope. You may cope so well that you are not aware that you are ill.

People with chemical dependency first learn to compensate for the problems created by the disease and then to adapt to the disease. When they compensate for the disease, they learn ways to make up for it. They learn to function while slightly intoxicated, perhaps by walking with their fingertips against the wall for balance. They learn to manipulate other people to do for them what they are

TRYING TO DROWN YOUR
TROUBLES AND PROBLEMS
ONLY TEACHES THEM HOW
TO SWIM. . . . .

unable to do for themselves. They learn ways to avoid the consequences of their using behavior.

Eventually people with chemical dependency adapt or change to accommodate mind-altering chemicals in the blood. Their bodies need the chemicals to function. Their lifestyle changes to make it easier to use. Their using changes, their belief systems change (what's wrong with a drink in the morning?), their behavior changes, and their social life changes (they isolate more and more) to use. They adapt to a drug-centered life. Using becomes the most important thing in their lives, and they change their entire way of living to allow the using to continue.

Because this happens slowly over a period of time, people with chemical dependency are not aware that they have compensated for and adapted to their illness. They can deny they are sick for a long time. Because chemical dependency is a chronic disease, there is a high risk of relapse; there is always the danger that it may recur. It is never cured. It can only be controlled. Unless measures are taken on a long-term basis to control the disease, relapse is likely. Many people with chemical dependency return to using at least once after they make a decision to stop. For many it is a way of life. *It will never happen again.* And then it does.

There are steps most people with chemical dependency go through in attempting to control their chemical use.

1. They practice unregulated using. There is no attempt to control until life becomes disrupted.

2. They attempt to control by changing the pace of drinking or using. They use the same amount but attempt to consume it more slowly.

3. They attempt to control by cutting the quantity of intake, by setting limits on how much they use. It may work for a while but not permanently.

4. They attempt to control by changing the frequency of use. They restrict the time of day or days of the week or social occasions when they will use.

5. They attempt to control by changing the type of drug used. They have not yet learned that the mind-altering chemical itself, not the type of drug, activates the disease. They switch from bourbon to beer, or from cocaine to marijuana, or from beer to Valium.

6. They attempt to control by using other drugs in combination with the drug of choice. They may take downers to reduce the reaction to uppers or uppers to reduce the reaction to downers.

7. They attempt to control by attempting periods of abstinence with the goal of returning to using. They come to believe that if they can stop for a month or six weeks, control will return. And they stop for a while. They prove they can stop, but they know they will use again. People with chemical dependency can do amazing things on a short-term basis. This proof of control is worth the pain of these periods of experimental sobriety. But in the long run things continue to get worse.

8. They make the decision to stop using permanently, but they refuse to change their lifestyle. They learn they can't use mind-altering chemicals safely. They've tried everything they know to control it and realize that control is not possible. So they stop. What's the big deal? They continue to pursue the lifestyle that requires drugs to make it complete. They find things get better for a while, and then things slowly become confused, frustrating. They have not yet learned that chemical dependency is a chronic disease that has symptoms that persist even with abstinence.

9. They make a decision to stop using permanently while pursuing a program to change lifestyle. The solution to chemical dependency is finally found. They stop using, learn about the illness, and change their way of living so they can comfortably adapt to the chronic symptoms of chemical dependency that persist even with abstinence. This is called sobriety—abstinence plus attitude and lifestyle change.

Because chemical dependency can only be arrested, not cured, the person with chemical dependency cannot expect to go back to using chemicals. Chemicals will reactivate the symptoms of the disease at any time. Total abstinence is necessary to control chemical dependency, but abstinence is not the only requirement. Remember that the person with chemical dependency has developed a way of life to accommodate the illness. Because it takes a long time to get sick, it takes a long time to recover. Recovery requires long-term, total treatment that promotes physical recovery (healing of the body), psychological recovery (healing of attitudes and beliefs), behavioral recovery (the changing of habits from supporting illness to supporting recovery), and social recovery (readjusting to a lifestyle of health rather than illness).

Chemical dependency is not only chronic, it is progressive. Without treatment it always gets worse; it never gets better. As it progresses, it affects all areas of life—physical, psychological, and social—and the life of the person with chemical dependency becomes unmanageable. Chemical dependency progresses through three stages: the early stage, the middle stage, and the chronic stage.

The main symptom of early stage chemical dependency is a growing dependence on mind-altering chemicals.[1] This growing dependence is based in large part on increased tolerance. In the early stage it is difficult to distinguish addictive from nonaddictive use because there are few outward symptoms. The body, however, is changing and adapting to the regular ingestion of the drug. People who are becoming addicted can usually use larger and larger quantities without becoming intoxicated and without suffering harmful consequences.

With many drugs the user experiences a positive personality change and may actually function better as the level in the blood reaches and remains within certain control limits. This is tolerance. During the early stages tolerance increases. People with alcoholism can drink large quantities of alcohol and behavior improves.[2] They are more sociable and more comfortable and demonstrate a higher level of social skills.

It is difficult for these people to recognize that they are addicted because they can "handle their liquor" (or marijuana or Valium). The earliest warning sign actually interferes with early diagnosis because it conceals the problem. While most diseases create immediate impairments in functioning, this disease appears in the early stage as a benefit, enabling the affected person to enjoy the euphoria of drug use without paying any of the penalties.

Because of positive experiences with chemical use, the person seeks it more and more often and physical and psychological dependence develops. As cells of the liver and nervous system change to tolerate larger quantities of the chemical, larger and larger quantities are needed to achieve the same effect. As the disease progresses, the person with chemical dependency is seeking to recover the good feelings of the early stage, but once gone they can never be recaptured.

The middle stage of chemical dependency is marked by a progressive loss of control.[3] Tolerance becomes dependence; want becomes need. As the cells of the body change to tolerate large quantities of the chemical, the change creates a need for the chemical. As the dependence increases, the person has less and less control over using and using behavior. There is a progressive loss of control in three different ways: loss of control over the beginning of using episodes, over behavior during using episodes, and over the end of the using episodes.

People with chemical dependency become less able to choose not to use. Not using begins to cause pain. The drug is used to relieve the pain created by not using. Addicted people are unable to function normally without chemicals. The length of time they can go without using decreases. They become preoccupied with chemical use. They begin to break their own rules about time and place; using earlier in the day, using alone, or sneaking around to use. They may experience severe anxiety when an unexpected situation interferes with their chemical use or the source of supply.

The urgency to use may be triggered by the anxiety that builds from the time of the last using episode. It may be triggered by a situation in which the person has used mind-altering chemicals in the past and with which use has become a habit. It may be triggered by lack of confidence in the ability to function without the chemical. Or it may be due to the physical symptoms of withdrawal from the chemical.

More and more often people with chemical dependency find themselves behaving while using in ways they would not choose while sober. This is the result of a change in values and judgment while using. At the time their behavior seems normal to them. But when they are sober and look back on their using behavior, they realize it was not behavior they would choose while not using.

Family and friends begin to notice problems: job problems, health problems, marriage problems, legal problems. They are apt to believe, however, that the person is just behaving irresponsibly. They are not aware that the addicted person is not choosing the behavior. It is part of the disease. The person cannot through will-power choose to use responsibly. The only alternative to continued problems and progression is treatment and total abstinence.

As the disease progresses, the loss-of-control point occurs earlier in the using episode. The limits of control begin to shrink. It takes less of the chemical before the person goes beyond the control level and experiences symptoms of intoxication.

The chronic stage of chemical dependency is marked by deterioration.[4] The main deterioration is physical. All body systems can be affected at this stage. In the chronic stage the person shows such physical complications as liver damage, malnutrition, and severe nervous system impairments. In the late chronic stage the tolerance for mind-altering chemicals is nearly nonexistent. All pleasure of using is gone. The person finds only a brief moment of relief before losing control. The loss of control becomes more and more dramatic, ending in more and more severe consequences. It is in the chronic stage that psychological and social disruptions become severe and life becomes totally unmanageable.

Sid does not know when his reaction to alcohol began to change. But there came a time when, once he started drinking, he soon lost control and usually passed out. Gone were the good old days when he reached a "click" point, mellowed out, and found the magic. He was no longer able to drink large quantities and stay in control. He missed the feeling when he drank that he could do anything. He was still looking for the magic, but he couldn't find it. He kept thinking if he did it right it would be there again. He made firm resolutions to limit the amount he drank, to stop before he lost control. Instead, he would drink until his boisterous behavior got him into trouble. He tried switching from beer to wine with the same result. He would periodically declare himself on-the-wagon, but the pain of not drinking quickly weakened his resolve. He was in pain when he drank and in pain when he didn't. His life was filled with problems, and drinking no longer brought relief.

Some psychological effects of chemical dependency are a deteriorated self-image, depression, anxiety, unreasonable fears, rigid denials, possible destructive behavior, and change in values. Mood swings are common as the person uses the drug to feel better but is unable to maintain the good feelings. As a result, problems in behavior begin to occur. The chemically dependent person begins to lose problem-solving abilities, life-planning skills, and performance skills. Activities that interfere with drinking and using are given up. Addicted people structure their lives to protect their using. Behavior becomes self-defeating.

These problems result in social problems. The person, because of fear and anxiety and guilt, begins to isolate from family and friends. Friends and acquaintances separate themselves because behavior becomes embarrassing or offensive. There is a loss of communication skills. There are strained personal relationships, and eventually work habits become unreliable and sporadic. Life is consumed by the need to use.

Step 1 of the Twelve Steps of Alcoholics Anonymous says, "We admitted that we were powerless over alcohol, *that our lives had become unmanageable.*" Because of the progressive nature of the disease of chemical dependency, because it always gets worse and never gets better without treatment, all areas of life eventually become unmanageable.

Points to Remember

1. Chemical dependency is a chronic disease.
2. Chronic diseases come on gradually over a period of time.
3. Because chemical dependency progresses slowly, you can compensate for and adapt to the disease.
4. Chemical dependency is never cured, only controlled.
5. Chemical dependency carries a high risk of relapse; there is always a danger it will recur.
6. Total abstinence is necessary to control chemical dependency.
7. Chemical dependency is a progressive disease.
8. Without treatment chemical dependency always gets worse, never better.
9. There are three stages of chemical dependency: the early stage, the middle stage, and the chronic stage.
10. In the early stage there is an increased tolerance.
11. In the middle stage there is progressive loss of control over using and behavior while using because of the increasing dependence.
12. In the chronic stage there is marked deterioration resulting in physical, mental, emotional, behavioral, and social problems.
13. In the late chronic stage tolerance for the addictive substance becomes nearly nonexistent and all the pleasure of using is gone.
14. Eventually all areas in the life of a person with chemical dependency become unmanageable.
15. Recovery requires long-term bio-psycho-social treatment.

Notes

1. James R. Milam, Ph.D., and Katherine Ketcham, *Under the Influence* (Seattle, Washington: Madrona Publishers, 1981), chapter 4.
2. Ibid, 52-56.
3. Ibid., chapter 5.
4. Ibid., chapter 6.

CHAPTER 4

Physical Effects

St. Augustine said, "Men go abroad to wonder at the height of mountains, at the huge waves of the sea, at the long courses of the rivers, at the vast compass of the ocean, at the circular motion of the stars; and they pass by themselves without wondering."

There is no greater wonder in the world than the physical body. How can hundreds of muscles, 60,000 miles of blood vessels, 10,000 taste buds, and 206 bones work in harmony to create a healthy human being?

The body is an intricate machine with many systems: the nervous system, the digestive system, the cardiovascular system, the respiratory system, the musculoskeletal system, the reproductive system, the immune system. Each system or group of organs, tissues, and cells performs a special function to keep the body fine-tuned and balanced and working in harmony. All systems work in cooperation. Each cell, each organ, each system—while performing one or more essential tasks—also blends with other cells, organs, and systems. Then, the complex organism of the human body functions not as a group of separate systems but as a whole, complete unit.

The body has a need to function in balance or be in homeostasis, each part functioning with another. When chemicals are misused

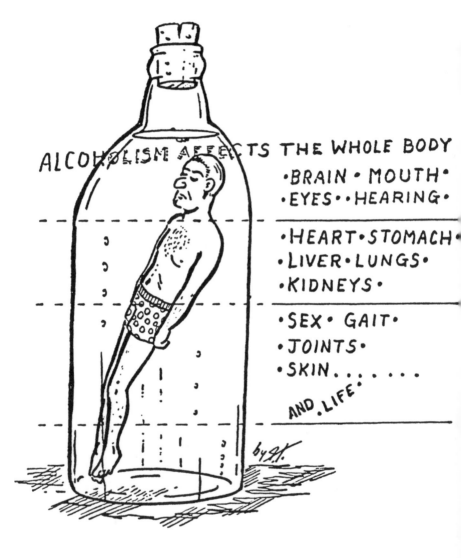

over a period of time, this delicate balance is interrupted. The body systems get out of step, eventually leading to the body's breakdown. Chemical dependency affects the entire body. Damage in one area affects other areas. Injury, change, and recovery affect the entire body.

The body is like a well-built house constructed of the finest materials. If the house is neglected and not cared for, then one part after another will begin to deteriorate. Because of the toxic nature of alcohol and other harmful drugs in the body, one system after another is affected as dependence or addiction progresses. At first the damage is acute and temporary. Then, with continued harmful drug use, damage becomes chronic and permanent. Acute damage means there is inflammation or short-term change in the various organ systems. The body can usually repair this damage. With prolonged chemical ingestion, the inflamed cells and tissues eventually die and are replaced by fibrous or scar tissue. This is permanent damage that cannot be repaired.

Effects on the Nervous System

The nervous system operates like a computer, relaying messages between your brain and other parts of your body. Nerves, made up of cells called neurons, receive information from the senses. The message then moves from one neuron to the next until the information reaches the appropriate place in your brain.

To work together, brain cells send and receive messages by way of brain chemicals called neurotransmitters. All thoughts, feelings, and sensations are sent by way of these neurotransmitters. There are different brain chemicals for different purposes. A cell usually produces one type of neurotransmitter but can receive many different types. The neurotransmitters are produced and sent by one cell and attach to the receptors of another cell.

Change in one brain cell slightly shifts the balance of all brain cells, all brain cell systems, and all body systems. Balance is the body's top priority. A cell changes function—to attain balance—according to the messages received from other cells.

Some neurotransmitters stimulate activity of a brain cell while others inhibit activity of the cell. So a cell may become more active or more quiet depending on the messages it receives. If a cell is bombarded by a particular message, it will become less sensitive to that message. If the message continues long enough, the structure of the cell actually changes to accommodate the new condition. It does this to protect the balance of the system.

Use of mind-altering chemicals over a long period of time changes this balance of brain chemistry. As the receptors are filled with foreign substances, the body's own chemical transmitters cannot stimulate the cell appropriately, leading to delayed, inappropriate, or even an absence of the desired reaction. Although the damage may be continuing, the consequences may not be apparent as long as the use of harmful chemicals is ongoing. But when drug use stops, the result is usually severe discomfort: drug craving, agitation, inability to experience pleasure, stress sensitivity, and a variety of other symptoms depending on the drugs used.[1]

The brain itself can also be damaged by long-term drug use—or in some cases even short-term use. Prolonged intake of depressants, inhalants, or PCP may shrink the frontal lobe cortex of the brain resulting in symptoms of chronic brain syndrome: confusion, disorientation, and lowered mentality.[2]

Korsakoff's psychosis and Wernicke's syndrome are conditions of irreversible brain damage experienced by some people with alcoholism. The major symptoms of Korsakoff's psychosis are severe memory problems and loss of insight and judgment. Wernicke's syndrome is characterized by a staggering gait, drowsiness, and paralysis of eye muscles.[3]

Cocaine psychosis and stimulant-induced psychosis are characterized by confusion, paranoia, and hallucinations. Continued use of cocaine may also cause the brain to become more sensitive to the drug, so even low doses can bring on seizures and death.[4]

The peripheral nerves in chemically dependent people are also affected by nutritional deficiencies, especially of the B vitamins. This leads to a degenerative condition of the nerves which causes numbness, tingling, muscular weakness, and paralysis.[5]

Effects on the Digestive System

The digestive tract is a tube that coils through the center of the body and changes your meal of meat, bread, and carrots into a form that will allow protein, fat, carbohydrates, vitamins, and minerals needed for energy and cell building to enter the bloodstream and eventually the body tissue.

This process of digestion begins in the mouth, where the teeth, tongue, and cheek muscles work together to grind the food into smaller pieces, mix it with saliva, and prepare it for the stomach. Enzymes in saliva get the digestion process started. A single enzyme can break up millions of food particles in a minute's time. Different enzymes break down various kinds of food.

Use of harmful chemicals can cause irritation and inflammation of the mouth. The mouth and dental structures are affected by the strength of the drugs used and by poor hygiene habits associated with chemical dependency. Chemical irritation produces burning sensations and inflammation of the lining of the mouth and throat. Inflammation of the tongue is also a problem. Dental cavities as well as gum disease result from lack of good nutrition and from poor personal hygiene. Mouth cancer is also common among smokeless tobacco users (even in very young users).[6]

When chewing is finished, food moves through the esophagus into the stomach. The esophagus is also subject to inflammatory reactions due to irritation from drugs. Alcohol and many other chemicals cause the stomach to overproduce acid, which irritates the esophagus wall when vomiting occurs. Cancer of the esophagus is not uncommon in people with chemical dependency.[7]

Bleeding at the point where the esophagus and stomach join sometimes occurs because of regurgitation of acid, which erodes the lining and exposes blood vessels that rupture. The lower esophagus can rupture, causing stomach contents to spill into the chest cavity. Vigorous coughing, severe vomiting, and seizures contribute to development of this most serious problem. Varicose veins (varices) of the esophagus develop from severe increases in the blood pressure within the vessel system of the liver. If the varices rupture, severe hemorrhage can occur (with bleeding sufficient to cause death within a few hours if not treated).

Three bands of muscles in the stomach work like a blender to break up bits of food while a powerful acid produced in the stomach helps dissolve the food. The stomach lining is protected from this powerful acid by mucus. Inflammation of the stomach occurs when alcohol and certain other drugs decrease the stomach's ability to prevent acid from backing up into the walls. Decreased food intake allows this acid to work on an empty stomach. As a result, the stomach lining is eaten away and ulcers easily develop.[8] Caffeine and aspirin are two of the more common causes of both ulcers and the inflammation that precedes them (gastritis).[9]

The stomach passes undigested food to the small intestine where it is absorbed into the bloodstream for use by the body tissues. Digesting and absorbing the nutrients needed by the body requires an area larger than the small intestine seems to offer. But the lining has many folds on which millions of fingerlike villi bristle with hairlike microvilli increasing the intestines' inner surface some 600 times. Alcohol and other drugs damage the small intestine which reduces its ability to absorb nutrients, leading to malnutrition.[10]

In the intestine, juices (enzymes) from the pancreas and liver aid digestion. In addition, these organs do dozens of other jobs. The pancreas secretes insulin, which controls the storage and use of sugar. Lack of insulin causes diabetes, a life-threatening disease. Inflammation of the pancreas, common in people with alcohol dependency, is a serious disorder whether acute or chronic and is a frequent cause of death in people with alcoholism. As the pancreas is damaged, some chemically dependent people release too much insulin causing hypoglycemia or low blood sugar.[11]

The liver processes nearly every nutrient that comes from the intestine. Every minute more than a quart of blood, carrying nutrients, flows to the liver. Liver cells package fatty acids into forms that can be stored and used for fuel. They convert amino acids to proteins, the building blocks for every cell in the human body. They break down complex sugars into glucose, the body's main source of energy. They consume worn-out red blood cells and recycle the iron. They detoxify poisons such as alcohol and harmful drugs. There are hundreds of other functions of the liver, so you can see that it is a vital organ. But it is the one most frequently and severely damaged by alcohol and other drugs.

The liver can be seriously impaired in chemically dependent people. Fatty liver, which impairs liver function, develops because of the liver's decreased ability to break down large amounts of alcohol and other drugs. Hepatitis, which damages liver cells, can result from the use of dirty needles. As liver cells die they are replaced by fibrous scar tissue. Cirrhosis occurs when fibrosis is advanced and nodules develop within the liver.[12] Cirrhosis is one of the ten leading causes of death in America.[13] Death from liver failure is one of the most gruesome ways to die, with seizures, coma, bloating, hallucinations, and a prolonged death process.

Effects on the Respiratory System

The respiratory system is a collection of highly efficient mechanisms that carries air to the lungs. During the course of a day we inhale up to 17,000 pints of air through the mouth or nose. The respiratory system not only takes in air but also cleans it. Air passes into the lungs through the windpipe. One branch of the windpipe enters each lung and divides into smaller branches. Each smaller branch ends in an air sac. In the lungs, blood vessels gather up oxygen, taking it to the heart to begin its trip through the body. The heart pushes blood that has completed its trip back into the lungs for a fresh supply of oxygen. Mucus-making cells that line your throat and windpipe help to protect your lungs from foreign matter.

The lungs of the chemically dependent person are subject to pneumonia (infection of the lungs usually due to bacteria or virus) and tuberculosis (a serious lung disease caused by bacteria) often due to a lack of personal hygiene, poor living conditions, and a decreased ability to fight infections. Lung cancer is no stranger to people with chemical dependency especially those addicted to nicotine, marijuana, or alcohol. Smoking is the major cause of lung cancer.[14]

Smoking tobacco or marijuana is also responsible for inflammation of the lungs and constriction of air passages, making it difficult to exhale. Smokers frequently experience chronic bronchitis (inflammation of the membrane that lines the air passages) and emphysema (a disease of the lung that causes structural changes in the air sacs where the exchange of oxygen and carbon dioxide takes place resulting in trapping of air in the sacs). Emphysema can also result from snorting or freebasing cocaine. Prolonged snorting of cocaine dries out the mucous membranes of the nose and erodes the cartilage separating the nostrils, which can result in serious infections.[15]

Effects on the Reproductive System

The endocrine system is composed of a network of glands that secrete specialized chemicals or hormones into the blood. The purpose is to maintain a consistent, balanced body environment by regulating metabolism and growth and influencing behavior. Sex hormones are produced in the ovaries and testes, which are also affected by hormones produced in other glands. Ovaries produce the female hormone estrogen; testes produce the male hormone testosterone.

With prolonged, heavy use of harmful chemicals, sex hormones are not properly manufactured or released. In males this results in reduced testosterone levels causing impotence. Females experience menstrual disturbances including heavy menstrual flow, pre-menstrual discomfort, and early menopause. They also experience higher rates of infertility, miscarriages, stillbirths, and premature births.[16]

Changes in reproductive functioning can often be reversed with abstinence and healthful living that allows for improvement in functioning of the endocrine system.[17]

The ovaries in a female also mature and release ova; the testes in a male produce sperm. When the ovum and the sperm unite, they become a single cell and begin development of a new human, creating more cells through cell division. Heredity is written on a chemical ribbon (DNA) that twists in a spiral of tens of thousands of genes which determine eye and hair color, body structure, even individual personality traits. Each egg and sperm is genetically unique. When damaged or altered genes occur in reproductive cells, they can be transmitted to future generations by heredity. There is growing evidence that multiple drug use can induce genetic mutations.[18]

The ingestion of alcohol or other drugs during pregnancy can affect the development of a fetus. Fetal alcohol syndrome is a leading cause of birth defects. Children with this condition may have any of a variety of defects including small head size, mental retardation, facial abnormalities, poor motor coordination, hyper-activity, reduction in size and rate of growth, and heart problems.[19] Babies frequently become addicted to the drugs their mothers ingest and may suffer withdrawal symptoms when they are born and for several weeks thereafter.[20]

Effects on the Musculoskeletal System

Bones are living tissue that need food and oxygen. About one half of each bone is composed of hard minerals, one fourth is water, and the rest is living cells and tissue. Every second, the marrow produces more than 2 million new red cells. It can increase pro-duction when the body needs additional oxygen. Bones could not move without the assistance of the muscles. When muscles contract, they get shorter and fatter. The ends of the muscles are made of strips of tough cartilage called tendons that grow onto the bone. The skeletal and muscular systems work together, allowing the body to move in many different ways and assume many different positions.

Bones and muscles are affected by nutritional deficiencies and the toxic effect of alcohol and other harmful drugs. The major problems are muscle pain, tenderness, and swelling. The muscles usually involved include thigh and upper arm, shoulder, and chest. With the chronic type there is weakness and muscle wasting.[21]

Effects on the Cardiovascular System

Nothing is more miraculous than the cardiovascular system. Blood—carrying oxygen and nourishment to every cell and removing waste and carbon dioxide—flows through every organ of the body, past every cell on a journey that stretches 60,000 miles. No cell in the body lies more than one millionth of an inch from this blood supply.

So many red blood cells (the oxygen-carrying cells) crowd the bloodstream of one person that if these cells were stacked one on top of the other they would reach up 31,000 miles. In one second we lose about 3 million red cells, but in the same second the same number is produced in the bone marrow. White blood cells defend against disease and infection, devouring bacteria, viruses, and other invaders as they move through the bloodstream.

Every 60 seconds, 1,440 times a day, the heart circulates the body's five quarts of blood throughout the body and back again, pumping 2,500 gallons of blood a day. The heart sends blood to every cell in the body, beating more than 1.5 billion times in seventy-five years. Alcohol and other drugs may disrupt this delicate process and affect the heart's ability to function as a pump. Diseases of the heart related to chemical misuse include congestive heart failure and rhythm disturbances caused by leaking of potassium, phosphate, and important enzymes from the heart muscle cells.

Folate deficiency anemia results from changes in bone marrow where most red blood cells are manufactured and is very common in heavy drinkers. Liver damage also plays a role in the development of this problem. High blood pressure is common in chemically dependent people who are three times as likely to have strokes as other people.[22] Atherosclerosis (a buildup of fatty material in the arteries) is common among cigarette smokers.

Effects on the Immune System

The human body has a marvelously efficient system of protecting the body from disease. This system works twenty-four hours a day to keep order and consistency among the body cells and organs. The immune system keeps balance by removing dead or damaged cells and by seeking out and destroying foreign organisms. It has the ability to recognize the "self" and distinguish between body tissue and foreign matter. It tracks down and destroys viruses, bacteria, and germs. Immunity develops when a particular virus or other microorganism gets into the body and the cells in the blood "remember" it and create plasma cells in large quantities, which protect the body from a repeated attack of that microorganism.

Infections are common in people with chemical dependency due to malnutrition, unsanitary conditions, and damage to the immune system. Intravenous drug users are at risk of AIDS, a disease that impairs the functioning of the immune system because the HIV virus that causes AIDS can be transmitted by contaminated needles.[23]

We have attempted to show you that the cells, organs, and systems of the human body work together in an almost unbelievably complex fashion. They work in harmony. Persons who use alcohol and harmful drugs upset the fragile balance of their bodies and disturb the natural interaction of the body systems, often creating complex problems.

This is much like upsetting the balance of the earth by polluting our water and air or cutting down the rain forest. Eventually the whole world is affected. Even throwing an empty can on the ground can make a difference. Our bodies are small ecosystems. Just as we can make a difference by cleaning up our environment, we can improve our health. In most instances, it is possible to restore the delicate balance of the system by removing toxic chemicals and rebuilding the body through healthful living.

Points to Remember

1. Each system of the body has a special function.
2. All systems work together.
3. Damage in one system affects the other systems.
4. All body systems are affected by the disease of chemical dependency.
5. At first the damage is acute and temporary.
6. Eventually damage becomes chronic and permanent.
7. Acute damage means there is inflammation in an organ system. Acute damage can be repaired.
8. Over a period of time, inflamed tissue dies and is replaced by scar tissue.
9. Scar tissue is permanent and cannot be repaired.
10. Chemical dependency results in long-term damage to the nervous system, the digestive system, the respiratory system, the reproductive system, the musculoskeletal system, the cardiovascular system, and the immune system.

This chapter has been reviewed for accuracy by Donald A. Potts, M.D., Associate Professor of Medicine, University of Missouri Medical School.

Notes

1. Joel C. Robertson, "Preventing Relapse and Transfer of Addiction: A Neuro-chemical Approach," *EAP Digest* (September/October 1988).

2. Carol J. Weiss and Robert B. Millman, "Hallucinogens, Phencyclidine, Marijuana, Inhalants," *Clinical Textbook of Addictive Disorders* (New York: The Guilford Press, 1991), chapter 7.

3. Jean Kinney, M.S.W., and Gwen Leaton, *Loosening the Grip* (St. Louis: Mosby-Year Book, 1991), 133-134.

4. Charles R. Carroll, *Drugs in Modern Society* (Dubuque, Iowa: Wm. C. Brown Publishers, 1985), 251.

5. Katherine Ketcham and L. Ann Mueller, M.D., *Eating Right to Live Sober* (Seattle, Washington: Madrona Publishers, 1983), 67.

6. Carroll, *Drugs in Modern Society*, 227.

7. Ibid., 121.

8. Ibid., 87.

9. Ibid., 260.

10. Ketcham and Mueller, *Eating Right to Live Sober*, 61-62.

11. Ibid., chapter 4.

12. James R. Milam, Ph.D., and Katherine Ketcham, *Under the Influence* (Seattle, Washington: Madrona Publishers, 1981), 78.

13. James E. Royce, *Alcohol Problems and Alcoholism* (New York: The Free Press, A Division of Macmillan, 1989), 63.

14. Carroll, *Drugs in Modern Society*, 224.

15. Ibid., 251.

16. Kinney and Leaton, *Loosening the Grip*, 123.

17. Ibid., 124.

18. Carroll, *Drugs in Modern Society*, 309.

19. Kinney and Leaton, *Loosening the Grip*, 125.

20. Milam and Ketcham, *Under the Influence*, 39.

21. Carroll, *Drugs in Modern Society*, 121.

22. R. P. Donahue, R. D. Reed, D.M., and K. Yano, "Alcohol and hemorrhagic stroke," *Journal of the American Medical Association*, 255, 2311-2314.

23. Carroll, *Drugs in Modern Society*, 17.

CHAPTER 5

Psychological Effects

As the body breaks down as a result of drug use, the mind and emotions are affected. As chemical dependency progresses, personality changes occur. These problems do not cause chemical dependency, but chemical dependency causes psychological problems. These changes and problems occur for a number of reasons.

Neurological problems, impairments of the brain and central nervous system, caused by chemical dependency include impairments in the ability to think abstractly, to concentrate, and to remember. They include overreaction to stress and lowered ability to tolerate stress. As a result of these impairments, people with chemical dependency begin to see themselves differently. Their self-image changes. They also begin to see other people and the world around them in a different way.

People with chemical dependency are affected psychologically by the need to use drugs. Their beliefs and values change, or seem to change, to protect chemical use. Using mind-altering chemicals becomes more important than activities that were once highly valued. All thinking is directed toward chemical use and not letting anything interfere with that.

Guilt feelings develop as these people repeatedly do things they vowed never to do again, things that do not conform to their value systems. There are two ways to get rid of guilt. You can stop doing what makes you feel guilty, or you can continue doing it until it becomes so routine you no longer feel guilty. Because people with chemical dependency find it difficult to stop what they are doing, they overcome guilt by changing their values to conform to their behavior.

Mood swings are common as people with chemical dependency use chemicals to feel better. Unable to maintain these good feelings, they become depressed and fearful, blaming others for their problems because it is too painful to blame themselves. Blaming themselves would mean they might have to change, and change might require giving up chemical use. People with chemical dependency believe they must have their drug of choice to survive.

Everyone has to make sense of life. People with chemical dependency have to make sense of their chemical use. They see life as they must to survive. They do not believe life can ever be different or that they can survive without using mind-altering chemicals. So they shape their values, their beliefs, and their images of themselves, others, and the world as they must to keep using chemicals.

Because people with chemical dependency do not believe things can ever change and because the reality of life is too painful to face, they use a common means of coping—denial. They simply refuse to admit that anything is wrong. They deny it to other people; they deny it to themselves. They convince themselves they are not addicted by rationalizing and justifying to make this "unreal" reality fit their lives. By disguising the truth they can allow their chemical use to continue.

Anne grew up in a family that didn't drink at all, and her value system included total abstinence as a lifestyle. She felt somewhat uncomfortable when she began drinking in college. But she was only drinking like everyone else, and it was certainly socially acceptable. She was soon quite comfortable with it. Most of the people she knew smoked marijuana so she was soon comfortable with that. She couldn't see any difference between smoking pot and drinking beer. Her roommate combined prescription drugs with drinking and that soon seemed perfectly normal, too. Gradually over the years Anne's drinking and pill use increased, but she always told herself she was all right because she was still able to take care of her home and her family. A person who has a drinking problem, she told herself, is someone who drinks before noon—and she didn't do that. After a while she was saying a person with a drinking problem was someone who drank before lunch—and lunchtime started coming earlier and earlier. One morning one of her children said, "Mom, why do we have to eat lunch so early? We're not hungry. Anne looked at the clock and saw that it was 9:30.

Many people have difficulty understanding denial because they believe it is the same as conscious lying. Denial is *unconscious* lying. People with chemical dependency lie to themselves. They convince themselves that something is true when it is not.

How do they do this? By their self-talk. They subconsciously repeat statements in their own minds until they believe them: *I don't have a problem. I never drink before lunch. I wouldn't drink this much if it weren't for my husband. I'm just tired.* These are a few of the repetitive, unconscious, untrue statements people with chemical dependency tell themselves. And you can think of many more, can't you? The problem is that people with chemical dependency do not realize these statements are untrue.

If you were to give a lie detector test to someone with chemical dependency and talk to him about his chemical use, the lie detector would show that he was telling the truth. Why? Because people with chemical dependency come to believe their self-talk. They lie to themselves so effectively that they no longer recognize the truth.

If you believe a lie, you begin to live the lie. If the lie happens to be *I'm a social user, and anyone who thinks I'm not must be crazy,* you have a problem. You look around and find a lot of crazy people in your life, people who think you do drugs too much because they use less than you do. How do you solve the problem? Easy. You push the crazy people who don't approve of your using out of your life and replace them with "normal people" who use socially like you do.

But denial does not change reality, only the way we see reality. The devastating effects of chemical dependency continue even though they are dismissed. Neurological impairment worsens, intensifying the denial. People with chemical dependency do not see the reality of life because their judgment is impaired.

They deny not only the disease but also their painful feelings. Pain is nature's way of causing us to seek healing. When pain is blocked by the denial process, motivation for recovery is also blocked. Anxiety, guilt, fear continue to grow unacknowledged.

People with chemical dependency lose touch with self-respect, love, and joy. Good feelings come only from getting high and from remembering the good things about using and ignoring the bad. Eventually chemically dependent people are unable to see reality. They are caught in a cycle of pain, using, and denial from which there seems to be no escape.

The Addictive Belief System

All people operate from a basis of what they *believe* to be true. It is the perception of truth, rather than the truth itself, that determines how we act. We all assume certain things to be true and act accordingly without thinking about them. We believe a chair will support us when we sit down, that a light will come on when we flip a switch, that our car will start when we turn the key.

One's most powerful basic beliefs are developed before the age of ten. Parents and other authority figures instill beliefs about self, others, and the world before one is old enough to think about these beliefs. Few adults ever stop to examine whether the basic beliefs they learned as children are true or false unless these beliefs cause problems later in life. Everyone develops some mistaken beliefs (beliefs not based in fact) and some reality-based beliefs. The more reality-based beliefs one has, the easier it is to make a successful transition into adulthood. The more mistaken beliefs one has, the more difficult it is to make that transition. The process of living alters some basic beliefs. At times life challenges beliefs and forces people to rethink and change those beliefs.

Sara grew up in a home where the belief was instilled that a woman did not work outside the home. Recently Sara's husband died. She needs to revise her belief, find employment, and develop a corresponding lifestyle. She may choose, however, to quickly marry another breadwinner to continue a familiar way of life based on her present beliefs.

When a belief causes enough pain, a person often examines that belief and changes it. At other times, denial and rationalization are used to maintain the belief even though the belief is causing pain. This may have disastrous effects.

Clarence had been shown his liver X-rays by his physician. The X-rays were positive for cirrhosis showing more than 50 percent liver dysfunction. Clarence continued to drink, justifying it because he still had 50 percent liver function. He died two months later.

Chemical dependency destroys reality-based beliefs and forces a person to adopt mistaken beliefs to survive. Chemical dependency is a disease of denial, misperception, and mistaken beliefs. Addicted people do not recognize the disease process that is occurring because they do not see reality as it is. They are confused, and they have good reason to be.

Many symptoms of chemical dependency contribute to the tendency to block reality from awareness. Some symptoms exist before the development of the addiction. Some contribute to chemical dependency. Many of them are caused by the disease.

Gradual Onset: Because chemical dependency usually develops gradually, the person is able to adapt to the symptoms over a period of time. Therefore, it is easier to push the symptoms out of conscious awareness than if they had come on suddenly.

Blackouts: Addiction to chemicals often includes blackouts or periods of time one cannot remember.[1] Blackouts erase experiences from memory as if they had not occurred, much like losing information from a computer because the computer was turned off before the file was saved onto a disk. Blackouts allow one to be totally unaware of some information necessary for a complete picture of reality.

Intoxication: Intoxication distorts perception and memory. An experience perceived by others as disgusting, harmful, or humiliating may be perceived by the intoxicated person as fun, exciting, and normal.

Nervous System Damage: If alcohol or other drugs have damaged the nervous system, causing unclear thinking, perception of what is actually happening will be distorted. Addicted people do not see their own behavior as others do.

Need to Use: The bio-psycho-social need to continue the addiction motivates the addicted person to justify using and to deny harmful consequences. This denial is a normal part of the addiction process. It is a coping mechanism that allows people with chemical dependency to use mind-altering chemicals while telling themselves that there is no problem. The truth about their behavior is too painful to accept. To look honestly at the situation and to acknowledge that the addiction is causing problems calls for the obvious next step: to stop using. For the addicted person that is not an acceptable option. It is less painful to believe that one's use is normal. So, to continue using it is necessary to deny the relationship between the addiction and problems.

Children of Alcoholics: Many recovering people are either adult children of alcoholics or have grown up surrounded by some other addiction. If you grew up around addiction, you grew up with inconsistency. It comes with the territory. When you grow up with the inconsistency of addiction and the game playing that does not permit you to discuss or even acknowledge the problem, you stop expecting the world to make sense. You come to believe that inconsistency and contradiction are normal. You stop trying to make the pieces fit and just pretend that they do. Pretending the pieces fit when they do not is denial. You do not see things the way they really are.

Withdrawal: The pain of withdrawal from addictive use contributes to the delusion that using creates pleasure. What may seem to be the pleasure of using is actually the relief of pain created by the addiction. Using is necessary for the person to feel normal. For the addicted user this creates the illusion that using is beneficial and contributes to well-being.

State Dependent Memory: People remember something best when they are in the same mental state as when they learned it.[2] If they learn something or develop a skill when intoxicated or high, they remember it better intoxicated than when sober. This creates the impression that they learn better when high, creating the illusion that using chemicals improves performance.

Misinformation: Incorrect, incomplete, or distorted information about chemical dependency allows mistaken beliefs to develop and to be maintained. Many people perceive a person with chemical dependency as being a "skid row bum." Therefore, if they themselves do not fit that picture, they do not believe they can be addicted. This type of misinformation keeps people with chemical dependency from recognizing their situation for what it really is.

With so much misperception, misinformation, and inadequate understanding, living with an addiction is much like throwing darts blindfolded. Dart throwers use visual feedback to adjust their throws to get closer and closer to the bull's-eye. When blindfolded they have no way of knowing how close they are getting to the target, so they have no accurate information on which to base change. With so many factors operating to "blind" them to what is really happening, they do not receive the information needed to make the adjustments necessary for healthy change. Recovery starts when a person begins to see through these misperceptions and can recognize the reality of addiction.

However, when people with chemical dependency enter recovery they still have mistaken beliefs that reinforce addictive thinking. Some developed in childhood and have been carried into adult life; others have been created by the progression of chemical dependency itself.

Although each person with chemical dependency has unique basic beliefs, some generalities can be made. If addicted people could be completely honest with themselves, their beliefs would be something like this:

Beliefs about Self: "I am no good unless I am using. My feelings are unpredictable and painful. It is only with chemical use that my feelings become manageable. I am all alone unless my chemical use temporarily allows me to make friends and be close to people. I am incapable of changing or improving myself except through use of chemicals. Without using I am incapable of facing life."

Beliefs about Others: "Other people either cannot or will not help me when I am in trouble. Others cannot understand me even when I try to explain myself to them. Even if they want to, other people are powerless to help me. My only protection against being alone is my use of chemicals."

Beliefs about the World: "The world is a painful, uncomfortable place. Life is tough, and my only pleasure is using. Without using life would not be worth living."

Beliefs about My Addiction: "Using chemicals is my only tool for coping with myself, other people, and the world. Without using I am unable to survive and function. My problems are not caused by my use; they are caused by the problems of other people and the world in general. I am the victim! To take away addictive use would be to remove my only pleasure in life. Without using chemicals I would have little or nothing worthwhile. My chemical use is me."

Comfortable sobriety requires that these beliefs eventually be identified and replaced with constructive beliefs. Recovering people must be challenged to decide, to choose, and to replace mistaken beliefs with accurate beliefs. What happens if they do not? Those who do not change their addictive beliefs judge everything in life by the standard of these beliefs. This causes them to experience the painful consequences of a victimized life.

Points to Remember

1. The brain and nervous system are affected by chemical dependency. These effects are neurological impairments.
2. The person's perception of self, others, and the world changes.
3. As chemical dependency progresses, using chemicals becomes the main focus of life.
4. When using chemicals becomes more important than anything else, people with chemical dependency begin doing things that conflict with their own values.
5. Beliefs and values change to protect chemical use.
6. Denial of the problem is a means people with chemical dependency use to cope with a reality too painful to face: they do not believe they can survive without mind-altering chemicals.
7. Denial of the disease of chemical dependency is part of the disease.
8. Denial is not conscious lying; it is unconscious lying to oneself.
9. Denial results in a way of life built on beliefs that are not true.
10. Denial blocks the motivation for recovery by blocking the painful reality of the user's life.

Notes

1. Jean Kinney and Gwen Leaton, *Loosening the Grip* (St. Louis: Mosby-Year Book, 1991), 144-146.
2. Isabel M. Birnbaum and Elizabeth S. Parker, eds., *Alcohol and Human Memory* (New Jersey: Lawrence Erlbaum Associates, 1977).

CHAPTER 6

Social Effects

The effects of chemical dependency are far-reaching. They aren't limited to the person with the disease. The lives of the people an addicted person lives with, works with, and associates with are affected and form an addictive relationship network. Alcohol and other drugs can destroy family and other cherished relationships.

As chemical dependency progresses it affects not only your body, mind, and feelings but also your actions, your performance, the way you function. In the early stages people with chemical dependency use mind-altering chemicals to improve behavior, but eventually they use in an effort to function normally.

As life becomes more and more drug centered, people have less and less control over behavior. They lose interest in activities that were once important. Getting ready to use, using, recovering from using become their life activities. Anything that interferes with those activities gets pushed aside. Life is consumed by the need to use. Drug-seeking behavior becomes a lifestyle.

Chemically addicted people progressively lose control over their behavior while using. They lose the ability to stop using before they become intoxicated. They may do embarrassing things, dangerous things, violent things, painful things. And each time it happens they swear to themselves they will never let that happen again. And time after time they do.

When using chemicals becomes more important than anything else, people with chemical dependency begin to violate their own value systems. While using chemicals they may do things they would not do sober. While sober, they structure their lives to protect their drug or alcohol use. They may break promises, forget commitments, lie, all to protect their using. They begin to do unreasonable things—hide bottles, get up in the night to smoke a joint, or buy liquor at several places to prevent anyone's knowing how much they buy.

As an addicted person becomes less able to function, employers and co-workers, family and friends, and other close associates must make sense out of the addicted person's behavior and find ways to cope with it. A lack of knowledge about addiction, along with the social stigma associated with chemical dependency, keeps most people from recognizing addiction in those they care about. They realize something is wrong but they don't know what.

As these people attempt to interact with the addicted person, they encounter that person's denial. People with chemical dependency are usually very convincing—using alibis, excuses, and rationalizations. Often they are masters of the blaming game, convincing friends and family that the problem is really the fault of someone or something else. In the early stages of chemical dependency, friends and family usually do not recognize the problem. They blame other things: job-related stress, in-laws, money, sex. Denial of the disease is sometimes as severe in close associates as in the person with chemical dependency.

The people close to an addicted person may actually begin to take responsibility for the problems and, consequently, assume responsibility for correcting them. As a result, they begin protecting the addicted person from the consequences of the addiction, which only makes the problem worse. Embarrassment, fear, and anger intensify.

As life becomes centered around drug use, people with chemical dependency isolate from others. They give up social activities that have been important to them because the activities interfere with their using. Friends and acquaintances separate themselves when the behavior of the addicted person becomes embarrassing or offensive. The family withdraws from social contacts for fear of how the person may behave. Children stop bringing their friends around; the spouse doesn't invite people to the house. Communication skills are lost as the person withdraws to use or get away from those with whom he has become defensive about using.

Addicted people become adept at blaming others as a way of taking the focus off their drinking or drug use. As the addiction progresses, they become more alienated from those who don't fit in or don't relate to the addiction—especially those who may express concern about the extent of the drinking or using. As the chemical use changes from just *wanting* to use to *needing* to use, a belief system is created that helps the addicted person guard the need for chemicals. People who are a threat to continued using may be avoided or completely rejected.

As problems accumulate, addicted persons will—usually without being consciously aware of it—begin to justify these problems or deny them entirely. Relating their life problems to their use of chemicals would leave them no alternative but to quit using. And that is not an acceptable option. Even when it is apparent to friends and family that chemical use is causing problems, the addicted person does not see it that way and conflicts arise.

As chemical use continues, family and friends are put into a no-win situation. If they point out problem behaviors, the addicted person becomes defensive and angry. If they say nothing, everyone is playing the game of "let's pretend nothing is wrong." People who care about the chemical user want to believe this is true and hope against hope that every using episode may be the last.

As the need for chemicals grows, addicted people become more and more alienated from friends and family and from anyone who represents a threat to their continued drinking or using. They become more self-focused (because of their need) and less involved with others. They have little need for people who do not support their use. They spend more and more time with those who will drink with them or support their drug use. These people provide a certain endorsement for their use. Friendships are based almost entirely on chemical experiences and provide a kind of family away from home—a "Cheers" environment where everybody knows your name and it's okay to drink or use.

Family and friends may begin to resent the time spent with drinking or using buddies. The addicted person then becomes more defensive and irritable toward family and friends who do not support chemical use. As more problems develop and stress levels rise, conflicts develop. Arguments occur, sometimes escalating into verbal or physical fighting.

To friends and family there may seem to be things happening that don't add up or make sense. There may be dishonesty and manipulation going on that are inconsistent and out of character for the addicted person. For the addicted person it becomes increasingly necessary to be dishonest because the truth exposes problems related to chemical use. It is easier just to avoid those who "don't understand" and to spend time with those who do.

As people with chemical dependency become unable to fulfill their roles in the family or on the job, others often take over their responsibilities. The person with chemical dependency allows this, even welcomes it (after all, it leaves more time to drink or use). But at the same time the person may resent this dependency and find other ways to be dominant. Attempts to be assertive may lead to aggression, unreasonable demands, or abuse.

Cliff had been a self-sufficient person who took pride in taking care of others, especially his family. He was a successful marketer with a large corporation. As his chemical dependency progressed, however, his family found they could take better care of themselves than he did. So they left and moved to another state. He found that he had no trouble attracting other women, but as one relationship after another ended because of his drug-related behavior he found himself alone more and more. He lost his job, but was able to get another right away (although it did not pay as well). But the job did not last long. One after another, he went through jobs like he had gone through relationships. He no longer associated with the successful people with whom he had once socialized. He took jobs that paid less and less and finally could find no job at all. He lost his car and his house. Recently his sister allowed him to move into the room over her garage. He would be dependent on her for shelter, food, and transportation. As his disease progressed, Cliff had gone from provider to dependent. His relationship with everyone in his life had changed because of his drug use.

Family members become so affected by chemical dependency that they too become unable to function adequately. To survive the pain brought on by the actions of the chemically dependent person, family members develop their own ways of coping, many of which increase and prolong the pain. Family life centers around the problem. Fear, lack of trust, guilt, resentment, and blaming replace the good feelings the family may once have had. A later chapter will discuss effects on the family in more detail.

Since the job is usually an area of great importance (because of the money and positive identity provided), it usually is the last aspect of life to be affected by chemical dependency. When they value and need their jobs, chemically dependent people struggle to protect them as long as possible. They put forth extra effort and find others who will cover for them.

Sometimes people who work with an addicted person become part of the addicted social system. They try to "help" by protecting the person from the consequences of his or her behavior. They take responsibility the person should take and cover so others won't find out. They make excuses for him or her, always giving the person another chance. The addicted person buys time with this protection.

But as chemical use progresses, a time comes when all the covering up will not help. The addicted person will use more and more, and work less and less. Eventually the person can no longer draw the line, and the addiction invades the last unaffected area, despite the added efforts. Absenteeism, tardiness, accidents, and low productivity lead to conflicts with supervisors, co-workers, and subordinates, eventually putting the job in jeopardy. Deterioration of this last area is often what motivates the person with chemical dependency to seek treatment.

Points to Remember

1. Chemical dependency has social consequences; it affects the lives of those who live with, work with, and associate with the person with chemical dependency.
2. The person with chemical dependency becomes isolated because of chemical use and using behavior.
3. Communication skills are lost.
4. The family is affected by fear, guilt, resentment, and their own ways of coping with the pain of chemical dependency.
5. When people with chemical dependency abandon their roles in the family or on the job, others often take over their responsibilities.
6. The job is usually the last aspect of life to be affected by chemical dependency.
7. Deterioration in the area of the job often motivates the person with chemical dependency to seek treatment.

CHAPTER 7

Recovery

Three things that must occur to free people with chemical dependency to recover:

1. They must come to believe they are sick.
2. They must come to believe they can recover.
3. They must take some action to allow the recovery process to begin.

Acceptance is the first step of recovery. Progress in recovery cannot be made until denial is replaced by acceptance. The first three steps of Alcoholics Anonymous and Narcotics Anonymous will help you with the process of acceptance.

Step 1 states: *We admitted we were powerless over alcohol, that our lives had become unmanageable.* [1] We have shown already how you are powerless over the way your body responds to mind-altering chemicals. We have shown how chemical dependency makes your life unmanageable.

The idea of acceptance or surrender may seem like weakness to you. Perhaps it seems weak not to be able to control your response to mind-altering chemicals and to be unable to manage your life. Perhaps it seems like giving up and not being willing to fight. This is not so.

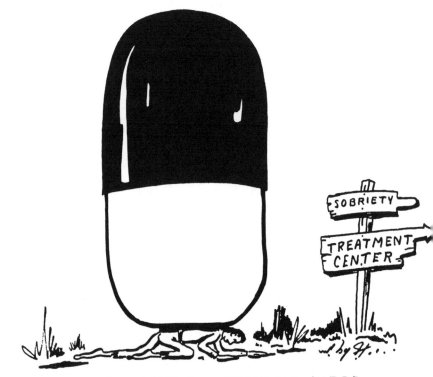

WE ADMITTED THAT WE WERE
POWERLESS OVER DRUGS...

To change something, you have to become aware that it needs to be changed. If you have problems because of drug use then something needs to change. Don't get confused between cause and effect. It is easy to allow yourself to believe that you use chemicals because you have problems rather than that you have problems because you use chemicals. If you have been arrested because you were driving while intoxicated, that problem is a direct result of your drinking. If you can't get to work on time on Monday morning because you have a hangover, that problem is a direct result of your chemical use. If you fell and broke your arm while intoxicated, that problem is directly related to your drug use. If you have problems because of your drinking, then you have a drinking problem. Something needs to change.

The question becomes: *What is within your power to change and what is not?* Acceptance of those things that cannot be changed enables you to do something about those things that can be changed. Can you change the way your body metabolizes alcohol? Can you change the way mind-altering chemicals affect your brain chemistry? Can you change your heredity that has set you up to lose control of alcohol or drugs if you use them? If not, then you cannot learn to use in moderation or to "drink responsibly." You cannot solve other problems and expect to be able to use "normally."

What you cannot change you need to *accept*. Until you accept that there are certain things over which you are powerless, you will find your life becoming more and more unmanageable. You will exert great energy and effort attempting to change what you cannot, while you lose control over what you do have the power to change.

Accepting powerlessness over mind-altering chemicals is not an easy step to take. When you admit that you cannot control the way mind-altering chemicals affect you, and that using them is creating serious problems for you, the next logical thought is that you need to stop using them. That is a frightening thought, and you will begin to argue with yourself. The part of you that is afraid to stop will tell you that you don't need to stop entirely; you only need to switch substances, or brands, or place, or time, or frequency. The part of you that wants to accept your powerlessness over chemicals will tell you that if you don't stop, your life will continue to be unmanageable, that you may develop serious problems or even die.

At this point the thinking part of you must take control. You need to look carefully at the problems that have developed because of your using and the ways that your life has become unmanageable. If people with chemical dependency finally admit powerlessness over their disease, they can then learn to manage the disease and restructure their lives to accommodate its limitations. Acceptance becomes strength.

Step 2 states: *We came to believe that a power greater than ourselves could restore us to sanity.*[2] As long as people with chemical dependency believe there is no power within or without that can make their lives better, they have no hope that their lives can change. They feel trapped by the "insanity" that controls them.

If you admit that you are powerless over your body's reaction to chemicals but have tried abstinence before and failed, your acceptance may leave you feeling hopeless. You have tried everything within you and you could not do it. What else is there to do? Try something outside of you.

When you come to believe there is more power available than the power you have used in the past, hope is born. With hope comes trust in that additional power. You begin to trust the power that can bring about recovery.

In *The Edge of Adventure: An Experiment in Faith*, Keith Miller and Bruce Larson[3] illustrate what it means to trust a power beyond what you have experienced before:

The following letter was found in a baking powder can wired to the handle of an old pump that offered the only hope of drinking water on a very long and seldom-used trail across the Amargosa Desert:

This pump is all right as of June, 1932. I put a new sucker washer into it and it ought to last five years. But the washer dries out and the pump has got to be primed. Under the white rock I buried a bottle of water, out of the sun and cork end up. There's enough water in it to prime the pump, but not if you drink some first. Pour about one-fourth and let her soak to wet the leather. Then pour in the rest medium fast and pump like crazy. You'll git water. The well has never run dry. Have faith. When you git watered up, fill the bottle and put it back like you found it for the next feller. Desert Pete.

P.S. Don't go drinking up the water first. Prime the pump with it and you'll git all you can hold.

If you were a thirsty traveler, would you trust Desert Pete—a person you didn't know—enough to risk priming the pump? Remember, if you drink any water, you won't have enough to prime the pump. Step 2 asks that you believe in a power that can give you something better than what you have. This is the hope of recovery.

Step 3 states: *Made a decision to turn our will and our lives over to the care of God as we understood him.*[4] This act of surrender allows the recovery process to begin. If the word "God" is difficult for you, underscore *as we understood him*. How do you understand God? What do you understand God to be? Your higher power can fit any description as long as it is a power that is greater than you alone.

Just allow that power within you or outside of you—that power you have not used before and have only now come to believe can restore you to health—to begin the process. This does not mean that you don't do anything. The main thing you do at this point is *choose*. You have the choice to keep trying to make it alone or to accept help.

There is a story about a little boy who was trying to move a large rock. He tried and tried, but it would not move. Finally he went to

71

his father and said, "I can't move that rock." The father said, "Have you done everything you can do?" The little boy assured his father that he had. "No, you haven't," the father answered. "You haven't asked me to help you."

You have this choice. You can continue to attempt to control what you are powerless over or you can allow a higher power and other people to help you.

In three steps you have moved from denial to surrender. You have come to believe you are sick; you have come to believe you can recover; you have taken action to allow the recovery process to begin.

Surrender is a difficult word for some people because it implies losing control. Remember that mind-altering chemicals control the lives of people with chemical dependency. These people are not in control of their lives. They may think they are, but they are thinking through the "smokescreen" of the disease. Only through surrender to this reality—and to the power that restores health—can they free themselves from the bonds that control their lives. They are then free to recover.

Modified First Three Steps of AA and NA:
>   Step 1: I can't do it alone.
>   Step 2: There is a power that can help me.
>   Step 3: I think I will let that power help me.

Points to Remember
1. To recover you must come to believe you are sick.
2. Acceptance of the disease—admitting powerlessness over mind-altering chemicals—is the first step in learning to manage chemical dependency.
3. To recover you must believe that recovery is possible.
4. Trusting a power beyond yourself opens the door to the hope that you can recover.

5. To recover you must take some action to allow the recovery process to begin.
6. Making a decision to turn your life over to that higher power is the action that allows the recovery process to begin.

Notes

1. *Twelve Steps and Twelve Traditions* (New York: Alcoholics Anonymous World Services, 1952), 21.
2. Ibid., 25.
3. Keith Miller and Bruce Larson, *The Edge of Adventure: An Experiment of Faith* (Waco, Texas: Word Books, 1974), 29.
4. *Twelve Steps and Twelve Traditions*, 34.

WE CAME TO BELIEVE IN A HIGHER POWER

COURAGE IS THE FEELING THAT ALLOWS
HUMAN BEINGS TO STAND UP AGAINST
FORCES THAT ARE ATTEMPTING TO TEAR
THEM DOWN. . . . .

CHAPTER 8

The Creation of a New Lifestyle

Fear not that thy life shall come to an end, but rather fear that it shall never have a beginning (J. H. Newman).[1] Recovery from disease affords a person the opportunity to create a new way of life, a new beginning. Disease imposes losses, but it is possible to look beyond the losses and recognize the potential gain. Oriental philosophy teaches that "in every loss there is a gain and in every gain a loss." Disease may take away certain aspects of a person's current lifestyle, but it also provides the challenge of building new and more meaningful ways of life. Many people with chemical dependency find life more satisfying and more meaningful after recovery than ever before.

As strange as it sounds to hear someone say, "I am grateful that I'm an alcoholic," many people mean it. Their addiction has taught them something about life because they chose to recover. The struggle with chemical dependency has taught them about their strength, their courage, the joy of giving and receiving help, and the depth of life that is possible despite the burdens of life.

This is what a person meant when after two years of sobriety he said, "I'm glad I have chemical dependency. I'm glad I was forced to face myself. I gained more from my struggle than I believed possible. I can see now, with hindsight, that I never knew myself nor my ability to care, struggle, and survive. I was out of touch with my values. It took the tragedy of my chemical dependency to force me to deal with myself."

To successfully battle an illness powerful enough to take life requires more than just medication, surgery, or other forms of treatment. It requires that one create a new lifestyle that does not allow recurrence of the illness.

Whenever people face the forced creation of a new way of life, they experience three distinct feelings. The first is a feeling of fear and dread, a doubting of the ability to cope and deal with the strange new world they are building. The second feeling is of loss, the emptiness experienced when saying good-bye to familiar habits, friends, and situations. The third is excitement generated by the prospect of facing something new. Unfortunately most people with chemical dependency focus on the fear and loss, totally ignoring the excitement.

Change, whether forced or voluntary, is always a two-sided coin. Fear is on one side, balanced by excitement on the other. To ignore the fear invites a dangerous plunge into the unknown. To ignore the excitement invites a fearful retreat into the comfort of old but self-defeating habits.

Recovery and Trust

You must always ask questions about your treatment, but you must come to trust the treatment system. You must learn to have faith in the process and trust that the treatment will help you get well. You must trust those who administer treatment. This is difficult because any reasonably intelligent adult realizes that people are fallible. But the hope of recovery requires that, despite human fallibility, you make the decision to trust the recommendations of someone else.

This trust in people is difficult for those with chemical dependency who have tried many times to recover on their own and who have failed each time. They carry with them a failure pattern deeply entrenched in their way of life. They are in the habit of failing, and this habit has built the belief that success is impossible. They have stopped asking for help and have unintentionally mobilized the people in their lives to support the failure pattern.

Most important, people with chemical dependency must learn to trust themselves. Their disease robs them of self-trust. They live in fear of their next failure. They avoid challenge and shrink their world through isolation and avoidance. They cover their inadequacies by denying their limitations and their feelings. They lie to themselves to preserve self-esteem.

Every newly recovering person has a fear of failure. To deny this fear and uncertainty is the first step toward failure. It is impossible to seek help for a problem that you have convinced yourself you do not have. In the darkness of denial fear grows.

You must believe that your own personal courage will be strong enough to withstand the demands the disease makes on you. Courage is the feeling that allows you to stand up against forces attempting to tear you down.

The person with chemical dependency must look within and separate the urge to use chemicals (the driving force of the disease) and the urge to recover (the basic human courage to fight back). Recovery demands that you look within and find that spark of courage that will give you the strength to fight back.

To recover, it is necessary to trust someone or something other than yourself. AA is based on this principle. They call this object of trust a "higher power."Trust does not exclude the possibility of pain. The reality is that we are often hurt most by those we trust most. To trust is to give another human being not only the power to help but also the power to hurt. Being human, we often accidentally hurt those we care about. You must enter treatment with your eyes open to the potential pain. You must ask yourself, "Do I stop trusting or am I ready to endure and see the depth beyond the pain?"

People can use pain as an excuse to stop trusting, or they can learn to look beyond the pain and learn that survival is possible. To expect that a trust relationship will protect you from the pain of life is unrealistic. It is wishful thinking.

Recovery and Action

Anyone can plan. Moving from thought to action is the giant step that requires courage, energy, resolve, and a willingness to accept change. It is tragic but true that pain is the universal motivator. Most people will not mobilize themselves to act until they experience considerable pain. The reason: With action comes risk, and people in this society are security oriented. Holding on to the certainty of today is easier than letting go and reaching for the promise of tomorrow.

People with chemical dependency are master planners. They plan, dream, and fantasize. As a matter of fact, they are often too busy planning to act, too busy planning to notice life falling apart around them, too busy planning to see that they are too sick to implement their plans. There is a saying that sums up this dilemma: *Life is what happens to us while we're making other plans.*

The stage for failure is set by the unwillingness to act. The goal of treatment is to help you move from thought to action, from concept to reality. Treatment helps you tap the courage, energy, and resolve you have within you. Once tapped, treatment directs that energy into a constructive course of recovery.

Recovery Is Facing the Future

I have seen the future and it is very much like the present—only longer (Kehlog Albran). The only way to face the future is by living fully today. Our faith in the future can only be acted on today. The purpose of yesterday is purely educational. Our past successes and failures serve as guidelines for today's actions and tomorrow's dreams. A history of failure contaminates our dreams and cripples our lives. The conflict is between the tomorrow that is desired and the tomorrow that is expected. History teaches us what to expect. The challenge of today is often sacrificed in favor of the memory of yesterday. If the memory of yesterday is more important than life today, a person is in despair.

Most people are so crippled by tragic expectancies that they cannot get in touch with what it is they desire. One of the first steps in recovery is to find out what you want from life, to escape from the trap of expecting less than you deserve, and to begin to look realistically at what is possible, beginning today. The answer to this dilemma is to believe, to have faith that things can and will get better. No matter how bad things look, by taking one small step at a time things will get better.

Recovery and Risk

Nothing in this world is guaranteed, including recovery. Recovery is a risky process. A person must be willing to take the risk of recovery. Through treatment the risks are minimized and the chances of success increase. Do the potential benefits outweigh the risks? The answer to this question becomes obvious when the consequences of untreated chemical dependency are considered. While treatment is risky, continued drinking or using has a definite and catastrophic outcome. A return to using is surrendering the human spirit to a mind-altering chemical. People with chemical dependency who return to using surrender their human spirit— their dignity, honor, courage, pain, triumph, and failure—in exchange for a magic chemical that, for a little while, allows them to escape the awesome realities of their humanness.

Points to Remember

1. The disease of chemical dependency may take away certain parts of life, but it provides the challenge of building a new, more meaningful way of life.

2. People with chemical dependency must learn to trust the treatment process and also trust themselves.
3. People can use fear of being hurt as an excuse to stop trusting, or they can look beyond being hurt to find that survival is possible.
4. Treatment helps people with chemical dependency go beyond planning to acting.
5. The only way to face the future is by living fully today.
6. Treatment is a risk and there are no guarantees.
7. Recovery is worth the risk.

Notes

1. John Henry Cardinal Newman, 1801-1890.

CHAPTER 9

Adjustments to Abstinence

The person recovering from chemical dependency needs to develop a new lifestyle to maintain sobriety. A way of life centered around using or drinking activities will not maintain sobriety. This requires the formation of new habits. It is not easy to change longtime habits. You must develop new patterns of living, build new friendships, find new sources of recreation and leisure, find a new place within the family, and learn to communicate in new ways. You must find new ways to cope with stressful living and to respond to social pressure to drink or use drugs.

Some painful reactions to so much adjustment at one time is normal. It is important to remember, however, that changes in habit get easier and easier. The first time you do something new it may be difficult, the next time not quite so bad. Each time it becomes a little easier until the new habit is as much a part of you as the old habit was. Then there comes a time when the old habits are no longer a part of that lifestyle at all and you become more comfortable with a drug-free lifestyle than you have ever been with drug-centered living.

State Dependent Memory

Anything that you learn is most easily recalled when you are in the same mental state in which you learned it.[1] This means that what you learned while using, you will remember more easily when using again and may have difficulty recalling when you are sober. This is state dependent memory.

If you started drinking or using at a young age, many social skills including communication skills, dancing, and the ability to assert yourself may all be dependent on chemicals. You may find it very difficult to function socially without alcohol or drugs. There may also be problems in expressing affection and in functioning sexually. You may have difficulty remembering how to do activities you have always done while drinking or using.

When sober, people with chemical dependency feel they should be able to do these things because they have done them many times before. When they attempt to do what was learned state dependently, they find themselves running into a brick wall. They can't do it in spite of their efforts. They feel that something is wrong with them, that they are crazy, defective, or incompetent. A minor limitation can be turned into a major crippler. They believe they cannot perform, and they become embarrassed and humiliated. As a result, they avoid situations in which relearning can take place.

Rather than admit to the limitation and handicap, most people with chemical dependency tend to rationalize: *Dancing isn't any fun anyway.* Or *AA meetings are enough, who needs to go out and have other good times?* This avoidance of relearning is tragic because skills that are learned state dependently are rapidly relearned with practice.

Sobriety-based Denial

Denial of chemical dependency while using is a normal part of the disease. All denial does not cease when you are able to say, "I am chemically dependent." Acceptance of the disease does not necessarily interrupt all denial patterns. Sobriety-based denial may continue. This may show up as denial of shortcomings or personal problems that interfere with recovery. For example,"As long as I am not using, why do I need to work on my anger?" You may deny the reality that you can never safely use mind-altering chemicals again or that you need to make a plan to prevent relapse. There may be denial of the need to change your lifestyle to support sobriety. Whatever form the denial takes, it may or may not be conscious. Most denial is subconscious and the person is not aware of it. A searching and fearless moral inventory as described in the fourth step of NA/AA will help you interrupt sobriety-based denial that can block progress in recovery.

Feelings

While chemical dependency is not caused by mental illness or moral weakness, psychological problems (problems relating to thinking and feeling) do result from the disease of chemical dependency. And most of these problems do not miraculously disappear by removing chemicals from the body. There is immediate relief from some problems, but others can only be overcome with time. Some thinking and emotional problems actually result from removing the chemicals from the body.

Other psychological problems arise as a result of the attitudes and lifestyle established while using. Sobriety means attitude and lifestyle change. Attitudes and habits are not established overnight, and they are not changed overnight. All change is accompanied by some feelings of stress. This is not always a negative experience. Some change is accompanied by feelings of excitement and pleasure. The important thing to remember is that the recovery period will be a time when you will be experiencing some new feelings, some excitement, some anxiety, some depression, some emotional growth, some good feelings about yourself and others that you may not have experienced before or for a long time.

In the early stage of recovery it is normal for many people to have what is sometimes referred to as the "honeymoon" period. It feels good to be drug free. The experience of attaining sobriety has brought some new insights and new sense of power and control. You have found out you are not a weak person but a person with a disease. You have made some new friends and are experiencing some good feelings about yourself and other people that had been long buried by chemical use.

It is good to enjoy these feelings and learn to hold on to them when things aren't going so well. It is important to understand that it is also normal to have some unpleasant feelings during recovery and that by identifying and understanding them you will be better able to use them constructively.

Mood swings are common in recovery. When you are feeling that life is wonderful, you may believe it is always going to be that way, that those good feelings are going to last forever. Then when you have bad feelings that you aren't anticipating, you may not be able to handle them. And down feelings may become severe depression. There may even be times when you feel like hurting yourself or other people. This doesn't mean those feelings are going to last forever. And it doesn't mean you have to act on them. It just means you need to look at those feelings and what can be done when you experience them.

Depression may cause you to hurt yourself in some ways that are not really obvious. It may cause carelessness so that you become accident prone. It may cause you to neglect your health so you become sick or to neglect your recovery program so you set yourself up to relapse. These are indications that you need to take a hard look at ways to improve your recovery program.

Ben had four years of sobriety. Although he had not gone to an aftercare program or to AA or NA, he had not used and had no desire or craving to use. But he was not happy. He had a good job. He had saved enough for a down payment on a house but couldn't get interested in looking for one. He had a new motorcycle that he never used. He told his boss that everything seemed meaningless. His boss told him he was on a "dry drunk" and needed to get back into treatment. Fortunately he took that advice. He told his counselor that he felt like a "bomb of anger." In treatment he recognized many unexpressed feelings and the need for a recovery program that included more than not using.

The worst thing you can do is to keep depression and self-destructive thoughts a secret. Unspoken thoughts continue to build until they are acted upon. Depression is the surface layer covering other feelings: guilt, anger, and unmet needs. When you are feeling depressed, ask yourself, "Am I feeling guilty?" Guilt that does not lead you to correct a situation is a way of punishing yourself. Energy is used to keep the guilt alive that could be used to eliminate the need for it. AA/NA Steps 4 through 10 will give you active methods for doing something about those things that are causing you guilt, and we will be talking about that in more detail throughout this book. Dealing with guilt is an essential part of preventing depression and maintaining your sobriety.

Looking squarely at guilt often uncovers buried anger. Anger is an involuntary response to some event that has occurred. Note the word "involuntary." You don't choose to become angry. You don't sit around and think about it and say, "I believe I will become angry." Anger is not a choice; it just happens.

Anger has purpose. The emotion of anger is a necessary survival tool, an energizer. It provides the energy to act in difficult times. Anger forces us in a direction. When you feel angry, the first thing to ask is, "Who or what am I angry with?" Anger is a tool that invites others to take us seriously. It is a way to let people know how strong our convictions are.

Once you experience anger, you must respond to it in some way. There are two things you can do. You can turn it inward and let it become guilt or depression. Or you can get rid of it. Sometimes an active response to anger is appropriate. It may be necessary to enable you to protect yourself or someone else.

But unplanned action designed to hurt others has a high risk of rebounding and causing painful consequences. A recovering person should always express anger in safe surroundings because of the tendency to overreact. Later you might say, "Well, what did I do that for? Why was I so angry?" You need to give yourself time and space to separate overreaction from justifiable anger. Anger is a lot like gunpowder or nuclear energy. Both are powerful tools. They are neither good nor bad. It is how they are used that counts. A powerful tool can be used to produce great amounts of good or vast amounts of destruction.

Anger can be dangerous if misused. Hence, it should be respected. Respected and not avoided. There is a difference in being careful in expressing anger and attempting to deny or avoid anger altogether. The denial and avoidance of anger can lead to guilt, depression, anxiety, episodes of lost temper, and uncontrollable rage. Unexpressed anger also forms the seedbed for ulcers, high blood pressure, colitis, hemorrhoids, and a variety of other stress-related illnesses.

Change

Change is stressful, but many people have a difficult time recognizing how stressful even relatively small changes can be. To help you recognize the impact change can have on day-to-day stress levels, try the following exercises:

Exercise One: If you normally wear your watch on your left wrist, change. Wear it on your right wrist. Notice how aggravating it is every time you look at the wrong wrist when you need to know what time it is. That aggravation is called stress.

Exercise Two: When you are putting on a shirt or coat, you have developed a habit of putting one arm in the sleeve first. Some people put the left arm in first; others put the right arm in first. Your assignment is to change. Every time you put on a coat or shirt, start by putting the opposite arm in the sleeve first. Notice any feelings or reactions? These feelings are stress. Have we made the point? Change = Stress.

During the first two years of sobriety, keep unnecessary change to a minimum. If there are necessary changes, be sure to plan carefully for them. The question is often asked, "What is necessary change?" The answer is simple. A change is necessary if any of the following exist: There is a situation that creates high levels of stress or pain that may interfere with the ability to stay sober. Change is forced on you by circumstances beyond your control. You become aware in sobriety that certain areas of your life seriously compromise your value system or sense of personal integrity.

Guidelines for Planning Necessary Change

1. In changing any life area, make the minimal change necessary to accomplish your goal.

2. Only plan to change one area in your life at a time.

3. Plan for changes to occur during periods when stress from other sources is low.

4. Avoid big changes by learning how to break down major change into small steps that can be accomplished over a period of time.

5. Plan for periods of rest in between changes.

6. Practice a strong program of relaxation during periods of change.

7. Intensify your recovery program (attend more meetings, spend more time with your sponsor).

8. Plan for the worst so you have confidence that no matter what happens, you can handle it.

9. Expect the best; keep a positive frame of mind by talking to yourself constructively.

10. Plan for "stress escapes," periods during the day when you can mentally get away from the stress.

11. Plan for fun activities that will reenergize you to face change.

12. Once you have determined that change is necessary and made the decision for change, follow through. Backing out and starting over again makes the change more stressful than necessary.

Here are some helps in maintaining change once you have decided it is necessary:

1. Change the way you talk to yourself. Say things to yourself that will support your new situation rather than the old situation.

2. Plan your change carefully in your mind. Successful change is first accomplished mentally.

3. Use memories to reinforce change. You must give up the "good old days" syndrome, the tendency to remember how good things were before. Search for those memories that will make change easier, memories of those things that are making the change necessary rather than the memories that cause you to want to bring back the past.

Time

Remember, no matter what you do you cannot make up for the time lost in the failures created while using chemicals. You will feel the pressure to make up for that lost time but you can't. The best thing you can do now that you are in recovery is take advantage of the time you have right now. Probably the most important NA/AA slogan is, "One day at a time," and you will retranslate that into one minute or one hour at a time during the course of your recovery, depending on your present stress levels. All you will ever have is this instant; use it the best you can.

The first awareness that people have of time in early recovery is that they have too much of it. They don't have any more time than they have always had, but now they are not spending it preparing to use chemicals, using chemicals, or getting over using chemicals. It is not that they have more time; it is just that it is being used differently. It is vitally important as recovery begins that the time gaps where you used to drink or drug be filled with those healthy activities recovery should be made of. If not, it is easy to gravitate back into what you know best, using chemicals. Let's now look at how you will be using your time differently.

The foundation of your time reorientation will relate to your treatment activities and your AA/NA meetings. These, at least for a while, will—along with your job—fill your days and evenings.

It takes a lot of time using these resources in the best way you can. You will attend counseling sessions, become educated about the disease of addiction, meet many new and supportive people, experiment with types of exercise, nutrition, and meditation, read new books, become a functioning member of your family again, and lay the foundation for a healthy lifestyle that you will build upon the rest of your life.

Another difficult habit to break with respect to time is using it for the long-term gain rather than for short-term gratification. What you do today that relates to your health and recovery program will determine your long-term success and happiness.

Time takes on a new perception with sobriety. You will find that drug-related behavior has taken so much of your time that you will need to develop a new awareness of how much time certain activities actually take. You may need help in setting up realistic schedules so you will not take on more than you can accomplish.

A daily quiet time is a vital activity of recovery. This is a time when, for fifteen to twenty minutes preferably during the morning hours, you can reflect through meditation, reading, or prayer on those aspects of life that increase your peace, strength, and serenity. As you learn—and it is a learning process—to feel quiet and serene inside, you will not be as prone to feel manipulated by the fast-paced world we live in.

Remember that time passes every second, minute, hour, day, month, and year, no matter what you choose to do with it. But if you use it to the fullest toward a healthy recovery, it will be time well spent, and it will be spent sober.

Cravings

The nature of drug cravings has never been fully established, but some people in recovery do experience obsession and compulsion to use chemicals. They feel compelled to use and develop definite cravings for the effect. These cravings can be responsible for a return to using when you least expect it. If you experience cravings, you should have a plan of action that can be used anytime the cravings occur. Your plan of action should involve other people and provide a place where using is not likely to occur. People who encourage using or places where drugs are readily available should be avoided.

People and Places

They say in AA/NA that to find sobriety you must change playgrounds and playmates. The people you associated with while using are tied to your addiction-based lifestyle. It is not that they are bad; you just have one central thing in common with them. Your relationship to a large degree is based on your using chemicals together. It is not a moral issue of whether these people are good or bad; it is a question of what works and what does not. If you choose to spend most of your time around old using buddies, their expectations for you to use chemicals can become stressful.

As for the "playgrounds," it has been said that no one frequents a house of ill repute to listen to the piano player. By the same token, you do not go to a tavern to have orange juice. Bars are not in business to sell orange juice. Even if a person attends the local "Cheers" establishment and drinks soft drinks for a while, it will not take long until the pressure to be completely at home becomes overwhelming and puts you in high risk of having something stronger.

Cathy enjoyed going into bars to listen to music and could see no harm in it. She had no desire to drink. One night as she was relaxed and enjoying the music she was no longer in Kansas City in 1990. It was 1968 and she was in New Orleans. In her mind she was drinking. She was no longer in recovery. The experience was so vivid for her that she discontinued her practice of going to bars to listen to music.

It is not so much a question of just not associating with your old friends or not frequenting your old hangouts. It is more a question of what new places you are going to and what new friends you are

91

meeting. Your playgrounds will change automatically as you meet new sober people.

Meeting new friends is probably one of the most uncomfortable things you will need to do in early recovery, but in the long run the most satisfying. It is through these people who share your goal of recovery and health that you will find the most lasting and enduring friendships.

Points to Remember

1. What is learned while drinking is most easily recalled while at the same blood alcohol level. This is state dependent memory.
2. In sobriety you may have difficulty remembering how to perform many tasks you learned while using chemicals.
3. Skills that are learned state dependently are easily relearned.
4. Sobriety-based denial may cause you to avoid doing those things that are necessary to your recovery.
5. If you experience cravings you should avoid people and situations that would make it easy to drink or use drugs.
6. People recovering from chemical dependency need to learn a new way of living that enables them to adjust to and overcome the limitations imposed by the effects of chemical dependency that persist into recovery.

Notes

1. Isabel M. Birnbaum and Elizabeth S. Parker, eds., *Alcohol and Human Memory* (New Jersey: Lawrence Erlbaum Associates, 1977), chapter 13, page 2.

CHAPTER 10

Developmental Phases of Recovery

Recovery from chemical dependency unfolds in phases. Recovery is a process, the process of learning how to live. It is a progressive movement through specific periods. Each phase of recovery requires the completion of specific recovery tasks that must be accomplished to prepare you for the next phase of recovery.[1] As recovery unfolds, the tasks change according to recovery needs. As a child grows and develops, the tasks the child needs to accomplish change. There are periods for sitting, crawling, standing, and walking. Each task is important and gives the child the skills needed for the next step. An ongoing recovery program is necessary to build a lifestyle that grows and changes in sobriety.

Building recovery is like building a house. You lay a strong foundation, but you do not stop with the foundation. You give the house a floor, and walls, and eventually a roof. Even after your house is complete you still need to maintain it to keep it strong and secure.

The developmental periods of recovery are transition, stabilization, early recovery, middle recovery, late recovery, and maintenance.[2]

Recovery: one step at a time.

Transition: During this period you learn from the consequences that you cannot use mind-altering chemicals safely. The pain of the disease becomes a teacher. As the disease progresses, the consequences of continued drug use become more severe until you are forced to recognize that your use of mind-altering chemicals is not normal. The tasks of recovery necessary to move from the point of denial to the point of getting help are

1. recognizing that you have lost control over your drug use;

2. acknowledging that you cannot control your use because you are addicted; and

3. making a decision to accept help to achieve sobriety.

The first task, recognizing loss of control, is accomplished by attempting to solve your problems without stopping drug use. When this does not work and you realize that your problems are related to your drug use, you attempt to control your use by changing the nature of your use: by switching substances; by changing frequency, quantity, or time of use; or by attempting temporary abstinence (with the intent to return to using as soon as you prove you can stop whenever you want).

When none of this works, you are likely to recognize that you are addicted. At this point you may believe that you can just stop and everything will be all right. The transition phase of recovery ends when you realize that you cannot stop by yourself and you need help. In some cases, treatment may begin before the transition period ends. Treatment may help you recognize that you have a problem and that you need help.

Stablization: The goal of the stabilization period of recovery is to gain control of your thinking, emotions, judgment, and behavior. The major tasks of this period of recovery are

1. recovering from withdrawal;

2. overcoming preoccupation with chemicals;

3. learning to cope without using alcohol or other drugs; and

4. developing hope and motivation for long-term sobriety.

There are two types of physical withdrawal: acute (short-term) and post acute (long-term). Acute withdrawal usually lasts from one to ten days. Post acute withdrawal symptoms will last for an indefinite period of time but can be controlled when you learn more about them. These symptoms may include difficulty in thinking clearly, managing emotions, remembering, handling stress, sleeping, and avoiding accidents. Stress intensifies these symptoms, and managing stress is one of the keys to managing the symptoms.

The stabilization period can be painful as you learn to cope with withdrawal symptoms. In the past you have used chemicals to cope with pain, so it is natural during this time to be preoccupied with chemical use. To overcome this preoccupation it is necessary to learn new ways of coping with pain and creating pleasure. You learn new ways of coping from treatment professionals, from AA or NA sponsors and friends, from reading material, and from your own trial and error. By studying this book you will find many alternatives for building a new lifestyle free of addictive craving, obsession, and compulsion.

Overcoming preoccupation with chemicals lays the foundation for developing the hope that recovery is possible and for motivation to take the steps necessary to let it happen. Interacting with other recovering people will strengthen your hope and motivation and give you support for moving into other stages of recovery.

Early Recovery: The major goal of early recovery is to change attitudes and beliefs about drug use that put you in risk of relapse. You do this by

1. changing your understanding of chemical use and the role it has played in your life,

2. exploring the purpose of your chemical use, and

3. learning to cope with life without drugs by learning new life skills.

The first step in changing your attitudes about chemical use is learning all you can about chemical dependency and addiction and then applying that knowledge to your life. Your counselor or AA or NA sponsor can help you look at your life to see how you have been affected by use of alcohol or other drugs. This helps you, also, to understand your purpose in using chemicals. What did they do for you? What do you feel you cannot do unless you use chemicals? In what situations did you use drugs to cope? Answering these questions can help you recognize and accept your dependence on drugs and to see what you need to do to live without mind-altering substances. This is the time that you develop the firm belief that you have chemical dependency.

Middle Recovery: The goal of the middle period of recovery is repair of damage to life caused by the addiction. The recovery tasks are

1. focusing on normal life issues rather than focusing on not using mind-altering drugs,

2. resolving the normal letdown feeling you get at this stage of recovery,

3. making amends to those who have been hurt by your addiction, and

4. making changes in your recovery program to support life balance and ongoing personal growth.

It is normal at this point in recovery to evaluate your life and your sober lifestyle. You may look around you and say, "Am I living my life the way I really want to?" You may need to make some major decisions and changes that support your continued growth and help you attain what you want out of life. You may want to make some changes in your job, your family life, your relationships, or your education.

If you fail to evaluate your life and your recovery, you can get "stuck" at this point, believing that it is not all right to change what has been working to keep you sober. Making amends and repairing the damage caused by your addiction increases your self-awareness and helps you evaluate what is important to you. Making changes in your recovery program may be necessary to support the changes you need to make in your life.

Jenny was what is sometimes called in AA a "two-stepper," a person who goes from Step One (acknowledging her life has become unmanageable because of her addiction) to Step Twelve (carrying the message). She had four years of sobriety and seemed to be doing well. She was active in AA and sponsored a number of people. She was a frequent speaker at AA meetings and enjoyed the fellowship of her AA friends. But she was so busy with all these activities that she never got around to repairing the damage that had resulted from her addiction. She did not look at herself or what needed to change in her life. She was shocked and surprised when her husband left her saying that nothing had changed in their relationship since she got sober. Nothing had been repaired in her life. She had failed to evaluate what she needed to change in herself and in her relationships. Despite several years of sobriety, Jenny had never completed the tasks of middle recovery.

In middle recovery you consistently pursue the resolution of long-term problems that have developed because of addiction. You come to believe that you can create a lifestyle in sobriety that will bring you greater pleasure than you received from chemicals. You adopt new values and goals that bring about a more meaningful and fulfilling life. You seek to establish or reestablish a sense of spiritual identity. The focus of your attention is drawn more and more to learning to live again in a way that generates a sense of serenity and peace of mind.

Late Recovery: The goal of late recovery is attaining lifestyle balance by overcoming problems that existed before addiction. These problems probably go back to your childhood, especially if you are the child of an alcoholic or grew up in a dysfunctional family. The recovery tasks for doing this are

1. recognizing that problems from your childhood are affecting the quality of your life and your sobriety;

2. making the connection between your childhood and the problems you are having;

3. breaking the cycle of family dysfunction by restructuring your habits of thinking, feeling, and acting to support healthy living; and

4. moving past long-term obstacles to live the lifestyle you really want to live.

Despite several years of successful recovery, Marilyn began to feel something was still missing. She had grown up in an alcoholic home and knew there were some painful issues that she had not faced or resolved. While she felt secure in her sobriety, she could see that her peace of mind was threatened by memories of her childhood. A series of counseling sessions helped shed some new light on her feelings about these memories. The sessions were difficult. But she could see that attitudes, beliefs, and behaviors she had developed to cope in childhood were not supportive of continued growth in sobriety. Because it was a painful time, she made some changes in her recovery program to reduce her stress, to ask for more support from others, and to take better care of herself. Because of this late recovery work she is aware that now she is free to choose different behaviors and attitudes that will improve the quality of her sobriety.

By the time you enter late recovery you should have a good recovery program in place and feel secure in sobriety. But you may have a sense that something is not quite right. You may not know what it is, but this feeling may cause you to feel depressed or anxious. These feelings probably relate to unresolved problems that did not come from your addiction but preceded it. These are issues that are usually best left until your sobriety is secure. But when the time is right, it is important to face and resolve them in order to continue growing in recovery.

Maintenance: The goal of maintenance is to live productively and enjoy life. In this period you are maintaining abstinence, you have completed the major tasks of recovery, and you have developed the competence to live productively. Chemical dependency, however, is a lifelong disease that is subject to relapse. Recovery can only be maintained by recognizing the lifelong need for a strong maintenance plan consisting of a daily program of ongoing recovery and personal growth. The tasks of the maintenance phase of recovery are

1. maintaining a program of recovery that helps you recognize the limitations imposed by your disease and be alert for relapse warning signs,

2. continuing to take personal inventory and when wrong promptly admitting it,

3. improving your conscious contact with God through prayer and meditation,

4. carrying the message of recovery to others,

5. coping with normal life problems and complications,

6. continuing to grow and develop in all areas of your life, and

7. coping with stuck points in recovery.

During this time you need to regularly review your progress with a counselor or sponsor and construct a network that makes it easy for you to get help if problems develop. The tasks of the maintenance period are tasks of caring for yourself just as you would care for the house you have carefully built. The house is complete; it is strong and sturdy. But it must be carefully maintained to keep it that way. You must regularly check the wiring, the fixtures, the roof, for wear or damage. And when you become aware of any damage, you must repair it right away to keep it from getting progressively worse.

Partial Recovery

Partial recovery is getting stuck in recovery and failing to complete the process.[3] It usually begins with a recovery task that seems insurmountable. Denial blocks the awareness that something is wrong and creates stress. Stress intensifies the pain of sobriety. The person may attempt to reduce stress and deal with pain by using a substitute addiction. The person begins to lose control of the recovery program. As this loss of control breaks into conscious awareness, the person reactivates the recovery program until he or she hits the same insurmountable task. A person may go through the same process over and over again, living always in partial recovery. At some point a person may fail to reactivate recovery and experience a relapse. Or he or she may choose to face the painful stuck point and continue in the recovery process.[4] A stuck point can occur at any point in the process. It can be total or partial, but for most people relapse is based in partial recovery. The Big Book of Alcoholic's Anonymous calls it "half measures." The key to full recovery is completing all the phases of recovery.

Points to Remember

1. The phases of recovery from chemical dependency are transition, stabilization, early recovery, middle recovery, late recovery, and maintenance.
2. There are recovery tasks for each phase of recovery.
3. During transition you learn from experience that you cannot use mind-altering chemicals without painful consequences.
4. Stabilization includes regaining control of thinking, emotions, judgment, and behavior.
5. During early recovery you develop a strong belief that you have the disease of chemical dependency by learning about the disease and how it has affected you.
6. During middle recovery you repair damage caused by your addiction and develop a balanced lifestyle.
7. During late recovery you overcome obstacles to healthy living that developed in your childhood.
8. During the maintenance stage you must maintain an ongoing recovery program that will enable you to live productively and to recognize relapse warning signs should they occur.
9. Partial recovery is failing to complete all the stages of recovery.

Notes

1. Terence T. Gorski, *The Relapse Recovery Grid* (Center City, Minnesota: Hazelden, 1989).
2. Terence T. Gorski, *Passages through Recovery: An Action Plan for Preventing Relapse* (Center City, Minnesota: Hazelden, 1989), 7.
3. Terence T. Gorski and Merlene Miller, *Staying Sober: A Guide for Relapse Prevention* (Independence, Missouri: Herald House/Independence Press, 1986), 93.
4. Gorski, *The Relapse Recovery Grid.*

CHAPTER 11

Symptoms of Acute Withdrawal

The choice to pursue a course of sobriety is the first step of recovery. But abstinence is not recovery, only the beginning. You did not become sick overnight, and you will not recover overnight. Recovery is a process that is experienced one day at a time.

Just as some symptoms of chemical dependency are triggered by consuming a mind-altering chemical, symptoms of the disease are triggered by abstinence. These sobriety-based symptoms emerge as a result of removing the chemicals from the body.

Withdrawal from chemicals has both immediate and long-term effects. Recovery from chemical dependency means detoxification or ridding the body of the toxin. Withdrawal also means recovery from neurological (brain and central nervous system) damage as well as organ (liver, heart, pancreas) damage. Knowing what to expect during recovery makes it more manageable.

Acute withdrawal symptoms are different for various types of drugs. It is impossible to describe in detail the withdrawal symptoms of a wide variety of drugs. Because alcohol withdrawal is by far the most frequent, we will describe it here and then give an

SLEEP DISTURBANCES

overview of the withdrawal symptoms of other drugs. Other sedative drugs produce withdrawal symptoms similar to alcohol.

When the blood alcohol level drops below a certain point, a person with chronic stage alcoholism experiences acute symptoms of withdrawal.[1] These symptoms are what cause people with alcoholism to drink again within a few hours of their last drink, eventually causing them to drink in the morning or even in the middle of the night. Unless they maintain certain blood alcohol levels, they experience withdrawal symptoms because the body has developed a need for alcohol.

If the person chooses to abstain or is unable to get alcohol, withdrawal symptoms may become severe and may last from one to ten days. There are two types of acute withdrawal symptoms. Type I has five stages. Stage one is marked by hyperactivity of the nervous system, which takes the form of the following symptoms: tremors, loss of appetite, sweating, nausea, vomiting, low stress tolerance, hyperactivity, confusion, poor memory.

The second stage is hallucinosis. Although persons know who they are and where they are, reality becomes distorted. There is the illusion that things are happening which are not. Objects may appear to move, noises may be heard, physical sensations may be experienced which, in reality, are not occurring. The person may be aware that things are not as they are perceived, but the strong illusion can create confusion, fear, and even panic.

The third stage is delirium and disorientation. At this point persons lose touch with reality and become confused as to where and even who they are. Hallucinations usually occur with the belief that they are real. The person is confused, excited, incoherent, and frightened.

The fourth stage is convulsive seizures. These are major seizures in which the eyes roll back, the body muscles contract, and the person loses consciousness. If the person is protected from injury, the seizures are not usually life threatening. Seizures are most likely to occur within forty-eight hours after the last drink, but can occur up to one week later.

The fifth and most serious stage of Type I is called delirium tremens (DT's). With good medical care DT's can usually be prevented. Symptoms of the other stages of withdrawal become severe: agitation and tremors, delusions and hallucinations. There is usually a fever along with fluid loss and physical exhaustion. DT's can be very serious, and death can occur. This stage of withdrawal always requires medical care.

The other type of acute withdrawal, Type II, is marked by internal anguish. Patients don't shake or vomit or hallucinate. They often report that they feel as though they are being torn apart inside, that they have a thousand butterflies inside, that their joints are vibrating, that they are about to explode. They want to scream, to run, to do something to get away. But they can't get away because the anguish is inside.

Hank never realized he was experiencing withdrawal when he went longer than usual between drinks. He just felt restless and jittery. He decided he had low blood sugar and that the sugar in alcoholic beverages helped him feel better. When he went into detox, he kept telling people he needed something sweet. But when he ate something sweet, he didn't feel any better. He wasn't having the symptoms that some of the other patients were having. He could hold a coffee cup with a steady hand. But he felt like he might explode. He thought if his hands were shaking he could do something to steady them. But what could he do to steady his insides?

If patients don't understand this type of withdrawal, they may think they are going crazy. They hide their feelings, and the feelings build up like a pressure cooker, sometimes exploding into violent activity. The violence is frightening for people experiencing it. They don't understand it. They feel guilty and upset. They fear it will happen again, and this increases the inner pain and anguish.

Withdrawal Symptoms of Other Drugs

It may be helpful to keep in mind that as a general rule symptoms of withdrawal from a drug will be the opposite of the primary effects of the drug. If you have been taking drugs that quiet the nervous system, then without these drugs you will feel agitated and stimulated. If you have been taking drugs that stimulate the nervous system, then without these drugs you will feel depressed and lethargic.

Symptoms of withdrawal from depressants (downers) such as sedatives, barbiturates, and tranquilizers usually include anxiety, agitation, tremors, nervousness, headaches, delirium, hallucinations, convulsions, and insomnia. Narcotics (pain-killers) such as heroin, codeine, and morphine create some of these same symptoms along with a hypersensitivity to pain.

Symptoms of withdrawal from stimulants (uppers) such as cocaine, amphetamines, nicotine, and caffeine can include lethargy, depression, tremors, confusion, and abnormal heart rates. Withdrawal from hallucinogens (mind benders) such as LSD and PCP and from cannabis (marijuana) is likely to include confusion, disorientation, flashbacks, and paranoia.

Withdrawal in General

Withdrawal can be serious and, without proper care, can result in death. When people with chemical dependency are admitted for detoxification, they are carefully observed. The main goals of hospital care during the acute phase of withdrawal are the prevention of complications and the assessment of damage in the body. These goals are accomplished in two ways: by medical management and by behavioral management.

The doctor usually orders medication to prevent the body from overreacting to the absence of the addictive substance. The medication used depends on the type of drug the person is addicted to. For alcohol and other sedative drugs, the medication used is a depressant that acts in a similar way to alcohol. The amount is gradually reduced to nothing. The doctor often prescribes vitamins that are needed by the nervous system for healing and which were destroyed by addictive using. The physician also orders tests such as cardiogram, X-rays, and blood analysis to rule out or confirm more serious body damage.

Most of the time the high anxiety, confusion, sleep disturbances, and memory problems that are part of withdrawal also require another kind of care called behavioral management. This mostly consists of individual attention, talking about the pain (physical and emotional), stress management exercises, and reassurance that what is happening is normal and will end soon.

The seriousness of any type of withdrawal should not be underestimated. The person suffers emotionally as well as physically from the experience and should not undergo withdrawal alone. Anyone suffering withdrawal symptoms needs support, and medical care should be sought if there is any question about the severity.

Points to Remember

1. In the chronic stage, the person with alcoholism must maintain a certain level of alcohol in the blood or will experience acute withdrawal symptoms.

2. The stages of Type I withdrawal are hyperactivity of the nervous system, hallucinosis, delirium and disorientation, seizures, and delirium tremens (DT's).

3. DT's can be very serious and always requires medical care.

4. Type II withdrawal is marked by internal anguish, a feeling of severe agitation that can result in violence if not managed.

5. Withdrawal symptoms will vary depending on the drug used, but as a general rule are the opposite of the primary effects of the drug.

6. All withdrawal symptoms should be taken seriously.

Notes

1. Jean Kinney and Gwen Leaton, *Loosening the Grip* (St. Louis: Mosby-Year Book, 1991), 147-150.

CHAPTER 12

Post Acute Withdrawal

After the symptoms of the acute withdrawal have subsided, the symptoms of post acute withdrawal (PAW) begin to emerge. Post acute withdrawal syndrome is a group of symptoms that persist into long-term recovery. For the person with alcoholism these symptoms surface seven to fourteen days into abstinence, after stabilization from acute withdrawal subsides.

Post acute withdrawal is a bio-psycho-social syndrome. The symptoms are caused by a combination of biological, psychological, and social factors. You may have inherited physical conditions that cause PAW symptoms. Or the symptoms may be a direct result of your addiction. The nervous system has been damaged by alcohol or drug use. Your body may have been damaged by lack of proper nutrition. Stress is also created by abstinence from chemicals when you give up an addiction-centered lifestyle. Post acute withdrawal affects thought processes, emotional processes, memory, and stress tolerance. Intelligence is not affected. It is as if the computer in the head is not functioning properly.

Recovery from the damage caused by the addiction requires abstinence, but the damage itself interferes with the ability to abstain. Because of this, everything possible must be done to control the effects of PAW while recovery is taking place. With

RECOVERY AS AN ACTIVE PROCESS OF
CONQUEST. . . . .

proper treatment and effective, sober living, it is possible to learn to live normally in spite of the impairments. But the adjustment does not occur rapidly. The symptoms of post acute withdrawal can be managed, but this takes time and some effort.

Here are some common symptoms that occur in sobriety.

Stimulus Augmentation

People with chemical dependency often find they are victims of a neurological condition called stimulus augmentation,[1] a heightened awareness of sounds, sights, or touch—whatever is going on in the environment. People with this condition have difficulty screening out background noises. This causes a tendency to overreact to stimulation such as sounds, lights, being touched, even to background noises like someone eating potato chips across the room. People with stimulus augmentation may feel pain more intensely than people without it.

If you have this condition you will have difficulty filtering out sounds and sights. You may feel bombarded and overwhelmed by visual and auditory sensations. You may overreact to them without understanding what has happened. You will also have difficulty concentrating because you will be distracted by your environment. Like the other PAW symptoms, stimulus augmentation is aggravated by higher stress levels.

In looking back on her recovery, Sue confided to her AA sponsor that after learning about stimulus augmentation she could see why her husband Don often became upset with her during some very important discussions. Her stress levels were high because of what they were discussing. Because Sue was overly aware of her environment, she oftentimes became distracted and couldn't concentrate on what Don was saying. Then he became upset and their discussion escalated into an argument. When they both understood stimulus augmentation and could compensate for this common symptom, they were able to communicate much more effectively.

Problems Thinking Clearly

There are several thought disorders a recovering person experiences when PAW is activated. While intelligence is not affected, the brain seems to periodically malfunction. Sometimes it functions well; sometimes it does not. This is confusing because you cannot predict when it will work all right and when it will not.

One of the most common symptoms is the inability to concentrate. This often results from the distractions created by stimulus augmentation. It is very difficult to concentrate when you are feeling overwhelmed by the environment and distracted by a variety of competing noises. Consequently, you may not hear something important that someone is telling you. It may be embarrassing to say you "weren't listening" and ask for it to be repeated. So you may let it go and create other problems for yourself because you did not get all the information.

Another common symptom is rigid and repetitive thinking. The same thoughts may go around and around in your head, and you are unable to break through this circular thinking to complete a logical train of thought. You are unable to put thoughts together in an orderly way. You may have trouble figuring things out step by step and have difficulty following a problem-solving process through to its completion.

Impairment of abstract reasoning is a common symptom of post acute withdrawal. This is the inability to deal with nonconcrete subjects such as love, commitment, death, and so on. An abstraction simply means something that you cannot hold in your hand, take a picture of, or put in a box.

Some recovering people have trouble with cause and effect relationships. They cannot recognize patterns that allow them to solve problems and use good judgment. You may have difficulty creating logical pictures in your mind. When you have problems, you may have a hard time figuring out what caused them and understanding the logical consequences of your behavior.

So what is it that happens to recovering persons experiencing thought process impairment because of post acute withdrawal symptoms? They have difficulty concentrating. They become preoccupied with a cycle of rigid, repetitive thinking. Even if they recognize this as a problem and can turn off those rigid, repetitive thoughts, they find they cannot complete a logical train of thought. They are unable to solve problems that might ordinarily seem quite simple. All of this can be distressing for the recovering person and can lead to the inability to function unless the person understands what is happening and has learned how to manage post acute withdrawal symptoms.

Memory Problems

Most memory problems occur because of the inability to concentrate. When you are distracted and unable to focus, you are more likely to forget what occurred. So you may forget to give Sally a message. Sometimes the information is there, but it is jumbled and confused. You may remember to give Sally the message but give it incorrectly. The problem may relate to the confusion you felt at the time the information was received. Information that is simple and straightforward is easily remembered, but complex or confusing information is more apt to be forgotten.

Sometimes short-term memory does not get translated into long-term memory. You may hear something and understand it; but forget it within twenty minutes. Someone may give an instruction and you know exactly what to do. But when you walk away that memory becomes clouded or may disappear completely. Even more frustrating, you may be told something, forget what it is, and then forget that you forgot. As a result, in your mind it never happened, and you begin to feel that something is seriously wrong with you. The harder you try to remember, the faster you forget.

Short-term memory impairment is activated by high stress, and we will talk about that later. Other memory problems in recovery may involve important events from your life, perhaps from childhood or possibly more recently. For an alcoholic named Dave this created a problem in AA.

"I have trouble presenting my story at AA," he said. "I have trouble remembering events that happened before my drinking days, let alone things that happened while I was drinking. So to put my life in story form is hard for me. I don't remember all of my story. I do remember that some things occurred, but I get confused about when they happened."

Because of memory problems in recovery, it may be difficult to learn new skills and information. You learn new skills by acquiring knowledge and building on what you have already learned. Memory problems make it difficult to build on your previous knowledge. Remember that reducing stress reduces the severity of memory problems.

Emotional Problems

Emotional overreaction is experienced by many recovering people. This is the tendency to blow up or exaggerate emotional responses beyond what is appropriate in a given situation. You may find yourself getting angry over what may later seem a trivial matter. You may feel more anxious or excited than you have reason to be.

Dan was a recovering alcoholic who was usually calm and easy to get along with. People often remarked about his gentle and easygoing manner. There were times, however, when Dan felt unable to control his emotional responses. He had three children, so it was often noisy in his house. "The noise," he said, "made me feel like a time bomb ready to explode. Sometimes I couldn't hold it in. I would slam doors or break things and then storm out of the house."

This upset Dan's family. His behavior was mystifying in light of the fact that they thought everything should be better since Dan quit drinking. Now they felt that must be the reason Dan was so upset. They were frightened by these outbursts, and his wife was angry

and hostile. Shortly after these occurrences Dan always felt re-
morseful, but the harm was done. He almost lost his family before
a counselor taught them about post acute withdrawal and helped
them learn management skills.

Emotional numbness is the opposite of overreaction. You do not
feel anything. You become numb. You do not recognize what you
feel. Even in situations in which you know you should feel anger
or love or remorse, you don't feel anything. Feelings and emotions
are shut off. You may know that you love your family, but you do
not experience that love emotionally. You may be in trouble and
not feel upset. Someone may yell at you, but you feel no anger.
You do not react because your brain is not allowing emotional
reactions to occur.

Carolyn was a recovering person attending a support group
made up of people with a variety of problems. She was the only
recovering drug-dependent person in the group. The other people
easily shared their feelings with each other and encouraged Caro-
lyn to do so. But she found it difficult to actually feel what she
thought she should be feeling. "I felt so empty," she said. "Other
people would get angry, or cry, or talk about how much they loved
their kids. But all I felt was numb. I tried to say the words sometimes,
but I didn't have the feelings behind the words."

Sometimes the other people pushed Carolyn to express the anger,
or fear, or joy that they were sure she must be feeling. This only
increased her confusion. She thought there was something wrong
with her. She dropped out of the group because she felt "different,"
thereby depriving herself of a much-needed source of support.

Sometimes strong feelings occur for no reason. You can experience an emotional reaction for no apparent reason. These emotional reactions develop with no stimulus, reason, or cause. You
may suddenly be overcome with depression or fear. Or you may
suddenly become anxious or agitated for no apparent reason. The
feelings are produced without external reasons.

Many people search for justification for what they feel: "If I am scared, there must be something scaring me. If I am angry, there must be something or someone making me mad. If I am depressed, there must be something terrible going on in my life." Many addicts create a crisis or problems to justify these feelings.

You can see, then, that mood swings are common in sobriety. You may overreact at one time, feel numb at another, or have emotional reactions you cannot explain. The mood swings may be the most confusing part of what happens because you do not know what to expect. If you do not recognize that these inappropriate feelings are caused by the sobriety-based symptoms of addictive disease you believe you are crazy or attempt to find justifications for your feelings by blaming other people or situations around you for "making you feel that way."

So people with emotional problems in sobriety tend to overreact. When things happen that require two units of emotional reaction, they react with ten. It is like holding the "times" key down on a calculator. When this overreaction puts more stress on the nervous system than it can handle, there is an emotional shutdown. If this happens, you become emotionally numb, unable to feel anything. And even when you know you should feel something, you do not. Or when you do experience emotions, they may be inappropriate for the situation. You may swing from one mood to another without knowing why.

PAW-Related Sleep Disorders

Many recovering people experience sleep problems.[2] Some are temporary; some lifelong. The most common problem in early recovery is unusual or disturbing dreams. These dreams may interfere with your ability to get the sleep you need. But they become less frequent and less severe as the length of abstinence increases.

Mike was a periodic drinker. Periods of sobriety usually lasted for several months. During the time he was not drinking, Mike had dreams that severely disrupted his sleep. His wife said, "I never realized the nightmares Mike was having had anything to do with drinking or not drinking. He would frequently jump out of bed, screaming in terror. When I was able to awaken him and calm him, he couldn't remember what he had dreamed, but he remembered being afraid. After a year of sobriety, he seldom had the dreams. Only then did I realize they were related to his drinking."

Even if you do not experience unusual dreams, you may have difficulty falling asleep or staying asleep. If so, you will probably feel sleepy during the day or always feel tired. You may not feel rested after a night's sleep. This may be because you do not get enough deep sleep. You may experience changes in your sleep patterns, sleeping for long periods at a time or sleeping at different times of the day. Even though some of these patterns may never return to "normal," most people can adjust to them without severe difficulty.

PAW-Related Psycho-Motor Disorder

A serious PAW problem—though perhaps not as common as the others—is difficulty with physical coordination. Common symptoms are dizziness, trouble with balance, problems with hand/eye coordination, and slow reflexes. These result in clumsiness and accident proneness. This is how the term "dry drunk" came into being. When alcoholics appeared drunk because of stumbling and clumsiness, but had not been drinking, they were said to be "dry drunk." They had the appearance of being intoxicated without drinking.

Stress

Difficulty in managing stress is the most confusing and aggravating part of post acute withdrawal. Recovering people often cannot distinguish between low-stress situations and high-stress situations. They may not recognize low levels of stress, and then overreact when they become aware of the stress they are experiencing. They may feel stressed in situations that ordinarily would not bother them. In addition, when they react they overreact. They may do things completely inappropriate for the situation and later on wonder why they reacted so strongly.

To complicate things further, all other symptoms of post acute withdrawal worsen during times of high stress. There is a direct relationship between elevated stress and the severity of PAW.[3] Each intensifies the other. The intensity of PAW creates stress, and stress aggravates PAW making it more severe. At times of low stress, the symptoms get better and may even go away. When you are well rested and relaxed, eating properly, and getting along well with people, you will probably appear to be fine. Your thoughts will be clear, your emotions appropriate, and your memory all right. At times of high stress, however, your brain may suddenly shut down. You may experience thinking problems, inappropriate emotions, memory problems, and intensified stress.

Thelma got a new job shortly after she began recovery. She was confident in her ability to learn the job and function in her new responsibilities. She did not have any trouble understanding what she was supposed to do when it was explained to her. But a short time later, when she attempted to do certain tasks by herself, Thelma could not remember how to do them. She was embarrassed to ask for more help because she thought she should be able to perform these simple tasks without help. Thelma frequently made mistakes when she tried to figure out what needed to be done. She started to feel anxious, and as her stress increased, her memory problems increased. In addition, she began having trouble concentrating when someone explained things to her. She got confused and her anxiety increased. "I couldn't figure out what was happening to me," Thelma complained. "I knew I had the ability to do the job. But the harder I tried, the worse it got. I was confused and upset and I didn't know where to go for help." After a number of serious problems developed, Thelma lost her job. She was bewildered about how this could have happened and began to think she was much less competent than she was.

Recovering people can learn to identify sources of stress and develop decision-making and problem-solving skills that will help them reduce stress. Proper diet, exercise, regular habits, and positive attitudes all play important parts in controlling PAW by stimulating the brain and the body to produce its natural pleasure chemicals. Relaxation can be used as a tool to retrain the brain to function properly and to reduce stress. Learning about the symptoms of post acute withdrawal, knowing what to expect, and not overreacting to the symptoms will increase the ability to function appropriately and effectively.

For this reason it is necessary to do everything possible to reduce the symptoms of PAW. When you understand and recognize the symptoms of PAW, you realize you are not going crazy. Because post acute withdrawal symptoms are stress sensitive, you need to learn methods of control when stress levels are low. Then you can prevent the symptoms or at least manage them when they do occur.

When their thoughts become chaotic and confused and when they find themselves unable to concentrate or to remember how they solved problems before, recovering people may believe they are losing their sanity. They are not. These experiences are a normal part of recovery and are reversible with abstinence and a recovery program. As your body and mind begin to heal and as you learn ways to reduce the risk of post acute withdrawal symptoms through lifestyle changes, productive and meaningful living is possible despite the very real possibility of recurring symptoms.

Points to Remember

1. Post acute withdrawal (PAW) emerges after the symptoms of acute withdrawal have subsided (seven to fourteen days into abstinence).

2. Post acute withdrawal symptoms include problems with thinking clearly, managing feelings and emotions, remembering, and managing stress.

3. Recovery from neurological impairment requires abstinence, but neurological impairment interferes with the ability to abstain.
4. There is a direct relationship between elevated stress and the severity of PAW. Each intensifies the other.
5. People recovering from chemical dependency can learn to manage PAW with proper diet, exercise, relaxation, and life management skills.
6. The symptoms of PAW will pass with continued sobriety.

Notes

1. M. Buchsbaum and A. Ludwig, "Effects of Sensory Input and Alcohol Administration on Visual Evoked Potentials in Normal Subjects and Alcoholics" in *Biological Effects of Alcohol*, H. Begleiter, ed. (New York: Plenum, 1980).
2. Jean Kinney and Gwen Leaton, *Loosening the Grip* (St. Louis: Mosby-Year Book, 1991), 140-144.
3. Terence T. Gorski and Joseph E. Troiani, *Self Regulation/Biofeedback and Alcoholism—An Applied Model* (Harvey, Illinois: Ingalls Memorial Hospital, 1978).

CHAPTER 13

Post Acute Withdrawal Episodes

Post acute withdrawal symptoms are not the same in everyone. They vary in severity, in how often they occur, and in how long they last. Some people experience certain symptoms; some people have other symptoms; some people, none at all.

Over a period of time PAW may get better, it may get worse, it may stay the same, or it may come and go.[1] The most common pattern of PAW gradually gets better until the symptoms disappear, and then it comes and goes.[2] If you know what to do and you are willing to do it, you can change your pattern of PAW so that episodes occur less and less often, and when they do occur they will be less of a problem for you.

The first step for most people is to bring PAW symptoms into remission—bring them under control so you are not experiencing them at the present time. Should the symptoms recur, the goal is to reduce how often they occur, how long they last, and how severe they become. You must remember that even when you are not experiencing symptoms there is always the tendency for them to recur. It is necessary to build resistance against them—an insurance policy that lowers your risk.

ANGER IS A LOT LIKE GUNPOWDER

The less you do to strengthen yourself against an episode of post acute withdrawal, the weaker your resistance becomes. It is like a tetanus shot. The longer it has been since you had one, the more at risk you are of becoming seriously ill if you cut yourself on a piece of rusty metal.

To reactivate PAW from remission, it takes a combination of a *high-risk lifestyle* and a *triggering event.* A high-risk lifestyle includes those things that you do or do not do over a period of time that lower your resistance. A triggering event is a situation that directly causes the PAW episode to occur. The triggering event is the straw that breaks the camel's back.

High-Risk Lifestyle

Conditions that put you in high risk of experiencing post acute withdrawal symptoms are usually lack of care of yourself and lack of attention to your recovery program.

Lack of Support Systems: Many people believe that as soon as their sobriety has stabilized they can make it by themselves. They do not see the need for professional counseling, therapy groups, or self-help groups. They do not maintain relationships that will allow regular contact with people who can help them stay aware of their recovery needs and help them look honestly at what they are doing and not doing that will produce unnecessary stress. Without continuous contact with people who are supportive of healthful and sober living it is very easy to begin fooling yourself into believing that you do not have an addictive disease, that you can handle whatever comes along, or that you do not need to do anything special to manage stress.

Poor Health Care Management: Problems with physical or psychological health make you more vulnerable to PAW. Improper diet, lack of exercise, and lack of sleep place your recovery in jeopardy. Poor health contributes to stress. You may be malnourished because of poor eating habits or because chemicals have damaged your digestive system so your body is unable to use the nutrients in your food.[3] Because of damage to the digestive system, many recovering people also experience hypoglycemia—low blood sugar.[4]

Hunger itself produces stress. Skipping meals or going for long periods without proper nutrition is never a good idea. But some foods that you may eat to avoid hunger may be stress-producing foods. You are placing yourself in high risk of experiencing a severe PAW episode if you

- do not eat regularly to prevent hunger,
- do not eat a well-balanced diet to repair and maintain your body, and
- consume stress-producing substances such as concentrated sweets and caffeine.

Lack of rest is also a condition to avoid in recovery. Fatigue is nature's warning that you are depleting vital body energy. If you do not respond to that warning by resting, you are putting a strain on your body and your emotions, that puts you in high risk. Remember that your body and mind are being repaired and they must have the proper rest to do that.

Exercise helps rebuild the body and keep it functioning properly while also reducing stress. Lack of proper exercise robs you of the natural pleasure chemicals in the brain. For the recovering person, lack of exercise is stress producing and a threat to sobriety.

High Stress Living: The inability to manage daily living creates high stress levels. If there are circumstances in your life that produce ongoing stress, you are in high risk of experiencing post acute withdrawal unless you learn how to relax and you practice relaxation skills regularly. The more stressful your lifestyle, the more risk you are in unless you do something to reduce the stress. You can learn to relax even in the midst of a stressful situation. Too many people, however, believe that the more stressful things become the faster, more urgently they must live. This greatly increases their risk of post acute withdrawal.

High Stress Personality Style: Some people have personalities that increase the risk of stressful living by the way they interact with other people. People who are extremely independent believe that they can't accept help from anyone. They believe they can make it by themselves and set expectations for themselves that they cannot fulfill. Other people have the belief that they cannot function independently. Such people do not recognize any personal strengths and rely on others to function. There are other people who appear to be extremely independent, but are actually deeply insecure. They act strong and confident while in reality feel weak and helpless.

To have a healthy recovery, you must recognize that you can function independently but that you need others for a balanced life. The Serenity Prayer offers excellent guidelines for reducing stress that is related to personality style: "God grant me the serenity to accept the things I cannot change, courage to change the things I can, and the wisdom to know the difference."

High stress results from expecting too much of yourself, or not enough. Or from expecting too much of other people, or not enough. It results from not using the strengths of others through cooperative relationships.

Lack of Spiritual Program: An empty life leads quickly back to a life centered on immediate gratification. An addiction is often thought of as a means of escape, a way to run away from pain or discomfort, but it is probably as often an attempt to *find* something. It is often an inadequate attempt to fill the emptiness. If removing addiction-centered activity is not accompanied by meaningful activity, abstinence is insecure.

Inner conflicts, self-doubts, guilt, fears, and anxieties place you in high risk. These can be resolved or reduced by a spiritual program and regular prayer and meditation. Unless you take time to be alone with yourself and with your higher power it is difficult to be at peace and to find serenity and meaning and purpose in living.

Triggering Events

A triggering event for the symptoms of post acute withdrawal can be anything that happens in your life that causes stress. Some of these stressful circumstances can be controlled and some cannot. A trigger may be physical pain, emotional pain, or a situation in day-to-day living. Some triggers are external, some are internal.

External triggers may be interaction with certain people or a troublesome situation you are involved in. It may be a family problem, a job situation, a financial crisis, a health problem, or a change in daily routine. Internal triggers may be the surfacing of painful memories, future projections, thoughts, or emotions. In early recovery you are more likely to be dealing with external triggers; in later recovery internal triggers are more apt to occur.

Of course, some stress is healthful. You cannot eliminate all stress from your life, even if you wanted to. But you need to be aware of stressful situations that can be triggering events. What types of events, situations, people, or memories might be triggers for you? You have to look at your own life—present and past—to determine what situations are stressful for you. You have to assess the everyday conditions of your life. Then you have to assess how you cope with those conditions. You also need to look within to see if there are some painful memories that you have not resolved that can become triggers.

If you are not taking care of yourself, if you are not managing high-risk lifestyle factors, a normal act of daily living can become the triggering event for a PAW episode. The lower the risk factors of your life the more fortified you are against stressful situations that may arise and the less likely they are to trigger PAW.

If you are taking care of yourself and managing your life in a low-risk way, you may be able to handle stressful circumstances without triggering PAW symptoms. Or if they do occur you can recognize them in time to bring them under control with proper self care. Sometimes you may choose to do those things that you know are triggers for you. After all, it would be a very dull life with no stress (boredom would probably become a trigger). But if you are careful and know how to manage the symptoms when they occur, you can live with some periodic episodes of post acute withdrawal without allowing them to get out of control.

With three years of sobriety Greg felt he was doing fine in recovery. And he was—until he got the flu. When he started feeling better physically, he began to feel quite stressed from having to stay in the house, being alone, and not being able to take care of regular responsibilities. Fortunately for Greg, he had learned about post acute withdrawal symptoms in treatment. He understood what was happening to him when he began to experience them. And he took immediate steps to relieve them and the stress triggering them. When he went back to work, he took special care to ease himself back into his routine and to protect himself from unnecessary stress until he was feeling back in control.

The more high-risk lifestyle factors there are in your life, the smaller the triggering event it will take to activate your symptoms. By lowering your lifestyle risk factors (immunizing yourself) you can handle major triggering events. One person may have a major PAW episode because the garage door gets stuck. Another may be able to handle a serious family crisis because of lower risk factors.

Because you cannot remove yourself from all stressful situations, you need to prepare yourself to handle them when they occur. It is not the situation that makes you go to pieces, it is your reaction to the situation.

Points to Remember

1. The symptoms of post acute withdrawal differ from person to person in how often they occur, how long they last, and how bad they are.

2. For most people the symptoms get better over time and then come and go.

127

3. By what you do, you can reduce the risk of experiencing post acute withdrawal symptoms or the severity of the symptoms if an episode does occur.
4. A high-risk lifestyle puts you in greater risk of experiencing an episode of post acute withdrawal.
5. Indications of a high-risk lifestyle are lack of support systems, poor health care, high stress living, high stress personality, and lack of a spiritual program.
6. A triggering event is a stressful occurrence that increases the risk of a post acute withdrawal episode.
7. A triggering event may be physical pain, emotional pain, or a situation in day-to-day living.
8. The more high-risk lifestyle conditions there are in your life, the smaller the triggering event it will take to set off your symptoms.
9. By lowering your lifestyle risk factors you can handle major triggering events without being in serious trouble.

Notes

1. Merlene Miller and Terence T. Gorski, *Lowering the Risk: A Self-Care Plan for Relapse Prevention* (Independence, Missouri: Herald House/Independence Press, 1991).
2. Terence T. Gorski and Merlene Miller, *Staying Sober: A Guide for Relapse Prevention* (Independence, Missouri: Herald House/Independence Press, 1986), 67-69.
3. Miller and Gorski, *Lowering the Risk.*
4. Katherine Ketcham and L. Ann Mueller, M.D., *Eating Right to Live Sober* (Seattle, Washington: Madrona Publishers, 1983), chapter 4.

CHAPTER 14

Grieving Your Losses

Part of acceptance is acknowledging that there are losses connected with your situation and allowing yourself to mourn. Choosing to recover is a first step that brings many changes: some big; some small.

Change, any change, means that something is different. Something (a habit or way of daily life) must be left behind and a new way learned. Even good change, desired change, means something is gone.

Your higher commitment to recover means that sometimes you must lose something you don't want to lose. This may be something you value. For example, you may value the friends you have, but it is in your best interest to change social habits to reduce the temptation to use. Changing social habits may mean that some of your friends will not understand and may not relate to you as they have in the past.

So, any major change or redirection in life creates losses. The feelings of deprivation you have in accepting what you can't change about your condition are normal. There really are things you have lost. You are deprived.

Accepting the truth of what you cannot change is allowing the losses to occur rather than trying to deter you from your chosen

Grieving our losses.

course. This means that you will leave behind some lifestyle activities and friends that may have been important to you. There really are things you have lost and will yet lose!

Understanding the experience you are having empowers you to choose again and again to continue in recovery. It prevents you from feeling like a victim. The information in this chapter is about the work of mourning. Mourning is adapting to loss.

It is sometimes helpful to think of mourning (or grieving) as something you do rather than something that happens to you or that you passively experience. Then you need not think of yourself as a victim, but a participant in a normal experience that results in healing acceptance.

The work of mourning has been divided into four basic tasks. This concept of mourning has been observed and reported by William Warden in his book, *Grief Counseling and Grief Therapy*.[1] Although we have numbered the tasks, they are not accomplished in any particular order. All four tasks are going on at the same time, and each task reinforces the others. Understanding the work of mourning will help you know how to help yourself and how to ask others to help you.

The first task we will talk about may seem self-evident, but often it is the hardest one to accomplish because we don't always identify what is going on as a loss. This is particularly true in losses that have been chosen. (If I chose the change, why am I grieving?)

Task 1: *Accepting the reality of the loss.* This means coming to realize that the loss has really occurred. The feeling of loss is not going to go away. There are many ways to help accomplish this task. It is important to name your losses so you can understand why you are in so much pain. Naming or discovering your losses is accomplished in many ways and blocked for many reasons. One really useful way to identify losses is to tell the story of the change.

Many people with major loss find themselves needing to talk about the experience over and over. This is a very natural part of making the loss real. Recognize that accepting the reality of what you have lost is part of the new life you have chosen. You are betting that the new life is better than what you are giving up. But to accept that, you must acknowledge what you are giving up. Make a list of what your new life is costing you. Balance what you will miss against what you will not miss. Talk about the losses. It is all right to say, "There are some losses here for me, and it hurts to give them up." As Macbeth said: "Give sorrow words; the grief that does not speak knits up the o'r wrought heart and bids it break."

Task 2: *Experiencing the pain of loss.* One major block to talking about the losses is a natural tendency to avoid pain. However, allowing the pain to occur is an essential step to acknowledging and even honoring what you have set aside. There is no way around, over, or under the pain. It has to be experienced. You have to walk through it. Instead of looking for ways to make the pain go away, it is important to acknowledge that you have lost your pain control (your drug) and allow yourself to feel the pain. There are many reasons why that is not easy to do.

In our society we generally see pain as proof that something is wrong, that there must be a problem, and, therefore, pain is something to get rid of. There is social pressure to avoid publicly admitting to having pain or suffering. Crying or experiencing painful feelings is considered a sign of weakness or self-pity. So we stuff the painful feelings away and try to pretend it doesn't really hurt. All in the name of trying to be strong.

Even as he said, "Yeah, everything is great," to his family, Sam felt confused, anxious, and uncertain. Fishing without beer was like breathing without oxygen. As Sam was able to share these feelings of vulnerability with his treatment support people and his sponsor, he was able to experience the pain of his losses without running from his feelings.

The mistaken belief that painful feelings should be hidden can lead to a decision to act like nothing is wrong and to try to pretend recovery is no big deal. You can see how risky this can be because it can lead to denial of feelings and denial of the need to care for yourself in your grief. Another way to look at the pain and suffering of recovery is to label it part of the normal cost of being alive.

To accomplish this essential task of the mourning process you have to let the pain exist. You may think that if you don't do something to make the pain go away, it will always be there, but that is not true. Much of pain is resistance. When you choose to stop resisting pain and let it happen, you are able to move through it. Being patient with yourself and allowing your pain to occur is not the same as wallowing in self-pity. Look at the pain you experience in recovery as a way of honoring the loss. Not everything in your past is bad or worthless. It is important to discover what in your life has been good so you can find new ways to experience the good.

How do you help yourself feel the pain? This is not easy for many people in recovery because they have learned to numb off and to distance themselves from feelings. First, understand that feelings are neutral; they are neither good nor bad. It is how you behave in expressing those feelings that can be helpful or harmful. You may be able to express feelings through telling your story to a trusted friend or your recovery partner, someone who is comfortable with feelings and will not block your tears or anger. Another way is to write in a private journal. There are many good methods of acknowledging your feelings. The important and most common block to overcome is the feeling of shame about having those feelings.

Task 3: *Adjusting to life without what you have lost.* Developing skills to live without what you have lost means adjusting to sobriety, learning to apply your recovery plan to your daily life, learning how to be comfortable at AA, and using your time in constructive ways. All the skills you are learning for living sober are important tasks in adjusting to life without what you have lost.

This gets easier as you do it, but it takes time. It takes energy and effort to make the adjustment, and for a while it is the focus of your life. During this time there are little unexpected losses. For instance, you may not have ever thought through the fact that now that you are watching your nutrition, meal preparation takes more thought and planning time. You need to pace yourself to deal with these new losses. Be good to yourself and remember to take one day at a time.

Someone once said that time is nature's way of keeping everything from happening at once. Lisa felt everything was. So many changes to make, so many activities and functions to fill her day. It seemed overwhelming. But gradually recovery activities began to be a normal part of her life. As she began to feel better, she began to value her new way of life.

Task 4: *Withdrawing emotional energy and reinvesting it in something new*. This is the time you take to detach from what you have lost and attach to something new. Reinvesting isn't about preventing yourself from going back to your old behaviors. It is about becoming fully involved in new ones—new ones that work better than the old ones. It is about letting go of the affection and even love for the old ways and finding a joyful way to live in the present. This is a time for turning your experience into an opportunity that will stretch you.

It seemed too much to face as Sam plodded along thinking of life without—without alcohol, without his old friends, without fishing, without his favorite places. However, with the help of friends and other people who desire a healthy lifestyle, he discovered a truth: There was a time to leave the losses behind and fix his sights on what he was gaining rather than losing. Yes, he had to recognize and accept his losses, but he also needed to focus on where he was going, on the opportunities now available that would eventually fill the void.

This reorienting of your life is an important part of the mourning process and of your recovery. Until you have done this you have not really given up your addiction and will still find yourself wanting it back. This is the part of grief work that allows you to release the sense of doing without and move to the appreciation of the abundance to come.

Acceptance comes from completing the tasks of grieving. Completion takes time, and time heals. But it is not just something you wait out. You participate in the process of acceptance as you complete the tasks of grieving.

Points to Remember

1. There are losses connected with change.
2. Recovery means change and, therefore, includes some losses.
3. Mourning is a process of adapting to loss.
4. There are four tasks of mourning: accepting the reality of the loss, experiencing the pain, adjusting to life without what has been lost, and reinvesting emotional energy in something new.

Thanks to Anne Welch, director of Hospice at Independence Regional Health Center in Independence, Missouri, for assistance with this chapter.

Notes

1. William Warden, *Grief Counseling and Grief Therapy: A Handbook for the Mental Health Practitioner*, 2nd edition (New York: Springer Publishing, 1991).

A MODEL FOR UNDERSTANDING STRESS

Developed By Terence T. Gorski M.A.

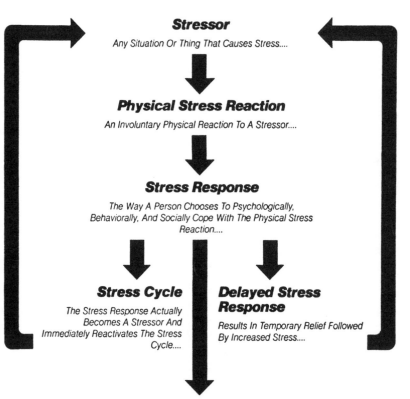

Stressor

Any Situation Or Thing That Causes Stress....

Physical Stress Reaction

An Involuntary Physical Reaction To A Stressor....

Stress Response

The Way A Person Chooses To Psychologically, Behaviorally, And Socially Cope With The Physical Stress Reaction....

Stress Cycle

The Stress Response Actually Becomes A Stressor And Immediately Reactivates The Stress Cycle....

Delayed Stress Response

Results In Temporary Relief Followed By Increased Stress....

Stress Reduction Response

Results In Pain Free Pleasure And Relaxation....

CHAPTER 15

Stress and Recovery

It is essential for every recovering person to recognize that there is a relationship between stress, post acute withdrawal, and relapse. There are many ways that your recovery is affected by stress and that stress in your life is affected by your disease. *People who have addictive disease are stress sensitive.* For some people this stress sensitivity is a physical preexisting condition that causes them to be more susceptible to an addiction. In other people the stress sensitivity is caused by the damage produced by the addiction. Whether your stress sensitivity preceded your addiction or resulted from it, you can be sure that it exists; and unless you take special measures to understand and manage stress, your control is in jeopardy.[1] Post acute withdrawal creates and intensifies stress, which intensifies the PAW. This creates a destructive cycle that can only be interrupted if you know how to manage and reduce stress.

Stressors: In your life there are many stressors. These are situations or events that cause you to react in a stressful way. Stressors may be noise, hurrying, your boss yelling, your children being sick, your grandmother's death, your car breaking down, losing your job, the phone ringing in the middle of the night, your son running away, stubbing your toe, losing your hair, moving, your daughter getting married, your dog dying, the alarm going off.

Some stressors are minor, others serious. What may be a stressor for me may not be a stressor for you. What may be a stressor at one time for you may not be at another time. What a stressor is depends on what you interpret as being threatening or anxiety producing as well as your perceived ability to cope with it. Is it a threat? Are you able to cope with it? Learning to recognize stressors and learning to cope with them is part of recovery.

For most people, change is stressful. Even if it is good change, it causes you to encounter that which is unfamiliar. The familiar is comfortable. Habits are difficult to change. Even when something new is exciting and stimulating it requires you to alter behavior. Recovery itself is a big change. You cannot recover without changing addictive-centered behaviors to behaviors that support sobriety. There are two rules of change in recovery: (1) avoid unnecessary change; (2) necessary change should be carefully planned.

Involuntary Stress Reactions: When stressors occur, your body reacts to them. This reaction is involuntary. You do not make a conscious decision to react. It just happens. This reaction is physical. You can feel it in your stomach or your head. Your muscles may become tight. Your respiratory rate increases. Your heart beats faster. Your body releases hormones and chemicals that change the way you feel. These reactions are preparing you to flee or fight. Your body will respond according to what you perceive as being threatening or anxiety producing.

Suppose you look down at your feet and you see a large, coiled rattlesnake. What is your reaction? Unless you are an unusual person, your heart rate will increase, your muscles will tighten, your breathing will speed up, adrenaline will flow, and your brain chemistry will change. But what happens if you look again and discover that the snake is not real? It is just a toy. You probably laugh in relief. Your muscles relax and the anxiety begins to decrease. The situation did not change, only your perception of the situation. Your body reacted to what you believed the situation to be, not what the situation really was.

What is or is not a stressor in your life depends on a great number of factors that determine how you see a situation. It is not how threatening the situation is that counts; it is how threatening it seems to you that counts.

Stress Responses: You respond to stressful physical feelings with a voluntary stress response. You may cry, laugh, yell, hit someone, slam the door, throw the alarm clock against the wall, walk away, smile, take a drink, call a friend, or choose to do nothing at all. Whatever you choose to do is your response.

Some ways of responding become new stressors. We call those *stress cycles*. If you hit your boss in the nose when he yells at you, your response becomes a new stressor. Choosing to respond in this way usually makes things worse rather than better.

One way of reacting that usually creates more stress is "stewing." You do not take any external action, but you continue to engage in internal behavior that magnifies the stress. You go over and over the situation in your mind. You lay awake at night thinking about it. You think about how you have been treated unfairly. Or you think about how embarrassed or stupid you were. You worry about what someone thinks about you or what someone might do. You do not take any action to change anything, but your stress increases and the worry itself creates new problems.

A *delayed stress response* is using some means to escape the stressor that causes the situation to become worse because of the delay. Most ways used to delay a stress response are potentially addictive. They enable you to escape the stress immediately but create pain in the long run. Using an addictive chemical will enable you to ignore the stressor or to escape from it. But the stressor does not go away, and the delay itself becomes a new stressor. Denial is usually a delayed stress response. You can reduce your stress by refusing to acknowledge that there is anything to be concerned about. But the situation is still there and will become worse because of the denial.

There are ways to respond that can reduce the stress. These are *stress reduction responses*. One way of reducing stress is to solve the problem that is the stressor. As you recover you should develop your problem-solving skills. Running away from problems may have been characteristic of your addiction, so facing problems and learning to solve them may be new to you. But it is eessential to your well-being.

Another way to reduce stress is to change your perception of the stressor. You can reduce your stress if you begin to see the situation that is a stressor for you in a way that is no longer threatening or anxiety producing. Here is an example. Imagine yourself in a traffic jam on a freeway. Traffic is stopped dead and you have no way to reach an exit. Are you getting restless, uptight, and anxious? Imagine yourself using that time as an opportunity for some quiet time. Think about how little time you have to be alone. Think how good it feels to be able to stop everything and not have someone interrupting your thoughts. Use the time for relaxation or to think creatively about an idea or a task you have been contemplating. Use the time to count your blessings or for prayer and meditation. Now does the situation seem so stressful? It is your perception of a situation that is stressful, not the situation itself. You can reduce stress by changing how you look at it.

Remember the Serenity Prayer: "God grant me the serenity to accept the things I cannot change, the courage to change the things I can, and the wisdom to know the difference." You can reduce stress by changing things. Or sometimes by accepting them and making the best of them. The key is learning to recognize which things are which.

There are natural stress reducers that you can use in your recovery. Some natural stress reducers are: daydreaming, laughing, playing, sex, exercise, storytelling, singing, and fantasizing. It is important to learn how to have fun and enjoy yourself. It will help you reduce stress *naturally*.

There are also relaxation techniques that you can learn that will reduce stress. Are you aware that your muscles cannot relax and be tense at the same time? You can *learn* to relax your muscles, and therefore reduce tension. You can also learn to form pictures in your mind that will help you relax. And you can learn to talk to yourself in a way that will reduce tension and increase your feelings of comfort and relaxation.

As you progress in recovery you can learn to use self-protective behavior to avoid unnecessary stressors. Putting your recovery first will help you make choices that will not only help you manage stress when it occurs but will help you *prevent* it from occurring. You can also learn to become aware of your involuntary stress reactions early so you can take action before serious problems develop. Recognizing stress responses that make things worse enables you to interrupt these responses with more helpful actions.

Some stress is necessary in life to keep you functioning. Otherwise, you would not take care of yourself or go to work or do anything for your family. But too much stress is harmful. Each of us has a level of stress at which we function best. Your best level is high enough to keep you productive and low enough not to hurt you or the people around you. Finding the level of stress that is useful without being destructive is important to your recovery. You can relapse because of too little stress (no constructive concern about your addiction), or because of too much stress.

Stress affects your body and your mind. It affects your thinking and feelings, your ability to remember, your sleep and daily functioning, and your physical and mental health. There is an alternative though. You can protect your recovery by developing stress management skills for a healthy, comfortable lifestyle.

Points to Remember

1. Because of stress sensitivity, recovering people must take special measures to understand and manage stress.

2. Stressors are situations or events that cause you to react in a stressful way.
3. Involuntary stress reactions are physical reactions to stressors (they are not chosen).
4. Stress responses are chosen responses to the involuntary reactions.
5. Ways of responding that create a new problem are called stress cycles.
6. "Stewing" over a stressful situation (going over and over it in your mind) usually increases the stress.
7. You can reduce stress by changing the situation, changing your perception of the situation, or learning to relax in spite of the situation.
8. You can prevent stress by avoiding unnecessary stressors.
9. Learning to recognize your stress reactions and self-defeating responses will enable you to interrupt them before serious problems occur.

Notes

1. Merlene Miller and Terence T. Gorski, *Lowering the Risk* (Independence, Missouri: Herald House/Independence Press, 1991).

CHAPTER 16

Situations that Complicate Recovery

From time to time certain conditions or situations can make recovery from chemical dependency more difficult. These conditions or situations must be dealt with directly, and special care must be taken to protect the recovering person from the consequences of them and from a return to drinking or drug use that might be triggered by them.

Coexisting Illness

Like anyone else, people with chemical dependency get sick. They may have acute illnesses such as colds or flu or they may have chronic illnesses resulting from chemical dependency or completely unrelated to chemical dependency. They may have diabetes, or arthritis, or perhaps an ulcer or mental illness. These conditions require treatment by someone trained in the treatment of that condition. But special care must be taken to protect against relapse into chemical dependency.

The coexisting illness may require medication. Yet any mind-altering drugs can lead back into addictive use. The first thing to do is to inform your physician that you are chemically dependent

WELL SIR, SINCE YOU DON'T HAVE A
DRINKING PROBLEM, YOU'RE JUST
NERVOUS, I'LL GIVE YOU SOME
VALIUM. THAT WILL CALM YOU
DOWN TILL THINGS IMPROVE....

and should not take any mind-altering drugs. Ask if there are any medications you can take that are not mood altering. If not, and medication is absolutely necessary, ask the physician to monitor the medication carefully with a time-limited supply. Inform your counselor or AA sponsor that you are taking the medication and ask their assistance in keeping it under control. If you experience withdrawal symptoms when you stop taking the drug, be sure you have special support until the symptoms are under control.

Chronic pain is a serious problem if you are chemically dependent. Chronic pain is a serious problem if you are *not* chemically dependent. But for the person with chemical dependency chronic pain creates special problems because of the stress that is produced by pain. If you have any condition that produces chronic pain—back problems, arthritis, migraines—it is our recommendation that you get special help. There are pain clinics where you can learn ways to manage pain—and the stress created by pain—without drugs. A person experiencing severe pain is often tempted to resort to the use of mind-altering chemicals for relief, but this will only prolong the problem and create other problems. Using chemicals is not a solution.

Polydrug Use

Another condition that complicates recovery is addiction to more than one drug. Addiction is a serious problem. The dangers of cross addiction and cross dependence are even more serious. When several drugs are used, the specific symptoms of chemical dependency are distorted. The combination of drugs changes or intensifies the reactions and creates unique symptoms of addiction, unique withdrawal symptoms, and unique sobriety-based symptoms. Cross addiction or multiple addictions complicate the recovery process.

If you are addicted to more than one drug, you need to have a special assessment to determine if any unique problems are present that will interfere with your recovery. And if those problems do exist, you may need specialized counseling from someone knowledgeable about the effects of the drugs on which you are dependent.

If illegal drugs have been used, the recovery process is further complicated by involvement in illegal activity. There may be criminal proceedings, incarceration, or legal problems that are not ordinarily encountered by the person addicted to alcohol or prescription drugs. In addition, special help may be needed to break away from a lifestyle that may have developed around illegal activity.

Substitute Addictions and Mind-altering Behaviors

People in recovery often use substitute addictions or mind-altering behaviors as a way to feel good or relieve pain after they have given up the substance that has been their primary source of pleasure or pain relief. Substitute chemical addictions may be using alcohol if you have given up cocaine, using marijuana if you have given up alcohol, using prescription drugs if you have given up street drugs. Recovery requires abstinence from all mind-altering chemicals. Switching from one drug to another is not sobriety. Beginning to use or increasing the intake of nicotine or caffeine is not helpful to sobriety and may be harmful to your health.

Your behavior has the power to change how you feel and to alter your moods. Changes in feeling and mood happen because these behaviors alter the brain's chemistry. Recent research indicates that mind-altering behaviors affect the brain in a way that is similar to the effect of alcohol and drugs.[1] There is much we do not know about chemical addiction and mind-altering behaviors. We are not sure in what ways they are alike and in what ways they are different. We *do* know that there are many similarities, especially in the reactions of the persons experiencing them.

The major difference between these behaviors and a chemical addiction is that an addiction to a chemical means you are putting a toxin directly into your brain. The chemical and the by-products of that chemical damage the brain and alter your brain chemistry, sometimes permanently. Behaviors can also alter brain chemistry, but even if used compulsively, are less damaging to the body and the brain than mind-altering chemicals.

While some people react obsessively and compulsively to alcohol or marijuana or cocaine, other people react obsessively and compulsively to their work habits, eating habits, or sexual habits. Or they may be obsessed with gambling or risk taking.

An abstinent alcoholic in long-term withdrawal will look for something to relieve pain and discomfort. Compulsive use of mind-altering behaviors may seem to be a perfect solution. The mind-altering behavior helps to manage the pain of long-term withdrawal but creates new pain as it becomes more and more compulsive.

If you are recovering from a chemical addiction and still act compulsively in other areas of your life, it does not mean that you are not in recovery from chemical dependence. But it does mean that you are going to have problems in your recovery that you would not have if you were abstinent from both drugs and mind-altering behaviors. The problems related to addiction-like behavior will make you uncomfortable in recovery and make it more difficult for you to function normally. And because the behavior provides a potential escape from pain and problems, you do not develop the problem-solving skills you need to deal with problems as a normal part of life. As a result, the compulsive use of a mind-altering behavior will increase your risk of relapse to chemicals.

Children of Alcoholics

Children raised in alcoholic families suffer long-term damage. The severity of damage will vary according to the age of the child when the alcoholism developed, the severity of the alcoholism, and the availability of healthy role models. People who are damaged by parental alcoholism are called Adult Children of Alcoholics (ACOAs).

Problems that have been observed in ACOAs include: poor self-esteem, depression, emotional detachment, aggression, irritability, guilt, poor coping skills, denial of feelings, lack of trust, hyperactivity.

It is estimated that 60 percent of all people treated for chemical dependency are ACOAs. Being raised in an alcoholic home does not cause chemical dependency, but ACOAs are at higher risk because of genetic factors.[2]

There is evidence that problems from childhood do not *cause* chemical dependency but can contribute to a more rapid progression, block early identification, interfere with the ability to respond to treatment, and increase the likelihood of relapse.

ACOA issues block early recognition of chemical dependency because children raised in alcoholic homes are used to so much dysfunction that they do not see their own chemical use as a problem. They have come to view high levels of emotional pain as normal, and chemical dependency must become severe before they recognize that something abnormal is going on. They have the concept that normal people use alcohol and drugs frequently and heavily. So when they use alcohol and other drugs they view their own dysfunctional behavior as normal.

Many children of chemically dependent parents have been abused and neglected. As a result, they are in chronic and severe psychological pain. They view this level of pain as normal. Chemical use brings temporary relief from the pain. People who have always been in severe pain when sober need to be severely dysfunctional before they recognize that chemical use is hurting them.

ACOA issues interfere with recovery because of the self-defeating behaviors learned in childhood. Children from dysfunctional families have trouble trusting and bonding with other people. The recovery process requires reliance on a source of help outside of self. In recovery ACOAs must learn a healthy dependence on other people, especially those supporting their recovery.

Therapy to resolve problems from childhood is necessary for recovery but is of limited value until a person has recognized chemical dependency as a primary condition, made a commitment to abstinence, and maintained a period of sobriety long enough to reduce the severity of post acute withdrawal.

People in recovery from chemical dependency who are also ACOAs may have a more difficult recovery because of the interrelationship between the two problems. Both issues must be addressed for full recovery. The full resolution of family-of-origin issues is possible for most chemically dependent ACOAs and will require one to three years of ongoing therapy. Resolution of these problems will provide greater comfort in sobriety, but there is no evidence their resolution will allow a return to social or recreational alcohol or drug use.

The question is always when to begin working on ACOA issues. Premature exploration can contribute to relapse. Failure to resolve these issues can lead to chronic distress in recovery. The general principle is to progress slowly from a primary focus on sobriety to a focus on ACOA issues.

Both short-term and long-term withdrawal symptoms interfere with the ability to think clearly and to respond appropriately to feelings. Stress intensifies these problems. Thinking about childhood problems causes stress levels to go up, thus aggravating post acute withdrawal symptoms. Therefore, symptoms of chemical dependency interfere with the ability to address ACOA issues, and stress from ACOA issues interferes with recovery from chemical dependency.

If you are a chemically dependent ACOA, care of yourself must include a strong focus on chemical dependency as the primary illness. Chemical dependency as a primary condition must have your full attention, to learn what you need to know and to make the necessary changes that sobriety demands. If attention is taken off recovery needs by focusing too soon on ACOA issues, recovery may be incomplete and the risk of relapse increased.

When ACOA issues are so severe that they interfere with the ability to maintain basic sobriety, they may need to be dealt with as soon as they pose an obstacle to recovery. In that case, the person should work closely with a counselor to protect sobriety while facing painful ACOA issues.

Situational Life Problems

From time to time there are major or minor crises in life that require special action to protect sobriety. Death, separation, financial problems, or family emergencies may be difficult, especially if alcohol or other drugs have been used as a way of coping at such times in the past. During these times you may need special counseling—grief counseling, family counseling, job counseling, premarital counseling—and special support to help you through the crisis and to help you maintain the structure of your recovery program.

A crisis that requires special attention is the accidental ingestion of alcohol or other drugs. You may unintentionally use a medication that contains alcohol or a sedative or a narcotic. Such ingestion can trigger a strong physical craving for alcohol or other drugs. Any time you use a mind-altering substance it will disrupt the recovery process. You should observe carefully the ingredients in everything you consume and you should seek assistance any time accidental ingestion occurs.

Points to Remember

1. Sometimes special problems require special care to protect sobriety.
2. Illness or pain can create stress that can jeopardize sobriety without special support and special ways of managing the problem.
3. Mind-altering medication should be avoided or, if absolutely essential, carefully monitored.

4. Cross addiction creates unique reactions, withdrawal symptoms, and sobriety-based symptoms.
5. Use of substitute chemicals or mind-altering behaviors for pain relief in sobriety can lead to new addictions or compulsions and increase the risk of relapse to the primary addiction.
6. People recovering from chemical dependency who are also children of alcoholics may have behaviors that interfere with recovery.
7. Resolution of ACOA issues is necessary for full recovery but should not be undertaken before sobriety is secure.
8. Any life crises or situational problems need special action to protect sobriety.

Notes

1. Joel Robertson, "Preventing Relapse and Transfer of Addiction: A Neuro-chemical Approach," *EAP Digest* (September/October 1988).
2. Terence T. Gorski, *Do Family of Origin Problems Cause Chemical Dependency? Exploring the Relationship Between Chemical Dependence and Codependence* (Independence, Missouri: Herald House/Independence Press, 1989).

LIFE IS WHAT HAPPENS TO US
WHILE WE'RE MAKING OTHER PLANS...

CHAPTER 17

Wisdom to Know the Difference

Wisdom for recovery lies in the words of the Serenity Prayer: *God grant me the serenity to accept the things I cannot change, courage to change things I can, and wisdom to know the difference.* Before you develop the serenity of acceptance or the courage to change, it is necessary to learn to tell the difference.

Learning about Chemical Dependency

Learning about chemical dependency and recovery will help you make responsible choices in relation to your condition. Numerous mistaken beliefs about chemical dependency can lead to trying to change what you are powerless over. When you learn that chemical dependency is a physical condition, you can give up trying to drink "responsibly" and *accept* your powerlessness over your body's reaction to mind-altering substances. When you learn that post acute withdrawal can be managed by reducing stress, you can take action to *change* some stressful situations in life. The more you learn about addiction the better able you will be to make responsible choices.

153

Chemical dependency is a self-managed condition. To manage it responsibly, ask questions, read books, learn all you can. Learn about the effects on your body and how you get well. Talk to your doctor, your counselor, and people who have been in recovery for a while. These people have information you need to tell the difference between what you can change and what you are powerless over.

Knowing Yourself

The wisdom to know the difference also lies in knowing yourself. AA/NA Step 4 says, "Made a searching and fearless moral inventory of ourselves."[1] This means being honest with yourself about yourself. The defense mechanisms used by people with chemical dependency that have enabled them to deny their chemical dependency have also enabled them to escape themselves, their thoughts, feelings, attitudes, values, and the reality of what they have become. Before they can determine what they can change and what they need to accept, they have to confront themselves, see themselves as they are, look squarely at their character, beliefs, and attitudes.

A searching and fearless inventory will be painful. You are going to uncover things you don't want to find. It is never pleasant to look at our weaknesses. But a thorough inventory also includes looking at your strengths. Surviving chemical dependency requires the development of strengths beyond those the ordinary person is required to use. The very strengths used to maintain chemical dependency can be used to maintain sobriety. But you must bring these survival skills with you into recovery and not discard them along with your chemical use. A searching and fearless inventory will enable you to separate your strengths from your weaknesses.

The first issue to look at is your denial itself. Are you being honest with yourself? Are you being honest with others? Or are you continuing to see things as you would like them to be? There are a variety of methods that people use to escape from the truth.

Denial is saying, *"No, it isn't so."* This is not lying; it is not deliberate. It is just refusing to face the facts. *"I am not addicted."* Or *"I do not resent the fact that I can never take another drink."*

Minimizing is making something less important than it is. *"I have a little problem but it isn't that bad."*

Avoidance is ignoring the problem and hoping it will go away.

Scapegoating is blaming others for our own faults. *"I don't have a problem; you do."*

Rationalization is a way of excusing ourselves with false reasons or by making comparisons. *"It's all right for me to go into bars now that I know I am an alcoholic. I will never drink again, no matter what."* Or *"Look at Joe if you really want to see irresponsibility. I'm in great shape."*

Compliance is agreeing to do something just to get someone to leave you alone (you don't really intend to do it).

Manipulation is getting others to do what you should do for yourself. *"If you don't do what I want you to, I will get high."*

Flight into health is blindly believing you are completely well and don't have to continue working on sobriety. *"Now that I understand my problem, I know I will never use again."*

You cannot make a searching and fearless moral inventory until you are able to be honest with yourself. With rigorous honesty you will become aware that some of your sober behavior—as well as your drinking behavior—is self-defeating or may hurt others. Without a willingness to be honest, these behaviors will continue to threaten sobriety. There will always be the attempt to feel better without thinking better or acting better. That makes drug use tempting because that's what drugs do. They allow you to feel better without changing your thinking or your behavior.

What areas of your life do you look at with a fourth step? Take what fits you, what seems most important for you to face. There is no particular set of questions that needs to be answered. There are guide books available. The *Hazelden Catalog*, from Hazelden Foundation of Minnesota, lists a number of guides for doing a fourth step. The "Big Book" of AA provides a guide for doing the fourth step. The National ACOA group in San Diego has a Twelve Step manual for ACOAs that goes into detail on how to do a fourth step. There are numerous approaches to doing it.

In considering what you need to look at, you might want to ask yourself some questions. Do you take responsibility for what is your responsibility? Do you allow others to be responsible for what is their responsibility? Are you considerate of others? Do you stand up for yourself when you need to? Are you accepting of imperfections in yourself and others? Do you see mistakes as opportunities to learn rather than as failure? Can you forgive others—and yourself?

In doing a "moral" inventory, the goal is to identify the "exact nature of our wrongs," not to make a list of every indiscretion ever committed. That's a confession, not a fourth step. It is important to write down the *nature* of the wrong not the specific details.

What is the character defect behind the behavior? It is not usually necessary or even possible to list each instance when, for example, you were being untruthful. The real issue is the character defect that results in lying. That's the nature of the wrong. Psychologists call character defects "personality problems." A character defect is a self-defeating way of thinking or behaving.

As you take inventory, remember to look for strengths as well as weaknesses. To help you do this, think first of things you like about yourself. Most people with chemical dependency find it harder to identify strengths than weaknesses. But you can overcome defects of character by using your strengths.

Just being honest with yourself is not enough. AA/NA Step 5 says, "Admitted to God, to ourselves, and to another human being the exact nature of our wrongs."[2] When feelings are kept inside, unexpressed, they are energized until they are acted upon. Admitting them makes them manageable, takes the power from them so they are more easily removed. In his book, *Life Together*, Dietrich

Bonhoeffer talks about the power of unexpressed feelings. Here is a paraphrased selection from the book:

The more isolated a person is, the more destructive will be the power of his wrongs over him, and the more deeply he becomes involved in them.... Wrongs want to remain unknown. They shun the light. In the darkness of the unexpressed they poison the whole being of a person.... They must be brought into light... openly spoken and acknowledged. It is a hard struggle until wrongs are admitted.[3]

It is self-defeating to keep what has been learned in a fourth step a secret. In AA they say, "We are only as sick as our secrets." Why? Because keeping a secret means living in isolation. Step 5 is the path out of isolation. It is this principle of admission that gives the statement "I am Mary and I am an alcoholic" its power.

Keep in mind that acknowledging character defects is not reciting a list of "sins." It is acknowledging the personality characteristics that lead you to do those things that are not in your best interest and that may be hurting others.

It may be terrifying to tell someone else your deepest thoughts and feelings and your most shameful behavior. You may fear humiliation or rejection. It is normal to have these fears. That's why it is important to choose someone you trust with whom to share your inventory, someone who will honor your confidence and treat it seriously.

Identifying Feelings

Step 4 and Step 5 mean being honest about your feelings as well as your behavior. The biggest problem most people have in identifying feelings is that they don't have words that describe their inner experience. There is something happening inside of them, but they don't have the words to tell it to someone else. There is a tool for finding words that can describe inner feelings. It is called a "feeling list."

Feeling List

angry	contrary	disgusted	happy	encouraged	joyful
warm	hostile	resentful	loving	friendly	irritated
caring	protected	frustrated	soft	concerned	interested
giving	impatient	revengeful	afraid	grateful	trusting
lonely	anxious	playful	strong	relaxed	sympathetic
proud	confident	independent	scared	overwhelmed	fulfilled
needy	hesitant	inadequate	sad	dependent	hopeful
weak	optimistic	responsible	wanted	envious	regretful
tender	inferior	discouraged	distant	isolated	contented
lonely	detached	amused	eager	depressed	despairing
aloof	excited	delighted	guilty	competent	pessimistic
pitying	grieving				

Life-Management Evaluation

To determine what needs to change in your life it is important to look at your *whole* life. A life-management evaluation takes a look at four basic areas of life: intimate/ family life; work life (career management); social life; and life skills.

Intimate/Family Life: This area applies to the people with whom you live in close day-to-day contact, people with whom you share residence or people with whom you spend significant amounts of time in informal living that is not work related.

Work/Career Life: This applies to people with whom you interact in meeting professional goals.

Social Life: These are people with whom you are involved in social activities but who are not part of your intimate or family life.

Life Skills: These are skills or activities you have to perform to keep your life functioning, tasks you need to accomplish to keep problems from arising in your life.

The idea of a life management evaluation is for you to review and evaluate your ability to function in each area. To do that, you need to ask yourself four questions about each aspect of every area.

1. Does it apply? Is this part of my life?
2. Am I pleased with it?
3. Is it impaired? Am I functioning well in this area?
4. How impaired is it? Mild (meaning I can manage it with effort)? Moderate (sometimes I can manage it with effort)? Severe (I cannot manage it)?

Now apply those questions to each category on the chart on pages 162-163. For example, apply them to your primary intimate relationship. First ask yourself if you have such a relationship. Are you pleased with the relationship? Is is functional? If not, how impaired is it?

How about your other relationships? What about your sex life? Are you pleased with it? Is it impaired? With effort can you function as you'd like (mild impairment)? Sometimes with effort (moderate)? Never (severe)?

Do you have children? Is your ability to function as a parent satisfactory? If not, how dysfunctional is it? How is your ability to manage finances? Your routine maintenance tasks? Are you satisfied with your recreational life? Do you know how to enjoy yourself?

The second section pertains to your work life. Are you presently employed? How is your relationship with superiors? Peers? Subordinates? Evaluate your job skills and performance, promotability, level of satisfaction in your job, security. Marketability refers to your ability to get another job. Is that limited because of your drinking history?

How functional is your social life? Do you and your spouse engage in social activities together? Do you have social activities as a family? Do you do things with people other than your immediate family? Do you do things by yourself? A hobby or fun activities?

How are your life skills in problem solving, time management, legal and financial management?

What Can You Control?

Many of the worries of our lives are needless concerns—matters that we can't do anything about. The following is reprinted from *Living With Stress*, published by Christopher News Notes:

Is concern over the past or future a major source of stress in your life? Consider the conclusion reached by a woman who came to the sudden realization that fears were ruining her peace of mind.

She took a pencil and made a tabulation of her worries, estimating as well as she could their nature and origin. These were her conclusions:

40% will never happen; anxiety is the result of a tired mind.

30% about old decisions which I cannot alter.

12%—other's criticism of me, most of it untrue.

10%—about my health, which gets worse as I worry.

8%—"legitimate" since life has some real problems to meet.

Adding it up, 92 percent of that woman's worries are unproductive. What would your worry balance sheet look like? You can control some areas of your life. And you can reduce stress in them.

As you look honestly at yourself—your lifestyle, feelings, disease, relationships, and beliefs—you will develop the wisdom to know the difference between what you can change and what you need the serenity to accept. Accepting what you cannot change empowers you to change what you can.

Because of her chemical dependency Diane lost her children and her driver's license. After treatment she was obsessed with getting her children back. She thought she couldn't get a job without a driver's license. And how could she get her kids without a job? She finally realized that no matter what she did she was not going to get a driver's license or custody of her children for two years. She accepted that. She got a job she could ride her bicycle to. The exercise helped her get in shape and improve her health. She rented a small apartment and fixed it up so she could have her children

160

with her on weekends. Developing the wisdom to tell the difference
helped her find the courage to change what was within her power
to change and the serenity to accept what she could not change.

Points to Remember

1. Before you can accept what you cannot change or change what you can, you have to learn to tell the difference.
2. Learning about chemical dependency will help you develop the wisdom to make responsible choices about recovery.
3. To develop the wisdom to "know the difference" it is important to look at yourself: your character, your strengths and weaknesses, your feelings, and your life-management skills.
4. AA/NA Step 4 enables you to look at yourself.
5. Step 5 allows you to share with someone else and God the results of your inventory.
6. Some people have trouble expressing feelings because they can't find the right words to describe their inner experience. A list of feeling words can help you if this is your problem.
7. A life-management evaluation can help you determine what areas of your life need care and attention.

Notes

1. *Twelve Steps and Twelve Traditions* (New York: Alcoholics Anonymous World Services, 1952), 42.
2. Ibid., 55.
3. Dietrich Bonhoeffer, *Life Together* (San Francisco: Harper & Row, 1954).

LIFE MANAGEMENT AREAS

	Does It Apply?		Am I Pleased With It?		Is It Impaired?		How Impaired Is It?			What was It Like Before Addiction?
	YES	NO	YES	NO	YES	NO	Mild	Mod-erate	Severe	
1. Intimate/ Family Life										
A. Relationship with Spouse										
B. Relationship with Immediate Family										
C. Relationship with Extended Family										
D. Sex Life										
E. Child Raising										
F. Financial Management										
G. Routine Maintenance										
H. Recreation										
2. Work Life (Career Management)										
A. Employment Status										
B. Relationship with Superiors										
C. Relationship with Peers										
D. Relationship with Subordinates										

	Does It Apply?		Am I Pleased With It?		Is It Impaired?		How Impaired Is It?			What was It Like Before Addiction?
	YES	NO	YES	NO	YES	NO	Mild	Moderate	Severe	
E. Technical Skills										
F. Job Performance										
G. Promotability										
H. Job Satisfaction										
I. Job Security										
J. Marketability										
3. Social Life										
A. Spouse										
B. Family Oriented										
C. Other Person Oriented										
D. Self- Oriented										
E. Activity Oriented										
4. Life Skills										
A. Problem Solving										
B. Planning										
C. Time Management										
D. Legal Management										
E. Financial										

PROBLEM SOLVING

DECISION   ACTION

CHAPTER 18

Courage to Change

With the process of recovery, there is the growing realization that with continued sobriety comes the freedom to choose. You are free to change your own behavior; mind-altering chemicals are no longer making your choices. With the freedom to choose comes responsibility. You are free to make responsible choices.

But you will find many things standing in the way of responsible behavior. Habits developed while using continue to plague you. Symptoms of post acute withdrawal may cause confusion and anxiety. Because of state dependent memory, you may have difficulty remembering how to use skills you learned and practiced while using chemicals. But if you do not exercise your right to make your own choices, the values of your old life or of other people are imposed on you. Making choices means taking risks. It takes courage to risk. It takes courage to change. You may make some mistakes along the way, but that's how you learn what works and what doesn't. Mistakes are not failure. They're just mistakes.

Responsible choices may require change to restructure your lifestyle and to develop responsible means of life management. The Serenity Prayer says, "God grant me the serenity to accept the things I cannot change, *courage to change the things I can*, and wisdom to know the difference." Responsible recovery means developing the courage to change the things you can.

Changing Yourself

In making a searching and fearless moral inventory and revealing the nature of your wrongs to another human being you have begun the process of looking honestly at yourself. AA/NA Steps 6 and 7 will help you make the changes that these steps have brought into your awareness. These steps say, "Were entirely ready to have God remove all these defects of character," and "Humbly asked him to remove our shortcomings."[1]

It takes courage to let go of old ways of thinking, feeling, and behaving. They are familiar; there is comfort in familiarity. Most of us have a tendency to say, "That's just how I am. I have always been that way"—as though that means we have to stay that way. Steps 6 and 7 tell us we can change. We don't have to be a certain way just because that is how we have always been.

Some people think that taking these steps means that all they have to do is turn everything over to their higher power to be fixed. Like the fellow who said he turned his bills over to God but God turned them over to a collection agency. The higher power provides insight into what needs to be changed and then gives courage to change it. But the leg work is up to us.

Turning character defects over to a higher power increases awareness of not only what we need to change but increases awareness that we do have the power to change. Nothing locks us into our character defects like the belief that we are powerless to change. One joy of recovery is recognizing the things you have the power to change that seemed hopeless before. It is important that you recognize that you always have a choice. If you have a list of things you "should" do, it may be helpful to change them to things you "can" do and remind yourself that you have a choice. Someone has said that if you only have one option you don't have any options. Look at your options and give yourself credit for your choices rather than feeling you are forced into certain actions because you "have no choice." You always have choices even when you don't know what they are.

You may recognize some things that need to change for some time before you learn what can be done about them. You may need some time to figure it out and to prepare yourself for doing it. Making these changes is a process. It doesn't happen suddenly. It occurs over a period of time. The recovering person takes one day at a time and is satisfied with progress. It cannot be overstated that recovery takes time. You can be reassured that it is taking place as you take the steps that make it possible.

Asking for Help to Change

Sometimes the courage to change lies in asking for help. This is not always easy. Sometimes we need the courage to say, "I know what needs to change, but I can't do it alone. Will you help me?" Sometimes it is a matter of saying, "I don't know *how* to do this. Will you show me?" No one can live exclusively by his or her own strength and intelligence. We need each other.

Many people are willing to accept help from others but don't know how to ask for what they need. They believe that others should know without being told. But we cannot expect others to read our minds. On an old Dick Van Dyke television show Laura says, "You just don't care." Rob asks, "About what?" And she replies, "If you don't know what you don't care about, I'm not going to tell you." It is not fair to others to interpret their lack of awareness of our needs as lack of caring. Have the courage to ask for what you need.

Changing Behavior

Many life-management skills have been lost during the period of chemical use. You may need to learn organizational skills to provide structure in your life. Structure is important in maintaining sobriety. You may need help in developing life-management skills.

Sometimes it is necessary to go to an expert to learn new skills. Perhaps you need help in financial management. Go to a financial adviser or to a friend who has those skills. Perhaps you need help in planning routine household maintenance or some family management.

Be patient with yourself in developing these skills. Try to keep it simple. Take things one at a time. A simple, uncluttered life is important. Regularity and routine may have disappeared from your life while you were drinking or taking other drugs. Just learning how to get yourself going and developing regular eating and sleeping habits—all new experiences without chemicals—may be all you can handle for a while. In AA or NA you will hear slogans like, "First things first," "Easy does it," "Keep it simple," and "One day at a time." This is helpful advice in learning to restructure your life.

Sometimes in these groups you hear people say, "Easy does it; but do it." This is good advice, too. Recovery doesn't just happen; you do have to do something. It is like walking up a down escalator. There is no such thing as standing still. You have to keep walking, or you will find yourself going backward.

Retraining

Impairments in thought and emotional processes are common in recovery. Retraining the impaired function may be possible through a sequence of progressively more difficult tasks that challenge the impaired part of the nervous system. Retraining means increasingly doing more tasks or work-up steps that will enable you either to rebuild the impaired area or to force an unused part of your brain to take over the function of the impaired part.

In some cases it becomes obvious that neurological damage cannot be repaired or the function transferred to another area. In this case retraining takes another form. Adaptation is a process of accomplishing the same thing by using other behaviors.

John's experience is an example of retraining through adaptation. He had impaired short-term memory. Although he could recall things immediately, the memory would dissolve within fifteen to twenty minutes. Through continued efforts at retraining with short-term memory exercises there was no significant improvement in his ability to remember. At this point he developed an adaptation technique using his ability to take notes, draw diagrams, and make sketches of key events, facts, and thoughts he wanted to remember. Notetaking helped him recall specific events that were important to him.

The person with chemical dependency suffering from state dependent memory may find that some knowledge and skills learned while using cannot be readily recalled in sobriety. However, skills that are learned state dependently are rapidly relearned through structured practice.

The primary method of structured practice of behavioral skills is called role-playing. In a role-play the person is asked to recreate in a safe place (in the controlled setting of a group or individual counseling session) the actual situations that demand the use of a skill he or she is attempting to relearn. The person is then observed while trying to relearn the skill and an appropriate sequence of work-up steps is developed.

The concept of work-ups comes from gymnastic training. The most difficult sequence of gymnastic moves can be learned if it is broken down into its basic movements and if each movement is practiced until the necessary strength and endurance are developed. All behavioral skills can be effectively relearned by breaking them down into small parts, practicing each part until it becomes habitual, and then assembling all the parts into the total action.

Even the most complex of life tasks can be broken down into the simple component steps necessary to get there. Skills training simply means breaking down skills into their simple components and systematically learning each component and then assembling them into a complex skill.

You can remember better when you are relaxed and when your mind is not on overload. Give yourself time and space. Try to remember one thing at a time. And give yourself a little extra time to remember things on demand. Say, "Give me a minute to think."

Try to avoid situations in which you have to remember something under pressure. If you can't avoid such situations, try to do something relaxing just before you need to remember. Anxiety is a block to memory.

Use memory tricks like, "Thirty days hath September." Write things down. Underline. Take notes. Have routines and habitual practices. Always keep items such as keys in the same place. Have a routine for getting out of your car and locking it. Create mental pictures and review them when you need to. Picture yourself in the place where you were when you heard something or used something. Visualize the page where you read something.

Avoid distractions when you are getting information you need to remember. It is impossible to remember what you didn't really absorb in the first place. Find a quiet, calm place to learn something new. Develop confidence that you can improve your memory. Fear of forgetting will block your ability to remember. Confidence will improve memory.

Prompt Problem Solving

A way to change difficult situations in your life is to learn some problem-solving skills that will help you handle these situations when they arise. A standard problem-solving process consists of the following steps:

Step 1: Problem Identification. First, identify what is causing the difficulty. What is the problem?

Step 2: Problem Clarification: Be specific and complete. Is this the real problem, or is there a more fundamental problem?

Step 3: Identification of Alternatives: What are your options in dealing with the problem? List them on paper so you can see them. Try to list at least five possible solutions. This will increase your chances of choosing the best solution and give you some alternatives if your first choice doesn't work.

Step 4: Projected Consequences of Each Alternative: What are the probable outcomes of each option? Ask yourself these three questions: What is the best possible thing that could happen if I choose this alternative? What is the worst possible thing that could happen? What is the most likely thing that will happen?

Step 5: Decision: Which option offers the best outcomes and seems to be the most reasonable choice for a solution? Make a decision based upon the alternatives you have.

Step 6: Action: Once you have decided on a solution to the problem, you need to plan how you will carry it out. A plan is a road map to achieve a goal. There are long-range goals and short-range goals. Long-range are achieved with short-range goals. One step at a time.

Step 7: Follow-up: Carry out your plan and evaluate how it is working. Revise it when you see that another plan would work better.

Self-protective Behavior

When all is said and done, you are responsible for protecting yourself from anything that threatens your sobriety. Reducing stress in your life and changing whatever you can that contributes to sobriety-based symptoms of addiction is of prime importance. You can learn new behaviors that can protect you from situations that put your sobriety in jeopardy. These behaviors can enable you to be firm in accepting your needs and not allowing other people or situations to push you into reactions that are not in the best interest of your recovery.

To protect yourself from unnecessary stress you must first identify your own stress triggers, those situations that might bring about an overreaction from you. Then learn to change those situations, avoid them, change your reactions, or learn to interrupt them before they get out of control.

Self-protective behavior means taking charge of potentially stressful situations, whether an isolated event or ongoing situations in your life. Perhaps it means choosing an alternative route to work to avoid rush-hour traffic. Or perhaps it means going in later and leaving later.

You may also change some of your activities, slow your pace of living. Eliminate some unnecessary activities or replace competitive ones with cooperative ones. It may be that competitive activities (handball, tennis) relieve stress for you. If so, you may want to add more of them. The point is to take charge of your own life. Make choices that will enhance recovery rather than jeopardize it.

Softening Your Environment

If you experience stimulus augmentation—the tendency to perceive everything around you more intensely—it is important for you to figure out what you can change in your environment to reduce the amount of stimulation you receive from the sights and sounds around you. Can you soundproof your home or workplace? Can you wear earplugs at times (especially to sleep)? Can you soften the lights in the places you spend the most time? How about using white noise? White noise is continuous sound (such as a fan or the sound of the ocean) that is soothing and helps cover disturbing noise such as traffic and sirens.

This is an example of the importance of asking for what you need from others. People who do not have stimulus augmentation do not know what it is like for you. They have no way of knowing unless you tell them directly. You may feel agitated when they eat potato chips in the same room with you. You may think they are inconsiderate. They may think you overreact to everything. To protect yourself from some of the sights and sounds that sometimes overwhelm you, explain to others what it is like for you. It is all right to ask for special consideration if you are also willing to make some concessions. If hearing someone eat potato chips bothers you, go to another room.

You may need to have a place you can go from time to time where you can hang a "Do Not Disturb" sign on the door. Make time for quiet activities. Go to the library, a church, a museum. Browse in a bookstore. Eliminate noisy, chaotic activities when you can. Speak softly and ask people to speak softly to you. Rid your life of clutter. Throw or give away items you don't use but that add to the perceived chaos around you. Turn off the radio or television. Make your surroundings as pleasant as possible.

When having a conversation, try to focus as directly as possible on the person you are talking to so as to avoid being distracted by other noise in the room. Also make it a practice to do one thing at a time. Avoid trying to read in a room where the television is on. Plan ahead for activities that may be noisy or chaotic and create ways to protect yourself as much as possible. Be considerate of others, but ask that they also be considerate of you.

Changing Habits

It is possible to break old self-defeating habits and to learn new productive habits that increase pleasure and serenity as well as enable you to better manage your life. However, breaking some of the habits connected with a lifestyle of drinking or using may be more difficult than you expect, simply because change is difficult. To change a habit requires becoming consciously aware of a behavior and choosing to do something different. Habits provide comfort because they are familiar. It is natural to revert to these behaviors without a deliberate effort to change them.

Tom had recently begun recovery. He was in a study group that regularly smoked marijuana. When he returned to the study group with six weeks of sobriety he was feeling no need to return to marijuana use. Yet when someone in the group lighted up and passed the joint, Tom had it in his mouth ready to inhale before he realized what he was doing. It was a habit that he had to consciously break.

To break habits it is necessary to unlearn the behaviors by replacing them with new ones. It is helpful if the new behaviors are enjoyable. Here are some suggestions for successfully changing a habit:

1. Find an enjoyable behavior to replace the undesirable one. Don't just try to "stop."

2. Practice the new behavior frequently as a method of "relearning."

3. Avoid risky situations in which you are more likely to revert to the old behavior.

4. Ask others for help and support.

5. Be realistic; give yourself sufficient time for relearning.

6. A mistake is not failure. Learn from your mistakes.

Remember you are in charge of your own life and responsible for your own recovery. You can change. And you are worth the effort. May you have the courage to change what you can.

Points to Remember

1. Recovery includes developing the courage to change the things you can.

2. AA/NA Steps 6 and 7 will help you change what you can with the help of a higher power.

3. Recovery may require learning or relearning skills to organize and restructure your life.

4. Sometimes courage lies in asking for help.

5. Retraining may help you overcome handicaps resulting from the symptoms of post acute withdrawal. It may enable you to rebuild areas of impairment, to force another part of the brain to take over functions of the impaired area, or to learn to adapt to the impairment by using other behaviors.

6. Skills that cannot be recalled because of state dependent memory can be rapidly relearned through structured practice, usually by role-play, practicing in a safe environment the skill you are attempting to relearn.

7. Developing skills in problem solving will enable you to handle difficult situations before they become stressful.

8. You can learn behavior that will protect you from an overre-action to stress that might put your sobriety in jeopardy.
9. To protect yourself from stress, you must first identify your own stress triggers and learn to avoid those situations, or interrupt those situations, before they become out of control.
10. If you experience stimulus augmentation, it is important to reduce the stimulation in your environment as much as you can.
11. To break habits it is necessary to replace them with new behaviors.

Notes

1. *Twelve Steps and Twelve Traditions* (New York: Alcoholics Anonymous World Services, 1952), 63 and 70.

REMOVING CHARACTER DEFECTS

CHAPTER 19

Serenity to Accept

God grant me the serenity to accept the things I cannot change....
If you are waiting for serenity to come as a result of conditions around you, you'll have a long wait. The world is far from ideal. It is our inner experience that determines how much serenity there is in our lives. We create our own serenity by our attitudes and our spiritual resources. Serenity is a choice.

You can fret about what you do not have the power to change—your heredity, the weather, what is past, what isn't here yet, other people. Or you can accept those things and reinvest that energy in that about which you can do something. Serenity is accepting what is and setting yourself free—joyfully—to experience the gift of life and the pleasures of sobriety.

Often it is not what is going on that is creating stress but your perception of what is going on. Learning to look at a situation differently can increase serenity even when there is nothing you can do to change it. Step back and refocus. Don't take things too seriously. A mistake doesn't mean you have failed. Focus on what you have learned that can help you in the future. Recall past successes to gain perspective.

Evaluate whether something is worth fighting for or about. Not every argument is worth trying to win. Some issues are not so critical in the long run. Stand up for values that are important. Learn to let go of lesser issues. Set yourself free from the anxiety of unrealistic expectations.

Choose your own goals rather than living as someone else expects you to. Live life at your own pace. You can't go full speed ahead all the time even when what you are doing is important.

Learn to live life one day at a time. Do one thing at a time. Concentrating on what is at hand, taking the next thing as it comes usually allows you to get more done with less anxiety.

Sometimes it helps you put your own situation in perspective to think of others or do something for someone else. Reaching out to others can take your focus off yourself and change your mood when you are down.

Serenity and Unpleasant Emotions

A person who is serene doesn't necessarily feel good all the time. Serenity does not mean you don't have any unpleasant feelings. It means you accept life as it is and do not expend excessive energy fighting against what you are powerless over. It does not mean that you do not get angry or afraid. Serenity means accepting and acknowledging *all* of your feelings. It is knowing that if you get angry you can handle it without hurting yourself or others. You can be serene and still be sad when your dog dies. Serenity is acceptance that your feelings are valid so you don't have to be ashamed or feel guilty about them.

Serenity is also knowing that what you feel and what you do about your feelings are not the same thing. You can be afraid and not run from what you are afraid of. You can be angry and not become violent. You can be sad and not give up on life. You can learn ways to express your feelings that are appropriate and heal-ing. You can be serene and cry at the same time. Having serenity means you are not a slave to your feelings. You can stop upsetting yourself about being human—a person who experiences pleasant and unpleasant feelings.

Self-Talk

We all talk to ourselves in our heads. We talk to ourselves in actual words and also in mental pictures. In fact, the person you talk to most is yourself. What you say to yourself affects your sense of well-being. You cannot experience serenity if you are giving yourself messages such as, "I can never succeed," "I'm afraid of what is going to happen," or "I can't trust anyone."

What you say to yourself affects reality. Suspicious people find proof of their suspicions all around them. People who expect others to be trustworthy find people they can trust.

You may think that you do not choose your thoughts, but you can learn to interrupt your self-defeating self-talk and replace it with messages that are constructive and encouraging. Instead of increasing anxiety, your self-talk can increase serenity.

First, learn to hear what you are telling yourself. Listen to your self-talk. When you hear yourself saying negative things, stop yourself. Ask yourself if what you are saying is really true or if you are perhaps making it true by your expectations. Then replace the message: "Oh, yes I can succeed. I already have quit drinking and made some positive changes in recovery." The point is, you can choose to think serene thoughts! Nothing increases energy and hope as much as hopeful and optimistic thoughts.

Living in the Moment

Perhaps the real secret of serenity is in living in the present— being present in the moment. There is little serenity in replaying what has already happened or waiting for some time in the future to enjoy life. If you are living for tomorrow you are missing out on today. Serenity increases as the experience of being present and comfortable in the moment increases.

"One day at a time" is a slogan learned in AA that is helpful in recovery because it teaches us to focus on the present. Sometimes it can be broken down to "one moment at a time." *Now* is all you have. The past is gone. You cannot change it. The future is not here yet. You cannot experience it. *The present is where life is lived.* Trying to live in the past or future robs you of the only life you have—the present.

Serenity in sobriety means learning to use your senses again, to become aware of your surroundings, to be mindful of what there is for your senses to experience right now. There is so much beauty in the world to see, hear, touch, smell, and taste. Using your senses to experience this beauty will enhance your appreciation of the world around you. Someone has said that we don't look *at* things as much as overlook them. During the course of your addiction your senses for the most part have been dulled into inactivity. They have been concealed by the chemistry provided by the drug. Now they need to come alive.

Awakening your senses can help you expand your awareness in your everyday life. This allows you to experience the serenity of the *present* and appreciation for the way things *are*. The experience of smelling a flower or chili cooking or a leather saddle, the sight of a blue sky or a puppy, the sound of children laughing can create a moment in time in which you are living *in* the moment rather than *for* the moment. This is serenity.

Relaxation

There are things you can do to reduce or escape the stress you feel when you cannot change a situation. These activities can also help you cope more effectively with the stressors of everyday living. Stress management consists of identifying stressors, responding in a way that does not create stress cycles, and learning to focus conscious attention on meaningful, pleasurable aspects of your life. Laughing, playing, listening to music, storytelling, fantasizing, reading, and massage are some methods of natural stress reduction. These are activities that help you be present in the moment.

Diversions allow you to relax by taking your mind off stressors and allow you to focus on the pleasure of the moment. Try body massage, a bubble bath, a walk by yourself or with a friend. Diversion is different from deep relaxation.

Deep relaxation is a way of relaxing the body and mind to reduce stress and produce a sense of well-being. Deep relaxation rebalances the body and reduces the production of stress hormones. What happens when you relax is the opposite of the "fight or flight" reaction. When you relax your muscles become heavy, your body temperature rises, and your breathing and heart rates slow down.

You can learn techniques to relax your body. The distress resulting from thought process impairments, emotional process impairments, memory impairments, and stress sensitivity can be reduced or relieved through proper use of relaxation.

To experience deep relaxation, create a quiet place for yourself. Separate yourself from the world in your quiet place. Lie on your back or sit in a comfortable chair with your feet on the floor. Close your eyes. Release distracting thoughts. Try to put background noises and sounds out of your thoughts. Breathe deeply and relax your body.

Actually, you do not make your body relax. You allow it to relax. You focus your concentration on one thing and allow distractions to drift from your awareness. With some relaxation methods, the focus is on the physical states you are trying to change—your muscles, body temperature, breathing, or heartbeat. With other methods you do not concentrate on your physical state, but on a color, a sound, or a mental picture or image. If you choose to focus on physical states begin with your muscles. Allow them to become heavy. Then concentrate on raising your temperature. You can do this by sensing a spot of heat in your forehead or chest and allowing it to flow throughout your body. Then think about your breathing. Let it become slower and slower. Breathe from your abdomen rather than your chest. Then feel your heartbeat and concentrate on slowing it down.

You can also relax by concentrating on something other than your physical body. Think of a color. Concentrate on that color.

Fill your mind with that color. Become a part of that color. Or feel yourself in motion—floating, tumbling, rolling. Get into a comfortable position, close your eyes, and repeat a pleasant word over and over to yourself. Or imagine yourself in a soothing environment such as beside a quiet lake or in a green meadow. These are all relaxation exercises you can do by yourself without the aid of a book or a tape.

You can also select a book that will offer you a variety of exercises from which to choose. Or you can purchase tape-recorded exercises.[1] Select a method that relaxes you and use it often. You will find it a helpful aid for reducing stress and creating peace of mind and serenity.

Here is a relaxation exercise you can do without a tape recorder:

Get comfortable and close your eyes. As you breathe in, say to yourself, "I am." As you breathe out say, "relaxed." Breathe in, "I am." Breathe out, "relaxed." "I am—relaxed. I am—relaxed. I am relaxed." As you practice this, allow your breathing to carry relaxation throughout your body. You can use this exercise whenever you feel the need for relaxation.

Another exercise you can do by yourself and without a tape is this:

Get comfortable and close your eyes. Select a word that is relaxing to you. It can be "flower," "peace," or "meadow" or just a word that has a pleasing sound to you. Repeat the word out loud a few times, whisper it a few times, then repeat it silently to yourself over and over again until you feel relaxed. If your mind wanders and you forget to say the word, that is all right. Just gently begin the word again when you become aware you have stopped saying it. After about twenty minutes, stop saying the word and gradually allow yourself to become fully alert.

A technique based on the passive repetition of phrases focuses on feelings of warmth and relaxation. The following phrases can be listened to and eventually repeated by you without the aid of another voice.

I feel quiet....I am beginning to feel quite relaxed....My ankles, my knees, and my hips feel heavy, relaxed, and comfortable....My solar plexus and the whole central portion of my body feel relaxed and quiet....My hands, my arms, and my shoulders feel heavy, relaxed, and comfortable...My neck, my jaws, and my forehead feel relaxed; they feel comfortable and smooth....My whole body feels quiet, heavy, comfortable, and relaxed....I am quite relaxed. My arms and hands are heavy and warm....I feel quite quiet....My whole body is relaxed, and my hands are warm and relaxed, my hands are warm, warmth is flowing into my hands, they are warm, warm....My hands are getting heavy and warm....My hands are getting warmer....My fingers are getting warmer....I can feel the blood flowing into my hands and fingers....I can feel the pulse in my fingers....My fingers are tingling with warmth....My fingers are growing and spreading out with warmth....My fingers are loose, limp, warm, and heavy.

This exercise uses emotionally cued words such as warmth, relaxed, heavy, and quiet that tend to trigger a flood of stored memories from the brain, which in turn are accompanied by pleasant feelings of relaxation. In addition, you can also imagine warm images such as floating on a rubber mattress on a quiet lake with the sun and breeze gently rocking and warming you.

Deep relaxation reduces your stress and helps you feel better. Relaxation exercises can help you manage post acute withdrawal symptoms. They can help you deal with some of the damage that alcohol or drugs have done to your body and mind. Some people do not practice relaxation techniques daily because they feel they are wasting time. Remember, it is important to the quality of your sobriety, or even sobriety itself, for you to take care of yourself. And that takes time. This will help you deal more effectively with the other important responsibilities of your life. You are important enough to spend time on yourself.

Breathing

There is a connection between breathing and your emotional state. Fear, anger, and frustration restrict breathing. Restricted breathing increases negative emotional states. Your sense of well-being can be enhanced by your breathing. When you calm your breath you calm your mind. Calming your breathing throughout the day brings a sense of peacefulness. The constitution of the blood is altered through oxygen exchange which, in turn, leads to more relaxed breathing. Try changing your outlook by changing your breathing. As you go through your day, start to notice how you breathe. Are you restricting it in any way? Breathe deeply and notice how much better you feel. Try the following breathing exercise:

1. While sitting or lying down, place your hands on your stomach and chest.

2. Sigh (audibly) several times.

3. Slowly and fully inhale through the mouth, filling the lungs comfortably from the bottom to the top. Imagine you are bringing energy into your body.

4. Without hesitation, allow the air to be exhaled through the nose, emptying the lungs from the top to the bottom in a comfortable manner. Visualize yourself releasing your tensions as you breathe out.

5. Repeat this procedure for ten to fifteen minutes, until you are totally and pleasantly absorbed with the breathing process and alert but not focusing on any other thoughts or processes. There will be a feeling of peace and serenity just in controlling your breathing process.

Points to Remember

1. We create serenity by our attitudes and spiritual resources.
2. Serenity is accepting that what is—is.

3. Serenity does not mean you don't have unpleasant feelings; it means accepting all your feelings.
4. The way you talk to yourself affects your sense of well-being.
5. Serenity increases as the experience of being present in the moment increases.
6. Diversions allow you to relax by allowing you to focus on the pleasure of the moment.
7. Deep relaxation is a way of relaxing the body and mind to produce a sense of well-being.

Notes

1. Tape: Relaxation By the Numbers, Independence Press, Independence, Missouri.

Now that I am sober, food really tastes better!

CHAPTER 20

Nutrition for Recovery

You have to have sobriety to be healthy, but you have to be healthy to have sobriety. Recovering and maintaining physical health is part of the total process of sobriety. Poor health contributes in many ways to difficulty in maintaining abstinence. Your eating habits have a lot to do with the level of stress you experience and your ability to manage the symptoms of post acute withdrawal. You may have substituted alcohol for food when you were drinking. Or you may have eaten properly, but your body was unable to use the nutrients that you consumed. Poor health contributes to stress, and malnutrition contributes to poor health.

Addictive living puts a great strain on your nervous system. Mind-altering chemicals have drastic effects on chemicals in the brain that influence mood. And so does lack of proper nutrition.[1] Deficits in these brain chemicals still exist with abstinence. It is not surprising, then, that so many recovering people experience depression, anxiety, and other emotional disorders.

Time will bring about some improvement, but abstinence alone is not sufficient to balance brain chemistry, rebuild damaged body tissue, and maintain good health. Improved eating habits should be established and practiced regularly and permanently. Your diet should contain a balance of vegetables, fruits, grains, proteins, fats, and milk products.[2] Ask a nutritionist to help you figure out how many calories you need each day and what quantities of each type of food you require.

You don't have to have extensive knowledge about nutrition to eat well, but some basic information will be helpful in making choices about nutrition that will improve sobriety.

Good Nutrition

Protein provides the body with the material it needs to grow, replace worn body tissue, fight infection, manufacture hormones and enzymes, and digest food. It is also a source of energy. Protein is made up of twenty-two amino acids, thirteen of which can be manufactured in the body. The other nine (essential amino acids) are supplied by what is eaten. If the diet lacks even one of these, muscle and tissue are lost. Another function of these essential amino acids is the production of brain chemicals (neurotransmitters) that affect mood and thought processes. The body stores very little protein, so it is important to eat it every day. About 8 or 9 percent of total calories should be complete protein (less than most people eat).

A complete protein contains all nine essential amino acids. Incomplete proteins lack one or more essential amino acids but can be combined for complete protein. Complete proteins are meat, fish, poultry, eggs, milk, and cheese. If you want to minimize these products in your diet (complete proteins are usually high in fat), you can combine incomplete protein foods to provide the essential amino acids. These are nuts and seeds, grains, certain vegetables, and legumes. You can also combine a small amount of a complete protein food with an incomplete protein: cereal and milk, chili made with meat and beans, pea soup with ham.

Carbohydrates are the body's major energy source and help the body use other nutrients. There are simple carbohydrates (sugars) and complex carbohydrates (starches, fruits, and vegetables). Complex carbohydrates are better for you than simple carbohydrates because sugars are empty calories. You get the calories without the vitamins and minerals. About 50 or 60 percent of your calorie intake should be carbohydrates and about 80 percent of those should be complex. It is nice to know that most carbohydrates are fat free.

Simple carbohydrates are candy, cookies, cake, pie, syrup, jelly, honey, sugared beverages (pop), sugar. Complex carbohydrates are fruits, vegetables, beans, peas, pasta, bread, cereal, rice, crackers, pretzels, popcorn, cornmeal.

Fat provides the most concentrated source of energy, supplies essential fatty acid, and enables the body to absorb vitamins A, D, E, and K. Only about 3 percent of total calorie intake needs to be essential fatty acids. Most people eat far more than this, much more than needed. You can eat more fat than other nutrients without feeling full. Fat contains more calories per gram than other foods, and it takes less energy to store fat calories than those that come from carbohydrates and proteins. So an excess of fat is harmful to your health. No more than 30 percent of your daily calories should be fat calories with the majority of these calories coming from unsaturated fats. If you want to lose weight you must consume even less fat.

Vitamins enable the body to use the protein, carbohydrate, and fat that fuel and maintain the body. A variety of food, particularly fruits and vegetables, is necessary to provide the body with essential vitamins. Too many of certain vitamins can be harmful, so be sure to use caution if using vitamin supplements. You should be aware that vitamin B12 (without which pernicious anemia develops) is available only in animal foods. However, many packaged foods such as cereal are fortified with this vitamin.

Minerals are necessary for the healthy development of bones and teeth, for carrying oxygen to body cells, and for muscle tone. They also help vitamins work efficiently. It should be noted that calcium—necessary for building and maintaining bones and teeth—is found primarily in dairy products, which are usually high in fat. In reducing the intake of dairy products to reduce fat be sure you are still getting adequate calcium (800 milligrams a day). Remember that you can eat low-fat dairy products (yogurt, skim milk) in order not to deprive your body of necessary calcium. You can also get calcium from green leafy vegetables such as broccoli and greens.

Water helps regulate body temperature, aids in digestion and elimination of waste, and is essential to the survival of all cells. You should drink six to eight glasses of water a day.

Fiber has no nutritive value, but it performs a useful role in digestion. Fiber contributes to good health and also is helpful in eliminating overeating. High fiber foods require more chewing, causing you to eat slower (slow eaters usually eat less). High fiber foods are also filling, causing you to eat less. (Too much fiber can be harmful by blocking the intestine, so don't go to extremes.) High fiber foods include whole grain breads, cereals, and pastas; brown rice; fruits and vegetables; legumes (beans, peas, soybeans, lentils); nuts and seeds. Refined grain products (such as white flour) are not high in fiber because the grain husk has been removed.

For additional nutritional information we recommend *The Tuft's University Guide to Total Nutrition* by Stanley Gershoff, with Catherine Whitney.[3] You should remember that the body—anyone's body—requires a balanced diet to provide needed energy to meet the demands put on it each day. As a recovering person, it is especially important for you to receive the proper nourishment to provide energy and reduce stress.

Nutrition for Reducing Stress

Hunger produces stress. Try to plan your eating schedule so you do not skip meals and so you can have periodic nutritious snacks. These snacks should provide energy without giving you excessive calories. Three meals and three nutritious snacks a day will stabilize your blood sugar throughout the day and keep you from feeling hungry. Snacks are an important way to combat fatigue and nervousness.

The body needs fuel to operate and needs to receive it early in the day. Eat breakfast. You will feel better, be more alert, and be more productive. Weakness and depression can result from lack of an energy source early in the day. Breakfast should be a good balance of the foods your body needs, but it need not be a conventional breakfast. If you don't want eggs or cereal, eat a baked potato or chicken casserole. We recommend fruit early in the day to give you a lift. You will have a better appetite if you do not drink coffee or smoke before breakfast.

You will probably find it beneficial to avoid foods that produce stress such as concentrated sweets and caffeine. Concentrated sweets such as candy, jelly, syrup, and sugar-sweetened soft drinks may give you a quick "pick up," but you may later experience a letdown accompanied by nervousness and restlessness. Have a nutritious snack before you feel hungry to prevent a craving for sweets.

Caffeine in coffee, tea, cola, and chocolate also causes nervousness and restlessness. Caffeine can easily become an addiction or a substitute addiction.[4] Caffeinism is characterized by irritability, headaches, nervousness, insomnia, or anxiety. It also contributes to the inability to effectively manage stress.

If you are drinking more than three cups of coffee (or its caffeine equivalent) per day, you are probably addicted. The caffeine itself causes stress, but you are also setting yourself up for the "short-term pleasure, long-term pain" created by any addiction. If you are addicted to caffeine, eliminate it entirely. Even if you are not addicted, keep your caffeine consumption to a minimum. Because recovering people are stress sensitive—they have a low tolerance for and overreaction to stress—they should be especially aware of those substances that have a tendency to increase feelings of fatigue, restlessness, and nervousness.

Make Eating Enjoyable

Nutritional recovery not only includes changing the foods you eat but also changing your eating behaviors. There are some guidelines for reducing stress that can make your eating time more enjoyable and beneficial. First, eat slowly. Your brain needs at least twenty minutes to know you have eaten. By eating slowly you not only allow for this to occur and for you to feel full but you also have time to relax while eating and can give yourself time to really enjoy your food. Next, don't eat and run. Instead, stick around after the meal to enjoy conversation or just relax. This allows for good digestion and also for relaxation. Plan your meals to allow for their enjoyment. Third, avoid noisy eating places. Since most recovering people struggle with stress sensitivity and stimulus augmentation, noise can be distracting and contribute to a stressful meal. It can be difficult to enjoy good conversation in the midst of noise. Plan for the right locations to eat, where noise levels are at a minimum. Finally, use your mealtime for friendly conversation, not problem solving. It can be tempting, especially in early recovery, to stretch problem solving throughout the day. Use meal times to converse and relax. Take advantage of the fact that in recovery your taste buds will come alive. Enjoy your food.

Weight

Many chemically addicted people are either overweight or underweight due to poor eating habits. Proper eating habits will probably correct an underweight problem fairly rapidly. A problem with obesity is not usually as easily corrected. A person can be overweight and still suffer from malnutrition. A weight reduction program should be undertaken carefully, with the help and advice of a physician.

Immediate weight loss in early sobriety may not be wise because of the stress related to dieting. This, along with the stress of adjusting to sobriety and a new lifestyle, may be more than you are ready to cope with. Talk to your doctor. It may be wise to establish and practice a good nutritional program along with making the other lifestyle adjustments necessary for recovery before thinking of losing weight.

When and if you decide to lose weight, do so sensibly. Beware of rapid weight loss diets. They can be harmful to your health and very stressful. Be satisfied with gradual loss. Continue to eat a balanced diet and avoid hunger. Increase your exercise as well as decreasing calories. It is the combination that makes for the most successful weight loss plan. A focus on good health rather than attaining a certain weight goal usually achieves the best results.

Remove All Mind-altering Substances

It should probably be stated that rebuilding the body cannot take place until alcohol and other mind-altering substances are totally removed. The alcoholic who substitutes pills or marijuana for booze, or the cocaine addict who switches to alcohol, will probably be substituting one addiction for another. Librium or Valium can trigger the same physical reaction as alcohol and produce the same consequences. The body is not free of harmful toxins if any mind-altering drugs are used.

The importance of good nutrition in recovery cannot be overstated. Physical health is important to your total well-being. Remember also that brain chemistry is affected by what you eat. Eat well to be well.

Points to Remember

1. Physical health is an important part of the total process of sobriety.
2. A balanced diet is necessary to rebuild a body damaged by alcohol, drugs, and malnutrition.
3. Nutritious snacks help sustain energy and combat fatigue and nervousness.
4. A nutritious breakfast provides a source of energy early in the day and helps prevent weakness and depression.
5. Concentrated sweets and caffeine cause nervousness and restlessness.

193

6. Nutrition for solid sobriety includes abstaining from mind-altering drugs.

This chapter has been reviewed for accuracy by Mary Muncrief, R.D., L.D., Diabetes Associates, Wichita, Kansas.

Notes

1. Joel Robertson, "Preventing Relapse and Transfer of Addiction: A Neurochemical Approach," *EAP Digest* (September/October 1988).
2. Stanley Gershoff, Ph.D., *The Tufts University Guide to Total Nutrition* (New York: Harper & Row, 1990).
3. Ibid.
4. John F. Blattner, *The Effects of Caffeine Consumption with Recovering Alcoholics and Its Relationship to Levels of Anxiety* (Santa Barbara, California: An Unpublished Doctoral Dissertation, Prepared for the Fielding Institute, 1985).

CHAPTER 21

Physical Exercise

Everyone needs a regular exercise program to be healthy and to feel good. The body that is not given sufficient exercise deteriorates. The heart, lungs, and circulatory system weaken; muscles lose tone; and the body generally becomes less efficient.

Recovering people especially need a good exercise program to rebuild the body, improve health, and also reduce stress and balance brain chemistry. Exercise produces chemicals in your brain that help you feel good. These chemicals are nature's own tranquilizers to relieve pain, reduce anxiety, and relieve tension.

Many recovering people have found exercise to be extremely helpful in freeing them from negative thinking and addictive attitudes. They have found it to be of value in reducing the intensity of post acute withdrawal symptoms. We know many recovering people who stop in the middle of their day's activities to exercise when they are feeling anxious or having difficulty concentrating . or remembering. After exercising they feel much better and are more productive (and easier to get along with). Researchers at the University of North Carolina—Greensboro found that aerobic exercise reduces alcoholics' depression and anxiety levels.

In *The Complete Book of Running*, James Fixx[1] tells about Kirt Freeman who worked with alcoholics. He noticed that they tend to

IN RESPONSE TO THE SUGGESTION THAT
RUNNING MIGHT BE HARD ON THE JOINTS,
ONE ALCOHOLIC REPLIED, ... IT IS, HARD
ON THE JOINTS THAT I NO LONGER FREQUENT.

lack any leisure activities other than drinking. One of his patients was a former high school sprinter who wanted to get back into shape. Freeman suggested he enter some track meets. He improved so rapidly that Freeman began urging other alcoholics to take up running and started an Annual Alcoholics Olympics in California. In response to the suggestion that running might be hard on the joints, one recovering alcoholic replied, "...it is, hard on the joints that I no longer frequent because it is more enjoyable to run six miles after work."

Here is what one recovering addict has to say about exercise:

Different forms of exercise have different payoffs for me. I have chosen these forms of exercise as strengthening contributions to my sobriety. Hiking or taking a long vigorous walk gives me "special time" to be completely alone with myself and my God, to meditate and to pray.

I find that movement of my body up hills and down inclines in the heart of nature allows me to think more clearly, often resolving issues or making short-range plans. I find that a walk enables me to break out of the dull stupor that daily routine can bring. Because I automatically feel good while walking, my awareness of my surroundings is also sharpened as if a newly discovered sense is emerging. I then begin to think in a more positive way about myself and my life. I feel more in control of my life. By the end of the walk I am ready to meet new challenges with a new sense of inner strength.

Racquetball or some "involvement sport" relaxes me in another way. It provides strenuous exercise with almost every muscle being used with complete awareness of my physical self. It feels good to reach out and slam the ball, providing a surge of power and energy and anger release.

Fellowship with my partner is also healthy and relaxing for me. Even though we are competing, it is all in fun. There is laughing, yelling, and just plain "letting go."

Swimming is my "special" activity. I know of no other recreation that allows me more feelings of surrender. When I let go and become part of the water, I seem to flow through it with my worries and tension dissolving. Exercise is a vital part of my sobriety program and improves the quality of my life.

As a recovering person, you should choose a form of exercise that is fun for you, something you enjoy doing. In the first place, if you don't enjoy it, you won't stick with it. But beyond that, you need fun in your life. Some activities that are satisfying to many people and will give you the physical exercise you need are walking, running, dancing, racquetball or handball, swimming, and tennis. Of course, there are many others, but these you can do alone or with one other person so you are not dependent on a number of other people to do them. Pick one you think you would especially enjoy, and set up a regular program to do it several times a week.

Different types of exercise are helpful for different reasons. Stretching and aerobic exercise will probably be most helpful for your recovery. Stretching exercises help to keep your body limber and to relieve muscle tension. Aerobic exercises are rhythmical and vigorous exercises for the large muscles. Aerobic exercises are intended to raise your heart rate to 75 percent of its maximum rate.

Aerobic Exercise

We recommend regular use of aerobic exercise. Brisk walking, jogging, swimming, jumping rope, and bicycling are common aerobic exercises. You might want to join an aerobic exercise class. Swimming laps is not only relaxing but is also considered to be one of the best all-around exercises for body toning and aerobic fitness. Dancing can also be aerobic, but remember it must be done vigorously. Aerobic exercise has many benefits to your health—your psychological health as well as your physical health. Here are some of the benefits:

1. Aerobic exercise stimulates the brain to release endorphins (chemicals that act as natural tranquilizers and pain relievers).

2. It relaxes you, reduces tension, and has a calming effect on the mind and body.

3. Aerobic exercise gives you energy and combats fatigue.

4. It strengthens your heart and lungs, improves circulation, lowers blood pressure, and lowers serum cholesterol. You are healthier and feel better.

5. Exercise helps you to better control your weight without dieting. It decreases appetite, raises the metabolism rate, and redistributes body weight.

6. You can improve your muscle tone, posture, and skin. Bones are strengthened and your body becomes more flexible.

7. You will sleep better.

8. You will develop a more profound sense of self-control and feel better about yourself and your life. Aerobic exercise contributes to a positive outlook and to making healthy lifestyle choices.

You should choose something that will allow you to achieve 60 to 80 percent of your maximum predicted heart rate. (But remember, if you are a beginner, increase the rate gradually.) To determine that rate, subtract your age from 225. For example, if you are 45, your maximum predicted heart rate is 180 (225 minus 45). Your beginning target is 60 percent of 180, or 108 minimum training rate, provided you are healthy enough to attempt to reach it. Do not attempt a training rate more than 70 percent in the beginning and do not go beyond 75 percent at any time unless you have a complete evaluation by a physician. Actually, before any exercise routine you should have a good physical examination.

Age	Minimum Rate	Maximum Rate
20	123	164
25	120	160
30	117	156
35	114	152
40	111	148
45	108	144

50	105	140
55	102	136
60	99	132
65	96	128

Walking

Research at the University of Massachusetts Medical School has found that walking can reduce tension and anxiety immediately. Walking is one of the most efficient forms of exercise and can be done safely throughout your life. It is also inexpensive and does not require special equipment other than good shoes. It offers the extra benefit of giving you time to reflect and organize your thoughts.

Walking can easily be incorporated into your daily activity. Maybe you can walk to work or to the bus stop, to the bank, post office, or to visit a friend. Try taking the stairs instead of an elevator. Walk around the airport while waiting for your plane.

You, of course, don't have to have a goal or destination for your walk. Sometimes you will want to set time aside for a walk around the block or in the park. You can enjoy the flowers and trees, people and houses. You can listen to music, compose a poem, or sort out your feelings or problems. Walking is good for creative thought, and you may find yourself coming up with all kinds of new ideas that never occurred to you in the hustle and bustle of your regular routine.

You may choose walking as a time to be alone. Or you may want to take someone along. It can be a time for pleasant conversation and for getting to know someone—perhaps a recovering friend. Walking in shopping malls has become such a popular pastime that there are now shopping mall walking clubs.

Stretching

Stretching exercises for warming up and cooling down will make your body more flexible. We recommend that you use stretching exercises throughout your day to relax muscles, reduce stiffness, and ease tension. There are many stretching exercises that you can do. We suggest you obtain a book that will instruct you how to do the appropriate exercises for the parts of your body that most need stretching.

It is especially helpful to relax the muscles of your neck and shoulders throughout the day. Many people store a lot of tension in this area. Raise both of your shoulders at the same time and slowly rotate them in a circle, backward and then forward. Then roll your head around several times in a full circle as you keep your back straight.

Another place that many people store tension is in the lower back. To strengthen and relax those muscles, lie on your back with knees bent and feet flat on the floor. Tighten your abdominal muscles, grip your buttocks together, and flatten your lower back against the floor. Repeat this several times. Then bring one leg toward your chest. Pull the leg to your chest with your hands. Slowly curl your head toward your bent knee and hold for a count of five. Repeat the exercise with the other leg. Then do the exercise with both legs simultaneously. If you do these exercises for a few minutes every day, you will prevent or reduce much strain in your lower back.

Easy Does It

After a physical examination it is important to start your exercise program slowly and work up to what your physician recommends. Remember, you have the rest of your life, a day at a time, to exercise. You have plenty of time, so make it a gradual process. Begin with modest goals and build gradually. If you have trouble breathing or get overly tired, cut back and build more slowly. You are usually the one who knows best what you can handle and how rapidly you can progress. The adage, "No pain no gain," does not apply! If it's painful, your body is no doubt rebelling because you are overdoing it. Overambitious starters often become quitters. It takes some discipline to make exercise a regular part of your life, but it should not be painful.

The most important thing about your exercise program is staying with it and doing it regularly. Most doctors and health experts will encourage you to exercise three or four times a week. But we recommend that recovering people exercise every day because of its value in reducing stress and raising brain chemistry. Any day that you do not exercise is a day that you are cheating yourself out of a way to feel more relaxed, be more productive, and have more energy.

Points to Remember

1. Everyone needs a regular exercise program to be healthy. Recovering people especially need a good exercise program to rebuild the body, reduce stress, and balance brain chemistry.
2. Exercise should be fun so you will stick with it.
3. Walking, jogging, swimming, jumping rope, dancing, and bicycling are common aerobic exercises that can improve recovery.
4. Stretching exercises can help you ease muscle tension when you are stressed or fatigued.
5. Begin an exercise program slowly and build up gradually.
6. It is important to exercise regularly and stay with it.

Notes

1. James F. Fixx, *The Complete Book of Running* (New York: Random House, 1977).

CHAPTER 22

Fun and Laughter

As you move into sobriety, probably one of the most essential ingredients to your sobriety will be the fun you make of sober living. Play is a necessary part of life and of recovery, and it is often neglected. In the past, fun has probably been associated with getting high. It now must come to include, one step at a time, all facets of life. Fun is not only a part of recovery; it is an essential ingredient of life. We all need time for having fun, laughing, being childlike and free. Learning to enjoy life naturally will take time and practice because in the past fun has occurred unnaturally through mind-altering chemicals. So it will take some time to convince yourself that you do have the ability to have fun, to enjoy and celebrate without altering your mood artificially. You have the ability to create pleasure in natural ways.

It is difficult to define play because it is not so much what we do as how we do it. Fun is usually perceived as something separate and apart from life. Fun is seen as the icing of life; as long as you get your work done you can then, and only then, have fun. We tend to think about fun in an either/or kind of way: you are working or you are having fun. Remember your school days when you studied for a part of the day and then went out for recess? You did what was important, namely work, and then you were rewarded with

play. So we have grown up with the notion that there is work over here and play over there, that it's unthinkable to mix the two together and have fun while working or learning. To get the most out of life—and this is what sobriety should be—it is important to begin in early recovery to have fun learning, laughing, loving, and working—to have fun living.

When one is using mind-altering chemicals, the brain learns to rely on the chemicals to feel good. Over a period of time as the addicted person uses more and more of a chemical, the brain shuts down its production of natural chemicals and becomes dependent on the mind-altering substance. So when the addicted person is not using the mind-altering substance, he or she is uncomfortable because his or her natural opiates are in short supply.

So a comfortable sobriety requires the use of alternative ways to stimulate production of the brain's natural "feel good" chemicals. Fun and laughter relate directly to the production of these natural chemicals. The reactivation of good brain chemistry should become a priority for any recovering person.

Norman Cousins in his book, *Anatomy of An Illness*[1] relates his experience of using laughter to overcome a chronic health condition that doctors had diagnosed as fatal. Research today indicates that laughter is directly related to overcoming serious illness by helping the body provide its own medications. Fun, humor, and laughter relate to the production of that chemistry that not only helps us feel better but directly relates to our healing.

Fun is first and foremost a change of attitude, reaction, and perception about yourself as you slow down and experience life in the present. This new perception, just as sobriety itself evolves, does not just happen. What has taken so long to develop as an addicted lifestyle does not just go away because you will it. It is like learning to walk all over again, but instead of walking past life you will walk into it. In other words, recovery is taking time to take time. Taking time to smell the flowers is not just a cliché but a lifestyle.

To gain some experience in "feeling good," it may be beneficial to schedule special times when you can step outside your routine and for a period of time just do something different. Fly a kite, go sailing, play a game, go to a movie, go shopping, browse through a book store, visit an art gallery, go fishing, go down a water slide, take a long walk, drive to one of those out-of-the way places to explore unique shops or landmarks, go to a baseball game, ride a roller coaster, go surfing, watch a Marx Brothers video, ride a jet ski, make a model airplane, paint a picture, catch a butterfly, take a walk with a child.

From time to time take breaks that add color, spontaneity, and some zaniness to life. Put on your favorite music, sing, dance around the room, let the child in you out. Have a water fight. Make yourself up like a clown. Get silly with the one you love. See what you can think of that is a little crazy and a lot of fun.

As you move back into your regular routine, you will be more refreshed, relaxed, and fit for whatever awaits you. As you move on with your sober life, you will become more adept at blending these times into your life and not think of them as separate.

Recovery is about replacing old, negative, stressful, and self-defeating lifestyles with new, creative, purposeful, successful, and fun lifestyles. Recovering people must always search out ways to alter brain chemistry naturally to feel good about themselves and other people. People in recovery can ill afford to live like so many other people—waiting for the weekend or counting the days until retirement.

Find people that you can have fun with, people that can let go and try new things. At one point in our lives the three authors of this book spent a great deal of time together. We not only worked together but had fun together. For a time one of us (Merlene) was so embarrassed by some of the crazy things that the other two (David and Terry) did that she tried to make them promise to behave before the three went out in public. Of course, the request fell on deaf ears. So she finally gave up and laughed at their craziness and even learned to share in the fun. It was not only beneficial for us individually, but we were more creative and productive together because we were friends and could laugh and have fun together.

Do you ever watch children having fun? They do not make a distinction between work and play. Play is their work. They play when they walk, talk, or when they are figuring out puzzles. They are constantly using their developing senses to explore as much as they can of this new world and, for the most part are happy with their exploration.

We can learn a lot from children about enjoying life. They can teach us things we have forgotten about being aware, spontaneous, and open to life. We can reclaim these childlike traits by living with the same eagerness to experience all that life has to offer. Recently we watched a home videotape of a child playing by the edge of a lake, captivated by the frogs, the mud, the little squigglies, and the nearby geese. He kept saying to the person with the camera, "Look at that big frog." Or "Help me with this fishing line." Getting no response, he finally looked up and said, "Would you put that thing down and come here?" What he meant was: *Stop taking a picture of life and come and experience it with me.*

You don't have to be a child or be with a child to do that. When did you get too old, too serious, or too busy to play? When did you stop noticing the frogs? When did you stop laughing at silly things? Someone has said that we don't stop playing because we grow old; we grow old because we stop playing. Life does not have to be dull and boring. Seek variety, be alive. Don't let society's messages to "act your age" or "grow up" or "stop being foolish" deprive you of the richness of life that play offers.

Celebrate with laughter. True enjoyment—as children demonstrate—is characterized by laughter. Laughter releases "feel good" brain chemicals and lightens our hearts. After we laugh we feel better, we think better, and we function better. Think of something that made you laugh so hard you cried or held your sides. Do you remember how good you felt for quite some time after?

You may be programmed to believe that playing is wasting time, that you need permission to play. Well, we give you permission. You must play for your health, your well-being, and your recovery. You will find that you accomplish more if you take time for play than if you neglect it.

Humor helps us adapt to change. Recovery requires a lot of change. Why not make it easier on yourself by seeing the humor and learning to laugh at yourself? Laughing at yourself allows you to give yourself permission to be imperfect. And when you can find humor in your own imperfections, it is easier to accept imperfections in others.

When we laugh, our perception shifts. We let go of feelings of judgment, blame and self-pity to embrace a more extended knowing of ourselves and others. Deliberately taking time to amuse and be amused allows us to sustain a great deal of change that would otherwise be overwhelming.[2]

Research also shows that laughter increases creativity and the ability to mentally organize information. If post acute withdrawal affects your ability to think clearly and to organize your thoughts, try a good laugh. Studies also show that humor, laughter, or mild elation enables people to remember, make decisions, and figure things out better. It seems this "feel good" stuff is just what a person with sobriety-based symptoms needs. Lighten up. Laugh a lot. It can only do you good.

Points to Remember

1. Laughter and fun are important aspects of recovery because it produces natural "feel good" chemicals in the brain.
2. Having fun requires learning to experience in the present.
3. You can learn a lot about having fun from children. They are aware, spontaneous, and focused on the present moment.

4. Laughter increases creativity and the ability to mentally organize information.
5. It also enables you to remember, make decisions, and figure things out better.
6. Fun helps you adapt to change.
7. People who experience post acute withdrawal symptoms need fun and laughter to help them manage the symptoms.

Notes

1. Norman Cousins, *Anatomy of An Illness* (New York: W. W. Norton & Co., 1979).
2. Jeanne Segal, *Feeling Great* (Van Nuys, California: Newcastle Company, 1981), 68.

CHAPTER 23

Rebuilding Relationships

Social recovery occurs as a person reorients his or her lifestyle around values that are not centered around using drugs. It involves a resolution of family, work, and social problems that were created by active chemical dependency. It also involves the development of new and more meaningful social networks.

Mending relationships broken by addictive behavior is a necessary part of recovery. Family problems, work problems, problems with friends and social acquaintances have arisen because of active chemical dependency. These problems do not just go away because you are no longer drinking or using. They must be resolved. The resolution of problems that were created by active chemical use begins by acknowledging that harm was done during that period.

Making Amends

AA/NA Step 8 says, "Made a list of all persons we had harmed and became willing to make amends to them all."[1] This may be an uncomfortable task. During your days of chemical use you developed the "ability" to excuse your behavior and blame others for problems caused by your behavior. It will be a new experience for you to look at how your behavior has caused pain for others and not allow excuses and blaming to interfere. It requires the same rigorous honesty that listing your character defects did to look at the past and acknowledge what harm has been done.

Are there friends to whom you have broken your word, friends that once depended on you? Have you caused your family anguish and fear because they love you? Have you embarrassed your children in front of their friends or let them down when they needed you? Have you broken your spouse's heart over and over again? Have you disappointed your parents? Cost your family money? Caused problems for people you work with? Have you physically abused anyone? Or destroyed or damaged someone's property? Acknowledging that you are responsible for these hurts is the first step in doing something about them.

It may be helpful in making your list to make three columns. In the first, list the people you have harmed. In the second, state clearly what you did that harmed them. In the third column, write down what you think needs to be done to make amends to that person. A willingness to make amends doesn't just mean saying you are sorry. It means being willing to fix what has been broken. It means acknowledging the harm that has been done and finding out what can be done to make it right.

The next step, Step 9, suggests that you make amends wherever possible (except when to do so would injure them or others).[2] Making amends removes guilt, rebuilds relationships, reduces pain. Making amends means taking the necessary steps to fix what has been damaged or to repay what has been taken. It involves saying, "I'm chemically dependent. My life has been out of control, and I have done things that I know have hurt you. I did these things because of my drug or alcohol problem, but I am still responsible. Now that I'm sober, I want to do what I can to make amends. So here is payment for the property I damaged. I know I cannot undo the emotional harm I caused, but I want you to know that I am sorry. Is there anything else I can do to make things right?"

It is important to evaluate the consequences of making amends. There will be cases when you cannot make amends openly because someone might be hurt by what would be revealed. But you can sometimes let someone know by your actions that you are sorry. Or you can do something quietly that touches their lives.

There are some things you can never make amends for, some debts you can never repay. Perhaps all that is necessary is to say you are sorry. Apologies as well as deeds can heal relationships. Some relationships will not be mended overnight, and it will take time for others to see that there really is a change in you that they can depend on.

Going to people to make amends opens up the possibility that you can be hurt. There are no guarantees that your apology and your attempt to make amends will be accepted. Remember that your primary objective is not to be forgiven but to try to the best of your ability to repair the damage that has been done. Others have the right to accept or reject what you attempt to do as well as the right to choose whether or not to forgive you.

Taking this step may be painful, but the goal of recovery is not to avoid pain. That was the goal of using mind-altering chemicals. Recovery requires rigorous honesty and responsible action—not always synonymous with pain-free living. Because of the possibility of having to deal with some painful situations—and because in the past you have probably used chemicals to avoid pain—it is important to do whatever is necessary to protect your sobriety while you are making amends to others. Rely on the supportive people around you and take special care of yourself.

It may seem that just forgetting about the past and going on from where you are would be less painful and less risky than making amends. But buried guilt will be more painful in the long run. Making amends is a freeing process. It releases you to leave the past, to let go of guilt, and to build new and better relationships with others.

Forgiveness

Forgiveness is a necessary part of resolving problems and healing relationships damaged by using. Destructive patterns of behavior established during active chemical use—blaming, rejection, anger, shame, guilt—need to be interrupted before new patterns can develop. Forgiveness is the tool of interruption. Forgiveness is a choice. It is the choice to let go of yesterday and focus on today. It may help you let go of some of your negative feelings to think of forgiveness as releasing expectations of perfection in others and in self.

Forgiveness is not only important for rebuilding relationships; it is also important to your own well-being. Unresolved anger and resentment intensifies over time until it can destroy you. The answer is forgiveness. You can't forgive yourself until you forgive others, and you can't forgive others until you forgive yourself.

Sometimes forgiveness is something that happens inside of you and may not require interaction with another person. You may resolve anger and resentment by writing a letter you do not mail expressing your feelings. It may help you to let go of the past to tell the person how you felt at the time the problems developed between you, and then how you feel now. It may bring healing to express how you feel about them and to express your desire to forgive them for their part in the situation. Writing down your feelings may help you recognize that we all make mistakes and that you may have contributed to the painful situation between you. Expressing how you feel may help you recognize that you are now strong enough to let go of painful mistakes on both sides and rebuild the relationship.

Communication

Rebuilding relationships involves learning new ways of relating and interacting with others even after you have made amends. Many social skills must be relearned. Many of your social skills were probably learned while drinking or using. It may be difficult to use these skills while sober. Other social skills have not been used for a long time because of isolation during active using. Communication must be reestablished.

Communication is a skill that is learned by practice. It is not a gift that some people are born with and others not. It can be taught and it can be learned, and it can be improved upon with practice. Rebuilding relationships is impossible without good communication skills. The following section on communication is taken from *Skill Development Program, Skill Building Manual for Students* by Ward Weldon, Julius Menacker, and Emanuel Hurwitz.

Communication is the ability to express your thoughts and feelings clearly and accurately to another and to receive the thoughts and feelings of another with understanding. We see good communication when the speakers reach a conclusion satisfactory to both of them—when they end feeling that they have really understood one another, or when they end just feeling good about having been able to say something that they wanted to say to another person.

Communication is never one way; it must be at least two way. Therefore, speakers who only think about their own feelings and their own ideas when they are in a conversation are not really communicating—they are only verbalizing.

Those people who are good communicators have such characteristics as the following:

1. They are good listeners. It is often true that the main ingredient in good communication is careful listening.

2. They help those speaking to them to be complete and accurate by giving them verbal and nonverbal encouragement while listening.

3. They do not dominate the discussion. There is sensitivity to the other person or persons in the conversation.

4. They give total attention to what is being said, rather than thinking about how they will answer what is being said.

5. They express themselves in ways meant to send meaning accurately to the others in a conversation, rather than to impress listeners with how smart they are.

6. They are sensitive to how much talking is needed to communicate well. They do not overtalk a point because they know this may cause listeners to lose interest.

7. They know how to stress the main points they want to communicate by the verbal and nonverbal emphasis they give to certain words or sentences.

8. They are open and honest in what they say but are also sensitive to the feelings of others in the conversation. They know that an angry listener is a poor listener.

9. They know they must be understood if they are to communicate effectively. Therefore, they are careful to speak clearly and in words that will be understood by the listener.

10. They try to identify feelings as well as thoughts of others in the conversations, and they make sure to check their interpretations for accuracy with others in the conversation.

Here are some ingredients of good communication that can be learned:

Affirmation: Looking for good in someone, focusing on the good, telling that person what you appreciate.

Active Listening: Listening is a choice. Active listening is listening fully to what someone is saying and not interrupting and not jumping to a conclusion of what that person is trying to say before you have let them say it. Sometimes it is listening just to understand what the other person is feeling without trying to fix things. It may be that he or she just needs someone to listen.

Confirming Meaning: We don't always know what others mean by the words they say; we have to confirm their meaning. It is asking questions, asking for more information, or restating what you think has been said. "Do you mean this? I hear you saying...." Sometimes words don't accurately express what someone is trying to say. Sometimes words make sense to the one saying them but can be misleading. Good communication requires that you make sure you understand what the other means.

Negotiating for Personal Needs: You have to be able to tell people what you need to get your needs met. Sometimes a person wants to be responsive to the needs of another but doesn't know how. You cannot expect another to read your mind. You cannot expect needs to be met without clear understanding of what the needs are. You cannot assume the other person knows. Sometimes one person will say to the other, "Well, if I have to tell you..." How else are others going to know unless they are told? It is important to learn ways to negotiate for getting needs met that are mutually satisfactory.

Conflict Resolution: This is using communication skills to resolve differences. This does not have to be "I win/you lose." It can be "I win/you win." This requires listening to one another and making some compromises.

Expressing Feelings

In attempting to express feelings to another person, people commonly begin what they say with the word "you" rather than "I." This tends to shift the focus of what is being expressed from what you feel to the behavior of the other person. You probably will find that sharing your feelings with someone else is easier when you use "I" statements rather than "you" statements (*I was worried when I didn't hear from you* rather than *You didn't call.*)

There is a difference between sharing feelings and sharing judgments. Sometimes it is difficult to recognize whether or not you are describing a feeling or a judgment. Feeling words are *happy, sad, excited, anxious* (see the feeling list in the chapter on serenity). If you can substitute the word "think" for the word "feel" in a statement, it is not a feeling but a judgment. For example, in the sentence, "I feel that you are wrong," if you substitute the word "think" it makes sense, "I think that you are wrong." It is a judgment not a feeling. But in the sentence, "I feel happy," you can't substitute the word "think" so it is truly a feeling sentence.

Or take the statement, "I feel there is no justice in the world." You can substitute the word "think" for the word "feel" and the sentence still makes sense. That is what you really mean. You think there is no justice in the world. That is a judgment. But if you say, "I feel lonely on cloudy days," that expresses a real feeling. It isn't a judgment; it is what you feel.

Can you identify which of these are feeling statements and which are judgments?

1. I feel excited about your promotion.
2. I feel your promotion is important.
3. I feel I am to blame.
4. I feel tolerance is a good virtue to have.
5. I feel intolerant.
6. I feel you shouldn't leave me alone.
7. I feel lonely when you leave me.
8. I feel competent to handle this situation.
9. I feel incompetent when you are around.
10. I feel you are not as competent as I am.
11. I feel anxious about your trip.
12. I feel you will not be safe on the trip.

If you identified 1, 5, 7, 8, 9, and 11 as feeling statements, you are learning to distinguish between feelings and judgments.

Social Networks

Recovery means developing new and more meaningful social networks. That means finding resources and making contacts that will enable you to meet new people who can offer more than just drinking company. As you replace chemical use with meaningful, enduring values and activities, you will want to associate with people who share those values.

NA or AA is a valuable source for establishing or reestablishing a meaningful social network. You will find that these people will understand not only your struggles but your need for deeper and more meaningful relationships. They will offer you friendship, support, acceptance, and encouragement. AA and NA also offer fun activities without alcohol or other drugs. Don't forget how important it is to learn to have fun—with people who do not center having a good time around mood-altering chemicals.

Being a social animal is different from being a "party animal." Becoming social is an art; being a party animal is nothing more than getting high or drunk, laughing a lot, acting crazy, and not remembering what you did or said. Reorienting your lifestyle around values not centered around using is an essential part of recovery. The values that you developed to allow yourself to keep using will not allow you to stay sober. A lifestyle conducive to using is not conducive to sobriety. Friends who encourage drinking or using do not encourage abstinence. Places where it was easy to drink or use are not places where it is easy not to. New friends, new activities, new social contracts are part of recovery.

Points to Remember

1. Full recovery involves a resolution of family, work, and social problems created by active chemical dependency.
2. Making amends to persons you have harmed is an important part of rebuilding relationships.
3. Forgiveness is a necessary part of healing relationships.
4. Communication skills must be relearned in sobriety; these skills are learned by practice.
5. Communication is the ability to express your thoughts and feelings clearly and accurately to another and to understand the thoughts and feelings of another.
6. Recovery involves developing new and more meaningful social networks.
7. AA is a valuable source for establishing a meaningful social network.

Notes

1. *Twelve Steps and Twelve Traditions* (New York: Alcoholics Anonymous World Services, 1952), 77.
2. Ibid., 83.

For Recovery you Need the Right Tools!

CHAPTER 24

Support Resources

Choosing to do the things necessary to stay sober and choosing behavior that will improve the quality of sobriety and the quality of life require support. One of the most responsible choices you can make is to get help. Just as you could not get sober alone, you cannot stay sober alone. There are people and resources available to support your efforts to build a responsible lifestyle.

Professional Monitoring

Ongoing professional care is part of healthy recovery. You will need a lifelong relationship with addiction counselors and other health-care experts. Participation in an aftercare program (or continuing care program) following primary treatment is good insurance. Through involvement in this ongoing treatment process you will learn more about your addiction and the skills you need for recovery. You will find support from other persons in the group. It is a place where you can get feedback on your feelings, thinking, and behavior as you progress in recovery. If you are involved in an aftercare program you will more readily recognize when your recovery is in trouble and get the support you need to take the necessary action to prevent relapse.

An individual "sobriety checkup" twice a year with your counselor can help you update your recovery program and provide progressional feedback. At least once a year have a medical checkup by a physician who specializes in alcoholism or addictions. A complete examination will help you determine if you have any physical problems and how they might be affecting your sobriety. Discuss with the physician what health-care services or medications you have received since your last checkup. Inform him or her about your nutrition and exercise programs and modify anything in your life that is not supporting a good physical health program.

If you develop any health-care problems, consider carefully whether they require professional monitoring and care. Surgery always requires special attention to your addiction because of the need for anesthesia and pain-killing medication. Remember, "Better safe than sorry." Contact your addictions counselor whenever you are seriously ill or considering surgery. Consult your addictions counselor when major changes occur in your life, such as marriage, separation, divorce, a birth or a death in the family, a job change, or a move. Major events that affect your life also affect your recovery program.

Helping Person

A "helping person" is any mature responsible adult who does not have a drinking or drug problem and who is willing to assist in your sobriety program. It is the responsibility of the helping person to spend fifteen minutes a day with the recovering person. The primary goals of helping person meetings are to support continuing sobriety, to provide daily structure, to provide daily sober human contact, to begin a process of social retraining, to monitor the stability of sobriety and the commitment to recovery.

With chemical dependency there is a tendency to isolate; and during that time of isolation, communication skills are lost. Meeting every day with a sober person and talking to him or her for ten to fifteen minutes helps you to regain those communication skills.

It also provides a daily structure. You are talking to someone every day who is part of your recovery program.

The helping person is someone you can talk to about how your program is going and whether or not you are having difficulties. It is somebody who cares about you and your sobriety and someone who can point out to you if your thinking starts to change and you are moving into relapse ways of thinking. That person may be able to help you just by noticing that your thinking is changing.

With your permission the helping person can also communicate with your therapist to let him or her know if you are having a problem. If you are on Antabuse and suddenly you refuse to take it, that is an indication that you are beginning to move toward relapse, and in a short time you may be drinking or using. The helping person can alert your therapist to the fact that you are having a problem.

Your helping person doesn't have to be someone who is well-educated in chemical dependency. It can be a neighbor or friend. The important thing is that the helping person not be actively drinking or using drugs. Another recovering person is fine as a helping person.

However, to choose someone that you live with, or even a relative that you are close to, is not usually helpful. The reason: In the course of daily living, people sometimes get into spats. If you are having an argument about something else and you don't want to see that person, that can cause problems.

A company nurse or a neighbor who understands the problem of chemical dependency and is willing to be involved can be a helping person. It doesn't have to be a good friend. It can be someone you respect and that you think would be willing to help.

Generally speaking, the helping person is someone who is close to you on a regular basis and that you can see daily. It doesn't have to be somebody in AA or NA, although many times people choose a helping person from among the people they know in AA or NA particularly if they have already been part of that community and have friends there. But if you are being treated for the first time, and you don't have anybody in AA or NA that you could see on a daily basis, then a friend or neighbor—anyone who is willing to make a commitment—can be a helping person.

If you cannot find a helping person, it is a sign that something is seriously wrong with your social life, and you need to do something about that problem. An alternative to having a helping person is to use a number of people who will talk to you on the phone for a reality-testing conversation.

Reality Testing Conversation

To be sure you are thinking realistically and clearly, it is helpful to have daily reality testing conversations. Find at least five people who are each willing to talk with you for ten to fifteen minutes (in person or by phone) once or twice a week. Consider fellow AA/NA members, your sponsor, friends, and others who need a partner for a reality testing conversation.

Choose people who will listen to what you have to say, who will take you seriously and affirm you as a person. Choose people who will give you useful feedback and who will respect the confidential nature of the reality testing conversation. Choose people who have more maturity in recovery than you. It is best not to select a family member or co-worker. Do select someone who has a knowledge of your addiction and your recovery history.

Contract with each person to listen to you. Report how your day progressed in a clear and understandable way. The other person will report what he or she heard you say. Discuss how accurate this picture of your day is. Discuss how you did in this reality testing conversation. Discuss what you can do differently.

The reality testing conversation should occur once a day for ten to fifteen minutes. Do not ask too much of any one person. Always remember that it is important that you *listen* to what is said. Do not feel pressured to defend yourself or immediately react to the person.

At the end of the conversation, always thank the person with whom you are having the conversation for making time for you. Return the favor—agree to listen to others.

Points to Remember

1. During your recovery there are people and resources available to support your efforts to build a responsible lifestyle.
2. A helping person assists in your sobriety program by spending fifteen minutes a day with you.
3. Helping person sessions help you develop communication skills. They provide someone who can point out warning signs that your sobriety program may be in trouble.
4. A reality testing conversation is a way to let others know how you are doing daily.

MEETS FORMER ADDICTS NORMAL AND HAPPY

CHAPTER 25

Alcoholics Anonymous

Alcoholics Anonymous and Narcotics Anonymous are the single most effective type of treatment for chemical dependency. More people have recovered from chemical dependency using these twelve step programs than have recovered using any other form of treatment. It is for this reason that Alcoholics Anonymous or Narcotics Anonymous needs to be a vital part of any recovering person's sobriety plan.

Many people, however, require more extensive help or more specialized help than AA or NA alone. People with chemical dependency often get physically sick, sometimes desperately ill. At such times the recovering person needs a hospital-based program to assist with recovery. There are other times when an individual is incapable of maintaining sobriety for long periods of time without the support of an inpatient setting. Again, in these cases AA or NA needs to be fortified and supported by professional treatment efforts.

Many times in the course of recovery the person with chemical dependency will confront specialized problems. These problems often include financial difficulties, marital problems, emotional or psychological difficulties, and so forth. The problems are often the direct result of chemical dependency. While these problems would respond and improve with an AA or NA program alone, it has been demonstrated that professional counseling and therapy can provide direct assistance in rapidly resolving these issues.

The most effective form of treatment combines AA and NA with professional treatment. The relationship between self-help and professional treatment is clearly explained in the pamphlet, *Alcoholics Anonymous in Your Community—How the Fellowship of AA Is Geared to Work in Your Community to Help Alcoholics.*[1]

Alcoholics Anonymous and Narcotics Anonymous are worldwide fellowships of men and women who help each other maintain sobriety and who offer to share their recovery experience freely with others who may have a drinking problem or other drug problem. The program they suggest consists of "Twelve Steps" designed for personal recovery from chemical dependency.

Several hundred thousand people with chemical dependency have achieved sobriety in AA or NA, but members recognize that their program alone is not always effective and that some may also require professional counseling or treatment.

These groups are concerned solely with the personal recovery and continuing sobriety of individuals who turn to them for help. They do not engage in research or medical or psychiatric treatment and do not endorse any causes, although members may individually participate in other organizations. They have adopted a policy of "cooperation but not affiliation" with other organizations concerned with the problem of addiction.

Alcoholics Anonymous and Narcotics Anonymous are self-supporting through their own groups and members and decline contributions from outside sources. Members preserve personal anonymity at the level of the press, films, and the broadcast media.

Selecting a Meeting For You

Some people say they went to an AA meeting and didn't like it, so they decided they wouldn't go anymore. Have you ever gone into a bar to do some serious drinking and found that you didn't like the people in the bar, you didn't like the bartender, and you didn't like the general atmosphere of the bar? Of course you have. When that happened, did you stop going to bars?

Of course not, you just went out and found another bar where there were people and bartenders and an atmosphere that you liked. The thing that most people don't recognize is that a typical AA meeting is attended by the same varieties of personalities that frequent the typical bars. As a matter of fact, many members of AA were going to bars not long ago. As a result, an AA meeting, similar to any bar, tends to attract people who match the character of the group. As a result, different meetings attract different kinds of people and have different types of group atmosphere.

What this means is that when you are seeking an AA or NA meeting that will benefit you, you must be prepared to shop around. The first meeting that you attend may not be the best meeting for you. You should be prepared to experiment with several different meetings and several different locations until you find a meeting where you feel comfortable and at home.

Attending Your First Meeting

Some people look for ways to be uncomfortable at their first AA or NA meeting. Here are some tips if you really want to find a reason for *not* going back.

Step 1: Find a meeting that is extremely far away from your home for fear that somebody, a friend, a relative, an employer might see you enter the meeting.

Step 2: Estimate the approximate amount of time it will take you to get from your home to that meeting and then subtract three minutes. In other words, if you think it will take thirty minutes to drive to the meeting, leave your home at twenty-seven minutes before the time that meeting is scheduled to start.

Step 3: Arrive late at the building where the meeting is being held. Be sure you do not get the exact room location for the meeting so you can spend another five to ten minutes looking for the meeting.

Step 4: Enter the meeting late and find the chair closest to the door. Pull the collar of your coat up, pull a hat down over your eyes, and sit there in silence during the meeting.

Step 5: Look at every person in the meeting and attempt to guess exactly what form of problems they have and exactly why you will not be able to relate to anyone in the room.

Step 6: Don't listen. Judge everything you hear critically.

Step 7: At the break between the speaker and the comments, sneak out the door and leave. If anyone stops you as you attempt to leave the room, just say "excuse me" and don't give them the opportunity to talk with you.

Step 8: On the way home review in your mind how unfriendly, uncommunicative, and basically unresponsive everyone was to you as a new member.

This may seem a bit absurd, but this is often the way people attend their first meetings. It is important that you understand that your first exposure to NA or AA can be very valuable to you if you follow more realistic guidelines.

Step 1: Plan to attend a meeting near your home. Check on the location before you leave, and make sure you know the exact room where the meeting is located.

Step 2: If possible, call the AA or NA office in your area (listed in the phone book in most cities) and attempt to find someone who will take you to your first meeting or who will meet you at the meeting. This way you will know someone and have a contact at that meeting.

Step 3: Plan to arrive about fifteen minutes before the scheduled start of the meeting. You will notice that one or two people arrive early to make coffee and to arrange a literature table. Ask them if this is the AA or NA meeting and introduce yourself by first name only. Be sure to tell them, "This is my first meeting. Could you introduce me?" Letting people know this is your first meeting will invite them to pay special attention and take special interest in you.

Step 4: Sit at your first meeting and listen. Listen; don't judge. It is easy to become critical and defensive. Don't do it. Just absorb what people are saying.

Step 5: When it comes your turn to comment, take the plunge. Say what is on your mind. Tell the group it is your first meeting, and if you are skeptical or have any questions, express that skepticism and those questions. It is also helpful if you mention you would like to talk about the program with someone for a few minutes after the meeting. You will be surprised how many people offer to talk with you.

Step 6: After some meetings, different members from that group go out for a snack. Attempt to include yourself with one of these groups. Exchange phone numbers with several members. Inquire about the program in general and the location of other meetings.

If you follow these more realistic guidelines, you will find that your first experience is a positive and a valuable one. AA has a statement entitled, *I am responsible.* "When anyone, anywhere, reaches out for help, I want the hand of AA always to be there. And for that, I am responsible."

The amazing thing is that members of AA and NA mean this. People will take your phone number, and you can take theirs. In AA there is a philosophy called the "dry dime." (Unfortunately in these inflationary times it is the dry quarter.) The philosophy of the dry dime simply means this: If you ever feel like taking a drink, call an AA member first, and they will help you to overcome that need to drink. *The help is there — all you need to do is reach out and use it.*

A good summary explanation of AA was written in 1947 and published in the *AA Grapevine*, a magazine for recovering alcoholics. It reads as follows:

Alcoholics Anonymous is a fellowship of men and women who share their experience, strength, and hope with each other that they

231

may solve their common problem and help others to recover from alcoholism.

The only requirement for membership is a desire to stop drinking. There are no dues or fees for AA membership; they are self-supporting through their own contributions. AA is not allied with any sect, denomination, political organization, or institution; does not wish to engage in any controversy; neither endorses nor opposes any causes. Their primary purpose is to stay sober and help other alcoholics to achieve sobriety.

The Types of Meetings

It is important to recognize that there are different types of NA and AA meetings. The major division occurs between what are called "open meetings" and "closed meetings." An open meeting is simply a meeting that is open to any member of the public who chooses to attend. Family members, friends, and interested community members attend to get an idea of what the AA or NA fellowship is all about.

Closed meetings, on the other hand, are restricted to attendance by admitted addicts or alcoholics only. AA states that the only requirement for membership is the desire to stop drinking. Any person who has a desire to stop drinking is welcome at any closed AA meeting.

As you become involved in AA or NA, you will hear about a number of different types of meetings. These include Step Meetings, Discussion Meetings, and Speaker Meetings. Let's explore some of these most common types of meetings.

A Speaker Meeting is a common type of meeting in which people are asked to come in and "tell their stories." One of the most important features of AA is the opportunity to listen to the stories of other people and the opportunity to tell your own story in front of an audience that will listen and understand. It is through the telling of our stories that we accomplish the primary purpose of sharing our experience, strength, and hope for recovery with each other. A complete NA or AA story consists of three parts:

Part 1: What it was like.

Part 2: What happened.

Part 3: What it is like now.

When you listen to a story, listen for these three parts. When people speak about what it was like, they explain to you what their drinking or drug use was like. They tell the progressive history of their addiction and the problems and difficulties they had. As they explain what happened, they share those experiences that caused them to decide to stop using drugs or drinking.

The most important part of stories is the "what it is like now" part. During this part members tell how they experience life sober. Listen carefully, for here you will begin to understand what methods of pursuing sobriety create serenity and happiness and which ones don't.

It would be totally untrue to tell you that everyone who uses an AA or NA program becomes serene, comfortable, and happy. This is not true. AA members are human. They are striving for progress toward spiritual happiness and comfort. They are not perfect and make no pretense at being such. However, there are certain methods of following a recovery program that work better than others. By listening to the mistakes of others, you can avoid those mistakes yourself. And by hearing the successes of others, you may be able to progress more rapidly in your own recovery.

A Discussion Meeting generally also uses a speaker, who introduces a topic for discussion. The speaker presents a lead or short summary on a particular topic of interest. These topics are related to some aspects of recovery but are almost unlimited in their variety. Topics may include resentments, loneliness, humility, honesty, acceptance, self-worth, simplicity, relationships with a higher power, making amends.

A Step Meeting is a specialized form of meeting. At a Step Meeting the task is to review the twelve steps. The essence of the recovery program of AA is captured in the twelve steps. Any discussion of AA would be incomplete without listing the twelve steps. See Appendix A for a list of the steps.

The Structure of Meetings

When you go to an AA or NA meeting, you can expect that the meeting will follow a general format. Usually the format is as follows:

1. *The Opening of the Meeting with a Quiet Time:* A quiet time is a few moments of silence or meditation designed to give you an opportunity to think clearly about what you want to accomplish during the meeting. It is a moment for you to remind yourself of the seriousness of this meeting and of your need to work a program of recovery.

2. *Introductory Statements and the Reading of How It Works:* Many times the chairperson will make a few introductory remarks welcoming you to the meeting and briefly explaining the program. The chairperson will then ask someone in the group to read Chapter Five from the Big Book (Alcoholics Anonymous) entitled "How It Works." The goal here is to remind everyone of the purpose and function of this meeting and to bring the twelve steps to mind.

3. *The Speaker or Lead:* Next, the chairperson will introduce a speaker who will either tell his or her story or introduce a topic for discussion. The story or the introductory comments will generally take twenty to thirty minutes. If it is a Step Meeting, at this time the book, *Twelve Steps and Twelve Traditions*, will be used, and the section describing the particular step will be read.

4. *Break:* After the speaker most meetings take a brief break for coffee.

5. *Comments:* In a closed AA meeting, every person present will have an opportunity to comment. A comment is simply that. You can say anything you want to say. This is your time. Every member of the group is free to pass. The general format of a comment is to say, "My name is John, and I am chemically dependent...." After

that introduction, you can say anything you would like. If you have nothing else to add, you can simply say, "I choose to pass." Usually, however, it is not a good idea to pass. People who stay sober usually comment. If you are not a little bit nervous or apprehensive about your comment, you are not being honest and your comment probably won't help. An AA or NA meeting is a time to speak what is on your mind, to get it out and on the table. The name of the game is honesty, and honesty begins in your comments. Say what you need to say at a meeting, and you will not have to get drunk over it at a later date.

6. *Collection:* NA and AA are self-supporting through their own contributions. At each meeting a basket is passed for contributions. You do not have to contribute if you do not want to. These groups are not in business to make money. The collection is used to pay for rent and coffee and to make a small contribution to the Central Office to pay the telephone bill, office cost, and literature costs.

7. *Closing with the Lord's Prayer:* At the end of the meeting the group members generally stand and close the meeting with the Lord's Prayer.

Sponsorship

The principles of AA and NA are simple but at first can be misunderstood. Therefore, they have developed a practice whereby a member with a great deal of experience with the program makes himself or herself available to a newer member. The sponsor's responsibility is to provide support during recovery, answer questions, discuss the various aspects of the program, assist the new members in identifying meetings that meet their needs, and direct them to appropriate literature and resources they may need to fully understand the program.

AA and NA sponsors are not therapists or counselors, nor are they responsible for telling other members how to work their programs. All members are responsible for interpreting the principles for themselves and developing their own programs based on those principles. The sponsor is merely a sounding board, a supportive friend, and a knowledgeable resource.

How to Find a Sponsor

Finding a sponsor is a personal and individual process. A person who may be an excellent sponsor to one individual may be a poor sponsor for another. It's important, however, that recovering people pay careful attention to selecting a sponsor with whom they can relate comfortably and who can successfully meet their needs.

There are some characteristics that should be present in a good sponsor. These are:

1. *A well-established personal NA or AA program.* A sponsor should practice what he preaches. Beware of any potential sponsor whose words convey one message and whose behavior conveys another.

2. *A sense of personal serenity and general well-being.* The test of any program is its effect on the serenity and well-being of the person who practices it. Sponsors can only teach new members to develop a program as they have developed it for themselves. If their personal programs do not result in personal serenity and well-being, they are apt to teach new members to make the same mistakes they have made.

3. *A thorough knowledge of the principles, steps, and traditions.* If a sponsor is to teach another person the program, it only makes sense that he or she understand the program. Be sure your sponsor really knows what he or she is talking about.

Changing Sponsors

The needs of the recovering person are different during various phases of recovery. One person may make a good sponsor during one phase of treatment but a poor sponsor as you progress through treatment. For example, one type of person makes an excellent sponsor for the newly sober person but may have difficulty relating to a person with two years of sobriety who is going through a divorce.

Don't be afraid to change your sponsor if you feel someone else can be more helpful. To discuss your needs openly with your sponsor is an essential part of recovery. A sponsor with a stable program will understand and respect your opinions and needs and assist you in meeting other members that can give you the support you need in a sponsor relationship.

Why AA or NA Is Recommended

AA or NA offers the recovering person many things that professional treatment cannot offer. It offers the person a readily available environment that is conducive to ongoing recovery and sobriety. AA is available twenty-four hours a day in every major city around the world. You are never farther away from a meeting than the telephone. In large metropolitan areas meetings are held at all times of the day and night. You can always have the phone number of someone who understands and will help you avoid that one drinking or drug episode, one day at a time.

AA and NA work, and they do not cost anything except time, energy, and a motivation to stop drinking/using. It is a place to meet other people who are interested in having fun and socializing without chemicals. Let's face it, we live in a chemical society. You need a place to go where you can find interesting people who do not drink or use drugs. Many people begin the social rebuilding process through friends and acquaintances they find at meetings.

We should note that AA or NA is not a substitute for life but a door to life. It is not an escape from the world but gives you strengths and resources to make your world and your life more meaningful and rich.

These groups offer a spiritual program for recovery. It is important to recognize that most people who maintain an active and comfortable sobriety have had a spiritual awakening as a course of their experience during the first one to two years of sobriety. By "spiritual awakening" we mean an awareness that there is a power greater than themselves that they can use to bring beauty and meaning into their lives.

Points to Remember

1. Alcoholics Anonymous or Narcotics Anonymous is the single most effective treatment modality for chemical dependency.
2. Many people need treatment in addition to AA or NA.
3. The most effective treatment combines AA or NA with professional treatment.
4. Alcoholics Anonymous is a worldwide fellowship of men and women who help each other maintain sobriety and who offer to share their recovery experiences freely with others who may have a drinking problem.
5. The program AA suggests consists of twelve steps designed for personal recovery.
6. Persons with chemical dependency seeking an AA or NA meeting may need to shop around to find the best group for them.
7. You can follow sensible guidelines that will contribute to making your AA or NA experience successful. The help is there; reach out and use it.
8. There are both open and closed meetings. An open meeting is open to anyone who chooses to go; a closed meeting is open only to alcoholics or addicts.
9. AA is available twenty-four hours a day in every major city around the world.

Notes

1. *Alcoholics Anonymous in Your Community—How the Fellowship of AA Is Geared to Work in Your Community to Help Alcoholics* (Alcoholics Anonymous World Services, 1966).

CHAPTER 26

Effects on the Family

Addiction is a family disease that affects all family members. All need treatment. Family members need to be actively involved in specialized treatment. Without realizing what has been happening to them, they have reacted to the presence of chemical dependency in the family in ways that have caused them to develop problems of their own.

The addictive disease creates impairments in addicts that may make it impossible for them to respond appropriately to the needs of the family system. It is natural for family members to compensate for this inappropriate behavior to keep the family functioning. They develop their own survival systems. They adapt and condition themselves to a new system of functioning that allows them to maintain sanity in the midst of chaos and confusion. They develop strengths that allow them to survive despite the progressing crisis of chemical addiction. But these strengths do not interrupt the disease process going on in the family, and they reduce the pain only momentarily. In fact, behavior that keeps the family functioning, paradoxically, is the same behavior that allows the problem to continue.

A Dip in Denial River!

Everyone Is Affected

Anyone whose life has become unmanageable as a result of living in a committed relationship with an addicted person has need of a personal recovery program. When persons in a committed relationship with an addicted person attempt to control drinking, drug use, or addictive behavior (over which they are powerless), they lose control over their own behavior (over which they can have power) and their lives become unmanageable. They develop symptoms of their own as a result of attempting to adapt to and compensate for the effects of living with addiction. Without treatment the symptoms will continue even if the addicted person gets sober or leaves the family.

When we attempt to control what it is impossible to control, we lose control over what it is possible to control. When we expend all our effort and energy attempting to change what we have no power over, we are not taking care of those things that we need to be taking care of to manage our lives. If you attempt to prevent a flood by trying to hold back the river with a stick, you are not getting yourself and your possessions out of the path of the flood, and you may be destroyed by it.

So it is with addiction. When people attempt to control the addictive using of another, they are focusing their energies on something that is not within their power to control and they usually lose control over their own lives.

Family members become dysfunctional by their attempts to cope with addiction in the only way they know. Their response is a normal response to their inability to cope with a situation they have no resources or tools to handle. Methods of preventing or reducing pain in the family do not make things better. Pain is nature's way of getting our attention, to get us to do something about the source of pain. Behaviors that reduce the pain of addictive behavior do not help things get better because they protect the addicted person from the consequences of his or her behavior.[1]

Everyone has to make sense out of life. When everything we have been taught to do to make life make sense *doesn't work* and we don't know anything else to try, we find ways to cope that at least create the illusion of making sense. In a family where addiction is present these ways of coping may help keep the family functioning through confusion and chaos. They help protect the image of the addicted person, protect personal self-esteem, free the family from guilt, and provide the myth of control.

To cope, family members may deny there is a problem. They may avoid facing it. Or they may excuse drinking or using by saying: *It's normal. Everyone does it once in a while. We're on vacation. It's New Years. We won't make an issue of it.* Often family members blame themselves: *If I was home more. If I controlled the kids better. If I watched the budget better. If I was a better provider.* Or they may convince themselves that the problems are the result of another problem—job pressure, phase in life, peer group, or loneliness.

Jim always took a certain pride in knowing that he provided for his family in some of the same secure ways he had been provided for by his parents. He was proud of his son's good grades and how well he did on his jobs. When Jeff began to have problems with drugs, Jim said, "Well, maybe he just needs a better job; that one is not paying him that well." So he got a friend to give Jeff a job that paid better. But Jeff lost the job two weeks later because he didn't show up for work for two days. Jim said, "Jeff is just bent out of shape over that girl he has been hanging around with these days." Jim tried to talk Jeff out of seeing the girl, but despite the good relationship Jim and Jeff had once had, Jim now found they were arguing and fighting on a regular basis. With each argument he became more convinced his son's problems were caused by "that wild girl." After Jeff and the girl broke up, Jim had to bail Jeff out of jail a couple of times and came to realize that Jeff's problems did not originate with the wrong job or the wrong girl.

These ways of denying the problem may work for a while but eventually the problems become too severe to hide. Someone has said that denying addiction in the family is like hiding a baby gorilla. You can do it for a time. But after a while it grows—and grows.

As these ways of coping fail, family members may try *controlling drinking or using* by canceling social events, pouring out liquor or hiding drugs, pleading, demanding, controlling the money. When those efforts fail, they may attempt to *control reasons for drinking or using*: he or she works too hard, doesn't get enough privacy, doesn't get enough love, doesn't get enough rest, doesn't eat right.

Enabling

When the family is unable to control drinking/using, they often attempt to control the *consequences*. This is called *enabling* because it allows the addicted person to continue drinking or using. Enabling behaviors are: protecting the addict, making excuses for the addict, buying into the alibis of the addict, covering up for the addict. Examples are: calling the employer to say the addicted person is sick when he or she is actually intoxicated or experiencing a hangover, covering bad checks, or getting a lawyer to beat a charge of driving while intoxicated. The addicted person can deny the problem as long as the family provides escape from the consequences and doesn't allow her or him to feel the pain.

Enabling is a sincere effort to help, to spare the addicted person pain and save the family from further disintegration. The family is using the only tools it knows. They see the situation as a series of separate unrelated problems rather than a chronic ongoing problem. They believe if they can get over *this* crisis everything is going to be all right. Once the crisis is over they bury everything until the next crisis. They do not know they are dealing with a *chronic* disease that keeps recurring until it is treated, a *progressive* disease that always gets worse without treatment.[2]

Progression of Family Disruption

The normal reaction within any family to pain, to crisis, and to the dysfunction of one member of the family is to reduce the pain, ease the crisis, and to assist the dysfunctional member to protect the family. These responses do not make things better when the problem is addiction because these measures deprive the addicted person of the painful learning experiences that bring an awareness that the addiction is creating problems.

In the early stages of dysfunction the behavior of a family is a reaction to crisis. Anytime there is a problem in the family the normal response by family members is to attempt to reduce the pain for everyone involved and to get over the problem as soon as possible. With addiction this response allows the problem to continue and to progress. But to react differently is to violate the value system of family members who believe it is their responsibility to take care of and protect the family.

When behavior intended to take care of and protect the family fails to solve the problem, the family tries harder. They do the same things only more so. They worry more and attempt to control time, place, frequency, and quantity of using. They cover up and rescue.

They do the same things, only more often, more intensely, more desperately. They try to be more supportive, more helpful, more protective. They take on the responsibilities of the addicted person, not realizing that this causes the addict to become more irresponsible.

Things get worse instead of better and the sense of failure intensifies the efforts of the family. Lack of self-esteem is common in families where there is an addiction. Family members have failed so many times and believe that the problems in the home reflect on their ability to take care of the family. They experience frustration, anxiety, and guilt. There is growing self-blame and lowering of self-esteem. So they try harder.

Lack of Direct Communication

Communication within the family becomes severely impaired. It is not surprising that family members stop communicating directly with one another. Without realizing it, they start practicing the unspoken "no talk" rule. This means there is an unspoken rule not to talk about anything related to the problem of drinking or using drugs. When so much thought, feeling, and activity centers around "it" and no one can talk about "it," what do they talk about? Very little. It has been said that there are two rules in families where there is addiction:

1. Nothing is wrong.
2. Don't you dare tell anyone.

This puts the family in the position of being unable to discuss anything, particularly what is going on in the family. Communication becomes a form of "game playing." Everyone plays the game, "Let's Pretend." Let's pretend we are a normally functioning family. Let's pretend nothing happened last night. Let's pretend we're not afraid. Let's pretend we're not angry.

Family communication is indirect and vague rather than direct and clear. Instead of discussing our financial situation I say, "I'm not upset. Why should I be upset? You never worry about money. Why should I?" No one talks about the real issues. Accusing, blaming, and defensiveness replace direct communication. Verbal communication may almost cease because everyone is afraid to talk about what is really going on. This situation is compounded when one has grown up in an addicted family and has come to believe that he or she does not have anything worthwhile to say.

Roles, Rules, and Rituals Change

When an addicted person abandons responsibilities in the family to drink or use, those roles will be assumed by another member to keep the family functioning. As one person becomes less responsible, others may become more responsible. As one member of the family abandons roles, other members take them over. If the spouse neglects certain responsibilities because of preoccupation with the problem, children may take over the role. Eventually children may be functioning in adult roles and adults functioning in child roles.

Rules in the family are changed to make drinking/using easier or to protect everyone from the consequences. *Don't bring friends home on Friday evening anymore. Don't ask questions. Don't play music when Mom doesn't feel good.* Some rules are unspoken but communicated indirectly. *Don't mention feelings. Don't mention drinking. Don't create reasons for using. Protect the family at any cost.*

Family rituals change to accommodate drinking/using. Mealtime and bedtime may be altered. No one is invited for Christmas dinner anymore. The family stops attending church. Family vacations stop or are centered around activities where drinking or using occurs. Traditions and rituals change as behavior interferes.

Children

Children are affected by chemical dependency in the family in a number of ways.[3] Some children aid and protect the nonaddicted parent; some defend the person with chemical dependency. Some attempt to stop or control the using. Many blame themselves. The roles children take to cope and survive in a family where there is addiction depend on their age, their birth order, the severity of the problem, and a variety of other factors. Some become problem children, getting into trouble in school or with the law. Some develop strengths that appear to be assets but may hide troubled feelings. No one knows they are deeply troubled; they give no indication that there is a problem.

Claudia Black[4] describes three types of seemingly well-adjusted children of alcoholics. Some children become *superachievers*. They assume added responsibilities at home, make excellent grades at school, become leaders, and provide structure for the rest of the family. The second type of child is the *adjustor*, the child who rolls with the punches and doesn't get upset easily, does not express a lot of feelings, follows directions easily, and is very flexible. The third type is the *placating* child who smooths things over in the family, tries to alleviate guilt of other family members, and is sensitive to the feelings of others.

Increasing Dysfunction

When the addicted person in the family is an adolescent, there are additional pressures that increase the dysfunction of the parents. Their feelings of failure, shame, and guilt are intensified by their sense of responsibility for the behavior of their children. When their children use drugs, parents often shift between feeling totally helpless and going to any length to "control" the behavior of a son or daughter. Efforts to control are usually ineffective, leaving parents feeling frustrated, angry, powerless, afraid, ashamed, inadequate, guilty, and hopeless.

Whether the chemical user is a husband, wife, son, daughter, father, mother, fiancée, or intimate partner, there is no consistency or dependability in any area of family life. Broken promises, unfulfilled expectations, and disrupted plans create tension and strained relationships. Family members are isolated and separated from one another by fear, anger, and confusion. Disruption of the family increases with the progression of the disease of chemical dependency.

At this point thinking and behavior are out of control in the whole family. They begin to realize that they are behaving irrationally but cannot stop it. The problems are so severe and disruptive that they are preoccupied to the point of neglect of other aspects of their lives. They neglect their own needs; their lives have become addiction-centered. In an attempt to control what they have no control over, their own lives have become unmanageable, leading to chaos and confusion and lack of consistency and structure in the entire family.

The things the family members have done in a sincere effort to help have failed. The resulting despair and guilt bring about confusion and chaos and the inability to interrupt dysfunctional behavior even when they are aware that what they are doing is not helping. The thinking and behavior of the family is out of control, and these thinking and behavior patterns will continue independent of the addiction. The entire family needs help to rebuild trust, reestablish communication, and learn how to feel good about themselves.

Points to Remember

1. Addiction is a family disease that affects all family members.
2. Family members develop their own survival systems that allow them to function in the midst of addiction.
3. The behaviors family members use to keep the family functioning allow addiction to continue.
4. Family members need to learn new ways of behaving to interrupt the dysfunction caused by addiction.
5. Addiction affects the ability of the family to communicate.
6. Roles, rules, and rituals are disrupted in families where there is addiction.
7. Without treatment dysfunction in the family will continue independent of the addiction.

Notes

1. Merlene Miller and Terence T. Gorski, *Family Recovery: Growing Beyond Addiction* (Independence, Missouri: Herald House/Independence Press, 1982).
2. Ibid.
3. Sharon Wegscheider Cruse, *Another Chance* (Palo Alto, California: Science and Behavior Books, 1989).
4. Claudia Black, *It Will Never Happen to Me* (Denver: M.A.C., 1981).

CHAPTER 27

Recovery of the Family

The family of the chemically dependent person must be part of the recovery program. They have been made dysfunctional by chemical dependency. The entire family needs to recover together. One of the first things to do is to redefine roles, rules, and family rituals. During active using, many people with chemical dependency are not able to fulfill their responsibilities in the family because of their preoccupation with using, so other members take over their jobs and their roles in the family.

In recovery the addicted person will want to take his or her share of responsibility in the family. But there may be some difficulties in doing that. Some addicted persons may never have balanced the checkbook completely sober. Because of state dependent memory, they may have to learn how to do certain tasks again. Other family members may have become so used to performing certain tasks that they now consider these their jobs.

It may take time to rebuild trust so that family members can feel safe in entrusting to a newly recovering person tasks that he or she was unable to fulfill responsibly in the past. Patience is necessary on both sides. The addicted person must be patient with other family members, knowing they have been hurt and cannot over-

NEW INTERESTS DEVELOP

come their fears magically because he or she is ready to resume some new responsibilities.

Treatment for the Family

Treatment for family members is available, too, and they should be encouraged to participate. They need support for their recovery just as the addicted person does. Individual and group counseling as well as Al-Anon, Naranon, Alateen, Families Anonymous, or Adult Children of Alcoholics can help the family to recognize how chemical dependency has affected them and to learn new ways to act and interact. The entire family needs to be aware that they are not alone and can find support from others with the same experiences.

For the family unit to recover, each family member must recover. The addicted person must eliminate alcohol, drugs, and addictive behavior from his or her life and learn to manage the sobriety-based symptoms of the disease. Other family members must interrupt their own illness progression and manage the symptoms that emerge with recovery. The family itself must learn new ways of functioning that support recovery rather than illness. Unrealistic expectations of how family life will improve with abstinence can interfere with the restructuring of family life.

The first step of recovery for family members is learning to tell the difference between what can be changed and what cannot. It is also identifying who is responsible for making the changes. Education about addiction and the effects on the family is a necessary part of doing that. Learning about addiction helps the family come to understand and accept it as a true disease. Then they can let go of a great deal of resentment, bitterness, guilt, and defensiveness and recognize what they can change and what they are responsible to change.

Individual Recovery

Recovery for the family means learning to accept and detach from the symptoms of addiction. It means learning to focus on personal needs and personal growth, learning to respect and like oneself. It means learning to choose appropriate behavior. It means learning to be in control of one's own life.

It means interrupting preoccupation with addiction and addictive behavior. The focus must move from the addicted person to self. There must be an emotional separation or detachment from the problem as family members confront the reality of their own illness and their own need for recovery. This is often referred to as "detaching with love."

Detaching is not full recovery, just the beginning of recovery. It is sometimes thought to mean acceptance of the addiction without caring, or acceptance without feeling. It is *not* not caring, *not* not feeling. It is not selfishness, not passive acceptance of a harmful situation. It is *releasing with love*. Releasing is not passive. It is something done *because* there is caring. It is by releasing addicted persons to experience the consequences of their own behavior and to take responsibility for their own lives that the door for change is opened.

At first it is necessary for each family member to focus on self and to build personal strength. It is important for each person in the family to understand and support the recovery of the others. A variety of problems are brought into recovery and recovery itself triggers new problems. Stress-related illness does not go away overnight and must be managed. There may be lack of trust that is the result of having been let down, disappointed, and betrayed over and over again in the past.

Denial of stress, denial of the need for lifestyle change, and denial of the chronic nature of addiction in the family can reactivate disease symptoms. Identity crisis is often a recovery issue for family members. Their lives have been centered around controlling using and using behavior (attempting to). When this is no longer a part of the lifestyle, an identity crisis can occur. "Who am I and what gives me self-worth?"

Often family members have lost confidence in their ability to make decisions and solve problems. They need to learn some skills for doing that and to learn to take care of their own personal needs. They may need to learn assertiveness skills. They also need to recognize their own needs and give themselves permission to do things for themselves. Nutrition, exercise, relaxation, fun, and personal growth are important in the recovery of family members just as they are for the addicted person. Spiritual growth is also important to personal recovery. Daily quiet time and spiritual fellowship support spiritual growth.

Children need their own treatment, treatment specific to their own issues, presented at a level they understand. This can be individual treatment or in a group with other children. Treatment should provide a safe place for children to express their thoughts and feelings. In this safe environment they should learn constructive ways of reacting to addictive behavior, learn not to blame themselves, learn they can't make the addictive behavior go away.

Restructuring the Family System

In most cases, the family must restructure roles, rules, and rituals to support recovery. Roles, rules, and rituals that developed to support drinking or using are not appropriate for recovery; those that existed before are out-of-date. And the family does not have the skills to restructure them. They don't know how to talk to each other, how to express personal feelings and needs, or how to listen to one another. In most cases they have not had direct communication for a long time.

Restructuring requires negotiation. Some people may want to maintain roles and rules developed while the addictive use was going on, while other people expect to resume roles and rules they had before or may want to establish new ones. A wife may have developed a new identity around a new career (taken to feed the family) and not want to give it up. A husband may want the wife to be a full-time homemaker. Children may have a loss of identity

253

if relieved of adultlike responsibilities. Renegotiating new rules, roles, and rituals requires communication skills.

Communication is the primary key to reestablishing family relationships. The family must learn to talk to one another, something they didn't do much during active drinking or use of other drugs. Communication skills are learned by practice.

The recovery of family requires *education* (learning about addiction and the effects on the family), *dedication* (commitment to personal recovery, recovery of each member of the family, and recovery of the family system), *communication* (developing the skills to express feelings and needs directly to one another and to listen to and respect the needs of other family members), and *perspiration* (takes effort, doesn't happen by itself).

Homeostasis is the tendency of a system to balance itself. What happens to one part affects all the other parts. If part is dysfunctional, the system compensates to keep functioning. After members of the family system recover, the system must attain a healthy balance that facilitates growth and self-worth in all its members.

Points to Remember

1. The family of the chemically dependent person must be part of the recovery program.
2. Roles, rules, and rituals need to be restructured.
3. Al-Anon, Naranon, Alateen, Families Anonymous, or Adult Children of Alcoholics are available to help family members recover.
4. Unrealistic expectations of how family life will improve with abstinence can interfere with the restructuring of family life.
5. It may take time to rebuild trust so family members can feel safe in trusting the chemically dependent person to perform tasks that he or she was unable to fulfill responsibly in the past.
6. To recover family members must learn to focus on their own needs.

7. Detaching with love is releasing another to experience the consequences of his or her own behavior.
8. Children need their own treatment, treatment specific to their own issues.
9. Learning to communicate can help the family restructure around recovery.

Abstinence Makes the Heart Grow Fonder.

CHAPTER 28

Recovery of Intimacy

Everyone has a need for intimacy: to be close; to touch; to share feelings; to give and receive support; to belong; to feel visible, wanted, needed, and appreciated. Recovering couples *especially* need intimacy to help heal the damage done by addiction that has left shattered egos and relationships and a tremendous void.

But the nature of chemical dependency is such that isolation becomes a part of the user's lifestyle. One of the first things lost in the family is the ability to communicate. Negative patterns will carry into recovery unless skills are learned that allow for change. The relationship that has developed because of the process of active dependency must be replaced by interaction that is part of the process of active recovery.

Recovering couples bring into sobriety conditions that interfere with intimacy. Sobriety-based symptoms of addiction—stimulus augmentation, stress sensitivity, emotional overreaction or numbness, and difficulty concentrating and remembering—can put serious strain on a relationship. And the symptoms that the partner of an addicted person brings into recovery—stress-related illnesses, lack of trust, lack of confidence, lack of self-esteem, and the inability to relax and enjoy life—also interfere with the ability to have an open, honest, and trusting relationship.

Remember that stimulus augmentation is a sensitivity to sight, sound, and touch. People with stimulus augmentation sometimes feel bombarded by the environment and are easily distracted by things going on around them, things that someone else might not even be aware of. Many of the things the recovering person does for relief from an overwhelming environment may seem like rejection to a partner unaware of the stressful feelings created by stimulus augmentation. And things the nonaddicted person does may seem like lack of consideration to the person overreacting to the environment.

Sometimes people with stimulus augmentation do not enjoy touching. This can put a strain on a physical relationship. Especially when there is a need for physical contact to heal some of the hurts that have resulted from addiction. Tension may also be created by memory problems and the tendency to be easily distracted. This may be interpreted by the partner as lack of caring or concern.

Characteristics that the partner brings into recovery can intensify the problems the addicted person brings. Lack of trust is a natural response to living with addiction. But intimate relationships require trust. The partner may have been disappointed so many times in the past that he or she is afraid to believe that this time things will be different. There is fear that the recovering spouse cannot be trusted with the checkbook, with the children, or with any major role in the family. It may take a long time to stop feeling afraid anytime an alcoholic is late coming home. The nonaddicted partner may need time to rebuild trust at a time when what the recovering addicted person needs most is trust.

Many recovering partners of chemically dependent people are unable to enjoy life because they have come to believe that it is their responsibility to worry about all the problems that have been going on in their family. For full recovery it is important to learn to enjoy life. This means learning to play, to laugh, to relax, and to have fun. This is not easy for people who have come to believe that it is their responsibility in life to worry. But it is important for health and wellness and for the ability to develop close and intimate relationships.

Painful memories often sabotage the present. There may have been so many hurts between two people who are dealing with chemical dependency that a lot of forgiveness and reconciliation is necessary before the painful memories can be put into the past.

Negative patterns will carry into recovery unless skills are learned that allow for change. The relationship that has developed because of the process of active dependency must be replaced by interaction that is part of the process of active recovery.

It can become easy not to accept responsibility for an intimate relationship. Both people focus on their own recovery and fail to support the recovery of the other. They learn about the symptoms of their own condition and what it takes to get well, but they learn nothing about the recovery needs of the other. They may make amends to everyone but each other. Their own recovery becomes a way of avoiding responsibility for the relationship. For the recovery of intimacy it is necessary that couples become aware of each other's needs and support the recovery program of the other. Recovery that is exclusive rather than inclusive cannot be full recovery. It is in the process of giving and receiving love that individual needs are met. The need for pleasure, freedom, and belonging are all met in relationships.

The ability to communicate will not come back magically because a couple is in recovery. It is *impossible* to be intimate without communication. A couple has to be able to share with one another what their needs are, what their feelings are, what their expectations are, what their dreams are.

The building of personal communication skills includes making amends, learning to say I'm sorry and learning to forgive. It means learning to be courteous to one another, to be pleasant to each other. It means showing respect and consideration. It may mean learning to put some things on the shelf that the couple isn't ready to tackle yet and being patient while they each progress in their own recovery. Recovery of intimacy is a road not a goal.

It is sometimes difficult for recovering couples who want to improve their relationship to know where to begin. They have to start where they are and build on what they have. You can't build on what is wrong. It is important to value and focus on what is good and strong and healthy. A small amount of intimacy can provide nurture that will allow it to grow. Small steps *toward* one another can interrupt destructive cycles. Hope encourages constructive change.

Intimacy may be physical, emotional, intellectual, or spiritual. *Physical intimacy* is an essential part of being close. Sometimes there are sexual problems in early recovery because of physical damage resulting from the use of chemicals over a period of time. These problems often go away automatically after a period of abstinence. It is important not to panic — stress will make the problem worse. Talk to your physician. If the problem is physical, he or she can probably help you or will refer you to someone who can.

We also need that sense of oneness that is *emotional intimacy*. This is an in-depth emotional awareness of one another and a sharing of meanings and feelings. Intimacy can also be the sharing of ideas and concepts. This is *intellectual intimacy. Spiritual intimacy* is sharing a purpose beyond ourselves. It is a closeness that develops around sharing of ultimate concerns, the meaning of life, and relationship to a higher power.

Intimacy is built on friendship, touching, and closeness. It is vastly improved by a relationship in which two people have the ability to have fun together. It is important to play together, laugh together, to be silly together. It is a marvelous way to reduce tension, get comfortable together, and mainly just enjoy life.

Of course, no relationship is conflict free and you wouldn't want it to be. We grow as we face our differences. Conflict offers us the opportunity to know one another better and to find out how we can meet each other's needs more fully. Conflicts don't have to mean fighting, although there is nothing wrong with fighting once in a while if you stay away from name calling, accusations that have nothing to do with what you are fighting about, and physical violence. But fighting isn't necessary to resolve conflicts. Sometimes it is a matter of getting things out in the open and looking for solutions or compromises that are acceptable to both.

Lack of self-esteem is especially common in recovering couples because one has used a chemical to attain a sense of identity and the other has developed a sense of identity around taking care of the problem. Intimacy is threatening to those who are unsure of themselves. Lack of self-esteem often leads to a demand for excessive protection or approval, needing someone else to tell you that you are okay. Or it sometimes leads to undermining someone else to raise one's own self-esteem.

One characteristic of a lack of self-esteem is a hungering for affirmation from others. Some people dream of finding this in romantic love. But the problems are inside, and no outside source can ever satisfy this hunger except momentarily. The hunger is for self-esteem and it can't be supplied by romance.

By now you are probably aware that chemical dependency is a disease. But perhaps we need to remind you. Sometimes we forget that we really are dealing with an illness and we expect too much too soon. A recovering couple needs patience. Recovery will take some tender, loving care and time. Recovery of intimacy is a process. Too often couples who have been overwhelmed by the enormity of their problem, think a big, complex solution is needed. That is not the case. There are simple skills to be learned, simple steps to be taken one at a time. Here are some steps you can take.

Believe that you can return to a complete and a full sex life. It may take awhile but it is worth it. If you continue to have problems after a reasonable period of time, see a good sex therapist. You may need some help in learning to communicate about sexual needs.

The pleasure that mutually fulfilling sex potentially offers is worth some effort to recover or develop.

Practice love. Change your feelings by what you choose to *do.* Remember, love is a choice.

Learn communication skills, both verbal and nonverbal. Practice with each other.

Ask yourself what you can do to improve the relationship independently of what your partner does. Most intense negative feelings in a relationship are signs of feeling helpless. You can always do *something* to change your situation. Start by changing one little thing.

Work on friendship together. Share activities. Share time daily, not to discuss the troubles of your relationship, but just to enjoy being together.

Learn about your own sobriety-based symptoms and the recovery needs of your partner. Learn how you can support his or her recovery while working on your own.

Do what you can to improve your own sense of worth while supporting the self-esteem of your partner.

Points to Remember

1. Everyone has a need for intimacy.
2. Recovering couples especially have a need for intimacy to heal the damage done by addiction.
3. Sobriety-based symptoms of chemical dependency—as well as symptoms experienced by the recovering partner—interfere with the ability to be intimate.
4. Intimacy is built on friendship, touching, and closeness.
5. Sexual problems in sobriety—whether physical or emotional— are usually temporary.
6. With effort it is possible to develop and enrich a healthy intimate relationship in recovery.

CHAPTER 29

Maintaining a Spiritual Program

Most recovering people agree that maintaining sobriety means maintaining a spiritual program. It is not enough to allow a higher power to help you *get* sober. Sobriety is improved by an ongoing relationship with a higher power. People in AA and NA call this "working a spiritual program."

People with chemical dependency repeatedly tell us that recovery is "spiritual." And they tell us there is a power that is available to them that seems to bring out their own strengths and resources, yet empowers them with new strength and awareness. This higher power gives their lives new meaning and new strength for recovery.

A spiritual program is a road map in the search for meaning. When you work a spiritual program, you consciously, actively attempt to get outside yourself, to transcend yourself, and to become a part of something bigger, greater, and more powerful than you alone.

Spirituality is a personal matter. It is not our purpose here to define a higher power or God. Rather, we are going to talk to you about those things that large numbers of recovering people have

A POWER THAT WE CAN CALL ON AND
USE EVEN WHEN ALL OUR OTHER POWERS
FAIL...................

found to be helpful in the process of their own spiritual growth and recovery. We are going to use the term "spirituality" to mean an active relationship with a power greater than yourself that gives life meaning and purpose.

Even though spirituality is individually defined it is interesting to look at the dictionary definition. As defined by Webster's, the word "spiritual" is derived from *spiritus* which means "of breathing," or "of wind" and means "an animating or vital principle held to give life...." This refers first to the major ingredient of life itself, namely breath or air, and to the force we feel throughout our being that seems to be central to life itself. We cannot see air, but we know that without it we die. The spirit part of a person allows for the air of life in the form of purpose and meaning to be breathed into all areas of life.

A recovering person is more in need of this breath of vitality—spirituality—than the average person. In the natural course of chemical dependency, certain defects fill the inner space reserved for that vital breath we are calling spirituality. These defects include anger, fear, resentment, and self-pity. The long history of relapse, the continuing sequence of struggle and failure, lead to personal demoralization. These people have often lost faith, hope, and confidence in themselves and their ability to improve. The only way out is to look outside themselves for strength and hope. Allowing a higher power to enter your life allows the work to be done that is necessary to remove these defects and have this higher power reclaim its rightful place in your life.

Spirituality is a vehicle by which recovering people can develop new confidence in their own abilities and develop a new sense of hope. Through a spiritual program, they can reach with hope and a positive attitude toward the future.

To have a spiritual program you must first accept the possibility that there is a power greater than yourself. You must recognize that you are not the beginning and ending of the universe. As James Royce says in *Alcohol Problems and Alcoholism*,

It is hard to imagine anyone so egotistical as not to recognize there is a power greater than himself. Belief in a higher power takes you out of the center of your universe and offers peace of mind and serenity through an awareness that there is a power that is not restricted by your weaknesses and limitations.[1]

Whether or not you wish to call your higher power "God" is your choice. You may prefer to use a term such as Universal Love, Divine Love, Spirit, Creative Power, or simply Higher Power. Whatever term you choose, surrendering to this power begins to fill the empty space that has resulted from addiction. It is not easy to surrender. Many people put surrender in the same context as weak or helpless, and oftentimes this idea of surrender keeps a person farther from it. But ask yourself the question: *Has what I have done in the past helped fill this void? What am I willing to do to fill it?*

Spirituality Is Not Religion

Spirituality and religion are not the same thing. Religion is a set of beliefs about the spiritual with practices based on those beliefs. Religion is simply a vehicle some people use to connect to the spiritual. Religion and a belief system can be part of one's spiritual program, but spirituality is greater than religion. Because of the guilt connected with addiction and because some people associate religion with condemning and judging, religious affiliation may not be sought, especially in early recovery. Some people, however, do find support in religious groups.

Spirituality is a process of growth similar to sobriety. It is defined through the process itself and within the experience of growth. This experience is different for every person because everyone's journey is different. To begin the spiritual journey you need only acknowledge the possibility that a higher power exists.

Conscious Contact with God

The next step is to consider the possibility that you can communicate with that power. Step 11 of AA says, "Sought through prayer and meditation to improve our conscious contact with God as we understood him, praying only for knowledge of his will for us and for the power to carry that out." You do not have to have any one image of God to increase your conscious contact. You do have to be open to the possibility of a higher power and be willing to experiment with communicating with that power. It is important to structure your life to allow time to be alone each day to interact with your image of a higher power.

This is spiritual discipline. "Discipline" is an uncomfortable word for many recovering people. They have lived lives of immediate gratification; discipline is the reverse of that. The purpose of spirituality is freedom from the slavery of self-indulgence. Becoming a person with spiritual depth takes some effort and lifestyle reorganization, but the rewards are great.

Prayer and meditation increase conscious contact with God, allowing that power to become a part of every aspect of life. Every aspect of your life that is touched by your higher power becomes spiritual. Prayer and meditation allow you to practice the presence of a higher power. It allows you to focus your mind on a higher power and on the meaning and purpose that this relationship gives you. In the book, *Celebration of Discipline*, Richard J. Foster says, "If we hope to move beyond the superficialities of our culture...we must be willing to go down into the recreating silences, into the inner world of contemplation."[2]

You cannot learn to meditate by reading a book. You learn by doing it. Prepare for specific times of meditation. Find a quiet place, free from interruption. Retreat to a place of solitude where you can relax with your higher power. Feel the serenity of that presence.

Meditation and prayer mean being quiet enough to get in touch with that power that gives new meaning to life. Being still is a skill that can be learned. Here are some meditation exercises you can easily use:

Close your eyes. Relax in a comfortable position. Clear your mind of everything but your breathing. Be aware of breathing in and breathing out. As you breathe in say, "I am." As you breathe out say, "with God." Breathe in, "I am." Breathe out, "with God." I am—with God. I am—with God.

For many people music is an aid to meditation. Select music that is relaxing for you. Sit back, close your eyes. Clear your mind of everything but the music. Allow yourself to experience the music as love. Allow it to embrace you with tranquility and serenity. Repeat to yourself, "I see and feel myself filled with universal love. I see and feel myself filled with universal peace. I see and feel myself filled with universal love and peace."

As you find other ways to pray and meditate, that increase your contact with your higher power, you will enrich your life and find your own understanding of spirituality. By experiencing this on-going transforming relationship, you will become more flexible and open to the ways in which you can experience your higher power.

Points to Remember

1. Most recovering people agree that maintaining sobriety means maintaining a spiritual program.
2. We use the term "spirituality" to mean an active relationship with a power greater than yourself that gives life purpose and meaning.
3. Spirituality and religion are not the same thing, although religion may be part of a person's spiritual program.
4. Prayer and meditation are means to improve your conscious contact with God as you understand him.

Notes

1. James Royce, *Alcohol Problems and Alcoholism* (New York: The Free Press, A Division of Macmillan, 1981) 306.
2. Richard Foster, *Celebration of Discipline* (San Francisco: Harper & Row, 1978), 13.

CHAPTER 30

Relapse Prevention

Many people do not make it after the first attempt at sobriety. It seems that they need one last experience at failure to convince themselves beyond a doubt that they are chemically dependent and cannot safely use. This is unfortunate because for many this last experience is terminal.

Even if the last experience is not fatal, it often carries with it irreversible consequences such as loss of job, loss of family, loss of friends. Remember, whenever people with chemical dependency use, they place themselves and those around them in serious danger because they can never be sure of what will happen.

We cannot overemphasize the seriousness of relapse nor the importance of realistically facing the possibility that it will occur. If you do not believe you can relapse, you probably will. Planning for relapse is the best way to prevent it. Failing to acknowledge the possibility increases the risk. While relapse is a real possibility, it is not necessary. With proper planning it can be avoided. You can learn to interrupt the relapse process before it is too late.

A wise person learns from the past. The past is often the best teacher. It teaches us what works and what doesn't work. The person with chemical dependency is wise to learn from past

RECOVERY IS LIKE GOING UP A DOWN
ESCALATOR. THERE IS NO SUCH THING AS
STANDING STILL; AS SOON AS YOU STOP
GOING UP YOU BEGIN MOVING BACKWARDS.

relapses. By allowing the past to teach you how to stay sober, you can avoid relapsing in the future.

Predictable and progressive warning signs occur in most people with chemical dependency before they begin using. Relapse is not the event of using. It is the process that leads to using. You don't have to do anything to begin the process. If you fail to do what is necessary to recover, warning signs will develop.

The warning signs will begin with minor changes in thinking and behavior. People with chemical dependency convince themselves that their disease is no longer a priority issue in life—other issues are more important. They make the decision to abandon new ways of living and to experiment with old behaviors. This experimentation reactivates old problem areas, including the extensive use of denial systems. A change in situation creates discomfort and makes a return to chemical use not only possible but desirable.

Many decisions reached in this relapse process force the person with chemical dependency to choose between positive alternatives and continued avoidance and denial. It is essential to remember that the person has many opportunities to interrupt this pattern. The more readily available the sources of help, the more likely the decision to reactivate treatment. For the recovering person, treatment must be as readily available as mind-altering chemicals if long-term sobriety is to be maintained.

Relapse does not begin with the first drink, pill, or joint. Relapse begins with feelings, thoughts, and behavior that reactivate denial, isolation, elevated stress, and impaired judgment. This pattern was identified in 1973 by Terence T. Gorski through the completion of clinical interviews with 118 alcoholic patients who met the following criteria: (1) They had completed a twenty-one- or twenty-eight-day inpatient treatment program; (2) they had been discharged with the conscious intention to remain permanently sober; and (3) their drinking and behavior eventually became out of control despite initial commitments to remain sober. The results of this clinical

271

THE RELAPSE SYNDROME

Internal Dysfunction

- *Thought Impairment*
- *Emotional Impairment*
- *Memory Problems*
- *High Stress*
- *Sleep Problems*
- *Coordination Problems*

External Dysfunction

- *Denial Returns*
- *Avoidance and Defensiveness*
- *Crisis Building*
- *Immobilization*
- *Confusion and Overreaction*

Loss of Control

- *Depression*
- *Loss of Behavioral Control*
- *Recognition of Loss of Control*
- *Option Reduction*
- *Relapse Episode*

research were compiled in the form of a relapse chart depicting the symptoms of a relapse.[1]

Relapse Warning Signs[2]

The following is a brief list of the common Phases and Warning Signs of Relapse. For a complete description, see *Staying Sober, The Phases and Warning Signs of Relapse*, or *The Staying Sober Workbook* (all available from Herald House/Independence Press).

Phase I: Internal Change

1-1. Increased Stress

1-2. Change in Thinking

1-3. Change in Feeling

1-4. Change in Behavior

Phase II: Denial

2-1. Worrying about Myself

2-2. Denial that I'm Worried

Phase III: Avoidance and Defensiveness

3-1. Believing I'll Never Use Alcohol or Drugs

3-2. Worrying about Others Instead of Self

3-3. Defensiveness

3-4. Compulsive Behavior

3-5. Impulsive Behavior

3-6. Tendencies toward Loneliness

Phase IV: Crisis Building

4-1. Tunnel Vision

4-2. Minor Depression

4-3. Loss of Constructive Planning

4-4. Plans Begin to Fail

Phase V: Immobilization

5-1. Daydreaming and Wishful Thinking

5-2. Feelings that Nothing Can Be Solved

5-3. Immature Wish to Be Happy

Phase VI: Confusion and Overreaction

6-1. Difficulty in Thinking Clearly

6-2. Difficulty in Managing Feelings and Emotions

6-3. Difficulty in Remembering Things

6-4. Periods of Confusion

6-5. Difficulty in Managing Stress

6-6. Irritation with Friends

6-7. Easily Angered

Phase VII: Depression

7-1. Irregular Eating Habits

7-2. Lack of Desire to Take Action

7-3. Difficulty Sleeping Restfully

7-4. Loss of Daily Structure

7-5. Periods of Deep Depression

Phase VIII: Behavioral Loss of Control

8-1. Irregular Attendance at AA and Treatment Meetings

8-2. An "I Don't Care" Attitude

8-3. Open Rejection of Help

8-4. Dissatisfaction with Life

8-5. Feelings of Powerlessness and Helplessness

Phase IX: Recognition of Loss of Control

9-1. Difficulty with Physical Coordination and Accidents

9-2. Self-Pity

9-3. Thoughts of Social Use

9-4. Conscious Lying

9-5. Complete Loss of Self-Confidence

Phase X: Option Reduction

10-1. Unreasonable Resentment

10-2. Discontinues All Treatment and AA

10-3. Overwhelming Loneliness, Frustration, Anger, and Tension

10-4. Loss of Behavioral Control

Phase XI: Alcohol and Drug Use

11-1. Attempting Controlled Use

11-2. Disappointment, Shame, and Guilt

11-3. Loss of Control

11-4. Life and Health Problems

Relapse Prevention Planning

Proper action on the part of the chemically dependent person and key persons in his or her life can prevent or interrupt relapse before the consequences become tragic. Planning for the possibility of relapse minimizes its destructive potential. People with chemical dependency can interrupt the relapse process at any time before chemical use is out of control if they are prepared to recognize and understand what is happening.

The person with chemical dependency is ultimately responsible for all behavior and decisions that accompany relapse. This person pays most heavily. Many people relapse because they don't understand the process and don't know what types of behavior changes are necessary to prevent it. And people close to them don't know how to help.

If you had heart disease, your family would know the warning signs and what to do in case of a heart attack. The same would be true if you were diabetic or epileptic. Any condition with high relapse potential should be treated with respect. This is true for chemical dependency.

Appropriate relapse prevention plans can give you and the concerned people in your life a sense of security. All involved can know that you are doing everything necessary to prevent relapse. You can develop a plan and a checklist of warning signs. As long as you follow that plan and watch for warning signs, you can be confident that recovery is following a successful course.

A relapse prevention plan should include the important people in your life. They should be informed of the potential for relapse and their responsibility and appropriate action if you demonstrate signs of relapse. The steps of relapse prevention planning are:

1. Stabilization: The first step in preventing relapse is stabilizing your sobriety. Until you are thinking clearly and your judgment and behavior are under control you cannot focus on the prevention of relapse.

2. Assessment: Do you believe that you are really chemically dependent and that you need to change your lifestyle? If you are not sure, you need to work on these issues before you are ready to develop a relapse prevention plan. You have to believe that you have a disease that is subject to relapse before you can do what is necessary to prevent that relapse.

If you have relapsed previously, then you need to cooperate with your therapist to assess that relapse and other relapse episodes to determine what contributed to the relapse process and what could have prevented it.

3. Education about the Relapse Process: You need to learn about recovery and relapse. You need to understand the sobriety-based symptoms and what it takes to manage those symptoms. You should review the thirty-seven warning signs of relapse and learn to describe examples of the general process and specific symptoms.

4. Warning Sign Identification: Develop a list of warning signs or indications that you may be in risk of using chemicals. The warning list should be developed from past experiences with relapse warning signs. Try to identify at least ten specific and clear indicators that you are moving away from productive and responsible sobriety and beginning to set yourself up for relapse.

5. Interruption of the Relapse Process: It is now important to establish new responses to the identified warning signs of relapse. Determine what you are going to do about each symptom when you recognize that it is occurring in your life.

6. Review of Recovery Program: Recovery and relapse are opposite sides of the same coin. If you are not in the process of recovering, you are in the process of relapsing. A good recovery program is necessary to prevent relapse. Has your previous recovery program been working for you? How can it be improved? A good recovery program should be based on what has worked for you and what has not worked for you in the past.

7. Inventory Training: Any successful recovery program involves daily inventory. AA Step 10 says, "Continued to take personal inventory and when we were wrong promptly admitted it." People with chemical dependency can learn to challenge themselves in their day-to-day living patterns. "Am I living up to my own standards and values? Are those standards and values realistic? Am I acknowledging my chemical dependency and managing its symptoms? Am I attending to my overall health needs?" For a relapse prevention plan you should design a special inventory system that monitors the warning signs of potential relapse. Develop a way to incorporate this inventory system into the fabric of day-to-day living. The key issue is this: You now know your personal warning signs. How are you going to determine if any of these symptoms are going on in your life?

8. Involvement of Significant Others: Make a list of all the people with whom you have regular contact. Select from that list those people you think would be important in helping you stay sober. Determine how each person has interacted with you in the past when you have shown symptoms of relapse. Has it been helpful or harmful to your sobriety? What could they have done that would have been more helpful to you? Now determine what you would like each of these people to do the next time symptoms of relapse are recognized. Bring these people together for a meeting. Explain to them your list of personal warning signs and form a contract with each person—what they will do when relapse symptoms are recognized and what they will do if you begin using chemicals.

9. Follow-up and Reinforcement: Recovery from chemical dependency is a way of life. Because relapse prevention planning is part of recovery, it too must become a way of life. For the recovering person it is especially true that there is freedom in structure. It is only in the habit and structure of a daily sobriety program that the person with chemical dependency can find freedom from addiction.

Remember that relapse begins long before the first using episode. There are warning signs and symptoms that pave the way.

These symptoms can act as early warning signals to people with chemical dependency and their families. By understanding the process, unnecessary pain can be avoided. Proper action by people with chemical dependency and the key people in their lives can prevent relapse or interrupt the relapse before the consequences become tragic.

Points to Remember

1. Many people do not make it after the first attempt at sobriety.
2. The relapse process begins long before the first use of mind-altering chemicals.
3. There are warning signs of relapse.
4. Proper action by you and the key people in your life can prevent or interrupt relapse before the consequences become tragic.
5. A relapse prevention plan is an important part of recovery.

Notes

1. Terence T. Gorski and Merlene Miller, *Staying Sober* (Independence, Missouri: Herald House/Independence Press, 1986), 156.
2. Terence T. Gorski and Merlene Miller, *The Phases and Warning Signs of Relapse*, Pamphlet (Independence, Missouri: Herald House/Independence Press, 1984).

CHAPTER 31

Balance in All Our Affairs

Twenty-five hundred years ago Plato said, "The part can never be well unless the whole is well." We have talked about physical recovery, psychological recovery, and social recovery. But none of the parts can be well unless the whole is well. The whole includes more than all these parts. There is something more that is part of a whole person. It is something called spirit. But it is more than just another part. It includes the body, mind, feelings, behavior, and relationships; and it joins them all into a whole. The parts cannot be well until the whole is well.

AA Step 12 says, "Having had a spiritual awakening as a result of these steps, we tried to carry this message...and to practice these principles in all our affairs."[1] Spirituality is a way of life that results from practicing the principles of sobriety and recovery "in all our affairs."

A Spiritual Awakening

A spiritual awakening occurs when the person with chemical dependency goes beyond the struggle of staying sober, and having found a meaning beyond himself, discovers the joys of *living* sober. This joy comes as a result of developing a lifestyle that frees the person from anxieties and stresses to experience the wholesome

IN HARMONY
WITH GOD, FAMILY, AND FRIENDS.

pleasures of all aspects of life. Personal growth with regard to attitudes, feelings, actions, family, job, hobbies, brings enriching pleasures that take you beyond just "not using." This means actively participating in life rather than being passively involved while hoping life will offer something good along the way. This is "practicing these principles in all our affairs."

Spirituality is not something separate from daily life. Spirituality encompasses all of life and allows you to bring new meaning to all your affairs. A spiritual awakening occurs as this new understanding becomes a part of your whole life.

The magic word is *balance*. Balanced living results from making effective choices while being open to new information and new skills for living. One cannot look to any one part of life for all the answers for spiritual growth. Because we are composed of many parts—bio-psycho-social—we derive strength and sustenance from many sources, all relative to our growing spiritual lives.

Balanced Living

Balanced living means that there is bio-psycho-social harmony in your life. It means you are healthy physically and psychologically and that you have healthy relationships. Balanced living means you are no longer focused on only one aspect of your life. It means you are living responsibly, giving yourself time for your job, your family, and your friends, as well as time for your own growth and recovery. It means allowing a higher power to work in your life. It means wholesome living.

Creating balance in all your affairs does not mean that you will not have good days and bad days. It does not mean you will not do things you will regret. That is part of growth. What it does mean is that you can cope with some bad times and bounce back from your mistakes, that you can deal responsibly with problems—sober. It means you are striving for progress and not becoming disillusioned by your inability to be perfect. It means you can accept your humanness and rejoice in your growth.

Living in balance means eliminating addictions and addictive behaviors—those activities that cause you to go to extremes and focus on the addiction at the expense of other important parts of your life. To achieve life balance, you may have to take action that is the reverse of addictive activity. You may need to do things that cause you some discomfort now to bring long-term pleasure. If you have neglected exercise, it may be necessary for you to experience some initial discomfort to gain the long-term benefits that come from exercise. With balanced living, immediate gratification as a lifestyle is given up to attain fulfilling and meaningful living. Practicing these principles in all areas of life means learning to do things today that produce positive consequences for tomorrow.

The quality of recovery is reflected in how day-to-day affairs are managed. Quality recovery requires proper health care so that the body functions well. Nutrition, rest, and exercise all receive the proper focus in your life to provide energy, manage stress, allow freedom from illness and pain, combat fatigue, and rebuild a damaged body.

Freedom from physical distress allows psychological growth. When you feel good, it is easier to think about your attitudes and values and to work on eliminating denial, guilt, and anger. Balanced living requires doing things to develop self-confidence and self-esteem and learning to feel good about yourself.

Having a balanced life means functioning as nearly as possible at your optimum stress level, maintaining enough stress to keep you functioning in a healthy way and not overloading yourself with stress so it becomes counterproductive. It means creating a healthy balance between work and play, and between fulfilling your responsibilities to other people and yourself.

Bringing wholeness into all your affairs means bringing the spirit of love into all your relationships. A balanced life requires a strong social network to nurture you and encourage a healthy, recovery-oriented lifestyle. A healthy social network provides a sense of belonging. It includes relationships in which you feel you are a valuable part. This network includes immediate family members, friends, relatives, group members, co-workers, counselors, employers, self-help group members, and sponsors.

With addictive living, life is usually self-focused. You have been concentrating on filling your own need for mind-altering chemicals and have been fighting the consequences of your relationship with drugs. Now *other* involvement is necessary—involvement with other people. With the involvement comes a renewed faith in the goodness of people. A higher power works through people, especially people engaged in causes like AA. You will not see new hope and different perspectives until you become involved in the lives of others.

It is helpful to develop friendships based in shared spirituality. These friendships need not all be through AA or other self-help groups. You may find it helpful to become involved in a spiritual program that is part of a religion or organized group. This can be an important adjunct to recovery. Many people feel it is a central component to finding the strength to continue in their recovery. The Big Book of AA says: "Though the family has no religious connections, they may wish to make contact with or take membership in a religious body....Being possessed of a spiritual experience, the alcoholic will find he has much in common with these people....he will make new friends and is sure to find new avenues of usefulness and pleasure."[2]

Carrying the Message

Through the healing that has occurred from practicing the principles of AA/NA and by learning to live a spiritual and balanced life, you will have the opportunity to pass the message on to others. As a spiritual awakening occurs, you realize that "to live is to give" and sense the urgency to carry the message. To keep moving ahead in recovery it is necessary to keep centered and balanced by "giving it away."

Once committed to recovery it seems we are always moving into new ways of reaching out to others. In fact, it has been demonstrated many times with many recovering people that we do not gain full spiritual lives without helping others in their recovery. When you share your message with someone else, the strength is multiplied through an implied understanding that the person you share with may someday do the same. For spiritual strength and growth, people must "give themselves away," sharing that special perspective they have of addiction and recovery and the hope of a newfound relationship with a power greater than themselves.

Points to Remember

1. These words from Plato have special meaning for the person with chemical dependency: "The part can never be well unless the whole is well."
2. Spirituality is a way of life that results from practicing the principles of sobriety in all your affairs.
3. A spiritual awakening occurs when the person with chemical dependency goes beyond the struggle of staying sober and discovers the joys of living sober.
4. Recovery is not complete nor continuous without carrying the message to others.

Notes

1. *Twelve Steps and Twelve Traditions* (New York: Alcoholics Anonymous World Services, 1952), 108.
2. *Alcoholics Anonymous* (New York: Alcoholics Anonymous World Services), 131-132.

APPENDIX A
The Twelve Steps of Alcoholics Anonymous*

Step 1: We admitted we were powerless over alcohol, that our lives had become unmanageable.

Step 2: We came to believe that a power greater than ourselves could restore us to sanity.

Step 3: Made a decision to turn our will and our lives over to the care of God as we understood him.

Step 4: Made a searching and fearless moral inventory of ourselves.

Step 5: Admitted to God, to ourselves, and to another human being the exact nature of our wrongs.

Step 6: Were entirely ready to have God remove all these defects of character.

Step 7: Humbly asked him to remove our shortcomings.

Step 8: Made a list of all persons we had harmed and became willing to make amends to them all.

Step 9: Made direct amends to such people wherever possible except when to do so would injure them or others.

Step 10: Continued to take personal inventory and when we were wrong promptly admitted it.

Step 11: Sought through prayer and meditation to improve our conscious contact with God as we understood him, praying only for knowledge of his will for us and for the power to carry that out.

Step 12: Having had a spiritual awakening as a result of these steps, we tried to carry this message to alcoholics and to practice these principles in all our affairs.

---

* *Twelve Steps and Twelve Traditions* (New York: Alcoholics Anonymous World Services, 1952).

APPENDIX B
The Twelve Traditions of Alcoholics Anonymous*

1. Our common welfare should come first: personal recovery depends upon AA unity.

2. For our group purpose there is but one ultimate authority—a loving God as he may express himself in our group conscience. Our leaders are but trusted servants; they do not govern.

3. The only requirement for AA membership is a sincere desire to stop drinking.

4. Each group should be autonomous, except in matters affecting other groups or AA as a whole.

5. Each group has but one primary purpose—to carry its message to the alcoholic who still suffers.

6. An AA group ought never endorse, finance, or lend the AA name to any related facility or outside enterprise, lest problems of money, property, and prestige divert us from our primary purpose.

7. Every AA group ought to be fully self-supporting, declining outside contributions.

8. Alcoholics Anonymous should remain forever nonprofessional, but our service centers may employ special workers.

9. AA, as such, ought never to be organized; but we may create service boards or committees directly responsible to those they serve.

10. Alcoholics Anonymous has no opinion on outside issues, hence the AA name ought never to be drawn into public controversy.

11. Our public relations policy is based in attraction rather than promotion; we need always maintain personal anonymity at the level of press, radio, and films.

12. Anonymity is the spiritual foundation of all our Traditions, ever reminding us to place principles before personalities.

* *Twelve Steps and Twelve Traditions* (New York: Alcoholics Anonymous World Services, 1952).

APPENDIX C
Alcohol Response Patterns

Terence T. Gorski, one of the authors of this book, through interviews with hundreds of alcoholics and nonalcoholics and by observing their reactions when they drink, has developed a theory that describes four typical ways that people respond to the ingestion of alcohol. The first type of reaction, pattern one, indicates a low risk of alcoholism. Pattern two indicates high risk of alcoholism. Pattern three indicates the presence of alcoholism. And the fourth pattern indicates the use of alcohol to escape problems or painful life circumstances.

Pattern One

People who are in low risk of becoming alcoholic, the pattern one drinkers, have a limited tolerance for alcohol. When they drink there is a feeling of relaxation, a pure sedative effect. Each drink increases the sedation of the central nervous system, and there is a gradual and predictable progression toward intoxication. These people know how much they can drink to experience a certain reaction, and because they know, they can control it. Because they know ahead what is going to happen to them when they drink, they believe everyone does and usually cannot understand why some people cannot control their drinking or drinking behavior.

Alcohol exaggerates the mood these people are in when they drink. If they are happy, they become happier. If they are sad, they become sadder, or if they are angry, they become angrier. Hangovers will occur in proportion to the amount of alcohol consumed; the more they drink, the worse the hangover will be. Drinking several days in a row usually causes them to become so ill that they cannot continue daily drinking.

Tolerance for alcohol generally does not increase over a period of time. Practice does not make perfect. These people cannot consume the amounts of alcohol needed to become addicted, and therefore, are in low risk of developing alcoholism.

Pattern Two

Pattern two drinkers are capable of drinking large quantities of alcohol frequently enough to create addiction, but they do not show definite symptoms of alcoholism. They have the potential of developing alcoholism and may actually be early stage alcoholics.

Like people who are in low risk, they have a sedative reaction when they begin to drink; there is a feeling of relaxation. As they continue to drink, however, they reach a "click point" and enter a period of control-level or tolerance-level drinking. They do not experience the usual indications of intoxication. They can consume large amounts of alcohol and still function well and feel good.

While these people are in the period of control-level drinking, negative moods are counteracted. If they are angry before they start drinking, the anger disappears. If they are depressed, they feel happier. If they are under stress, they can use alcohol to reduce the stress. They learn to use alcohol to cope with stressful situations and do not learn to handle problems in other ways. There is not a physical need to drink, but as they use alcohol more and more frequently to feel good and to relieve stress, a strong psychological dependence may develop. Severe physical damage can occur while people are in the period of control-level drinking because they are unable to feel the damage being done by alcohol. State dependent learning occurs while in the period of control-level drinking.

Pattern two drinkers experience rapid onset intoxication. In pattern one there are progressive warning signs of intoxication. This is not the case in pattern two drinkers. They become intoxicated very rapidly and without warning. At times they may suddenly pass out, or they may become very agitated or violent. Because these episodes of loss of control happen infrequently, pattern two drinkers tend to ignore or minimize them. Because of high tolerance, they can mask and ignore physical damage and developing addiction, and they generally don't notice early warning signs of alcoholism.

Pattern Three

Pattern three drinkers, people with alcoholism, react to the ingestion of alcohol much like pattern two drinkers except that there is a feeling of agitation that develops after the first drinks and results in an urgency to drink more. Alcoholics are powerless over this compulsion. They usually "gulp" the first few drinks to quickly reach the "click point" and relieve the feeling of agitation. When they reach control level they feel better, behave better, and do not appear intoxicated in spite of high blood alcohol levels. They take pride in the ability to "hold their liquor." As the tolerance for alcohol increases, the body changes and adapts to higher levels of alcohol and dependence develops.

There is no longer just a tolerance for alcohol but a need. These people no longer drink because they want to but because they need to. People with alcoholism are not aware of the developing need for alcohol. They are usually in control, feel good while drinking, function better than when sober. But alcoholism is a progressive disease. It takes more and more alcohol to reach the click point and fewer and fewer drinks before becoming intoxicated. The period of control decreases and they get drunk more and more frequently. People with alcoholism are powerless to control the response of their bodies to alcohol and over the ability to control drinking behavior.

Pattern Four

At times people who may be any one of the first three patterns drink in a way that can be described as oblivion drinking. We will call this pattern four because oblivion drinking makes it difficult to determine whether these people are pattern one, two, or three. These people drink with the intent to get drunk. They use alcohol to escape physical or emotional pain. They have psychological,

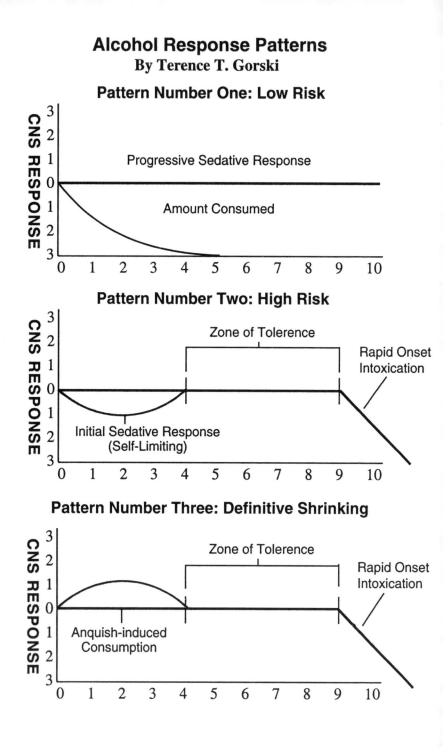

behavioral, and social problems because of drinking whether or not they are physically dependent on alcohol. Drinking affects their thinking, feeling, behavior, or social life, even if there are no physical symptoms. These people are dependent on alcohol to relieve pain. Pattern four drinkers may or may not be physically addicted to alcohol, but there is no doubt that they have developed a dangerous dependence. They need help to recover, and they must remove alcohol from their lives to resolve the problems it creates. Any type of dependence on alcohol requires treatment and abstinence for recovery.

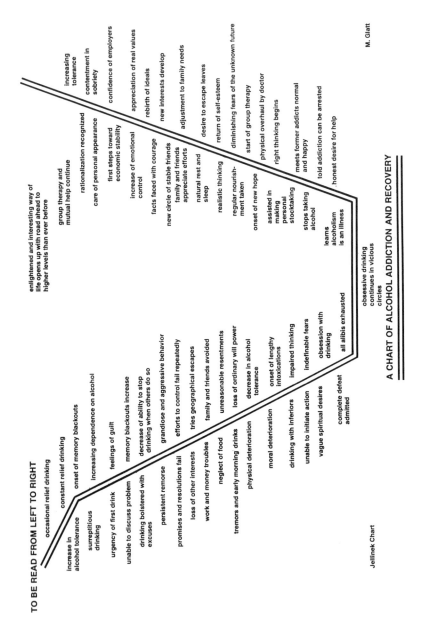

TO BE READ FROM LEFT TO RIGHT

Jellinek Chart

A CHART OF ALCOHOL ADDICTION AND RECOVERY

M. Glatt

292

APPENDIX D
Symptoms of Alcoholism
Based on the Jellinek Chart

A system of determining whether or not a person may be alcoholic is based on the Jellinek Chart developed by M. Glatt and based on the symptoms described by E. M. Jellinek in *The Disease Concept of Alcoholism*.[1] A description of the symptoms follows. If you are wondering whether you have the disease of alcoholism, ask yourself if you have ever experienced these symptoms.

1. Occasional Relief Drinking
Alcohol is used to get relief from some problem. It may be relief from a physical situation; or it may be from psychological discomfort or from a behavioral habit or social situation that is bringing pain.

Have you experienced this symptom?

_____ Never _____ Sometimes _____ Often

2. Constant Relief Drinking
As alcohol works to bring constant and continual relief, the habit of using alcohol as a problem-solving mechanism develops.

Have you experienced this symptom?

_____ Never _____ Sometimes _____ Often

3. Increase in Alcohol Tolerance
As alcohol is used more and more for relief, there is an increase in tolerance for alcohol, so it takes progressively more and more to get the same level of relief. While initially three drinks might give a comfortable feeling, eventually it will take five, then seven, and then nine.

Have you experienced this symptom?

_____ Never _____ Sometimes _____ Often

4. Onset of Memory Blackouts

Alcoholics may begin having blackouts at this point. A blackout is a period of time the alcoholic cannot remember, a complete loss of memory.

Have you experienced this symptom?

_____ Never _____ Sometimes _____ Often

5. Surreptitious Drinking

The alcoholic begins hiding alcohol consumption, camouflaging heavy drinking to avoid confrontation with the consequences.

Have you experienced this symptom?

_____ Never _____ Sometimes _____ Often

6. Increasing Dependence on Alcohol

There is an increasing physical dependence on alcohol. More and more life areas become associated with alcohol. Social life plus alcohol equals pleasure. All kinds of situations become related to alcohol consumption.

Have you experienced this symptom?

_____ Never _____ Sometimes _____ Often

7. Urgency of First Drink

It becomes necessary to gulp the first few drinks to get the blood alcohol level high enough to bring relief.

Have you experienced this symptom?

_____ Never _____ Sometimes _____ Often

8. Feeling of Guilt

The alcoholic begins recognizing that there is something wrong but not understanding what is happening, begins to feel guilty about it. Drinking-related behavior violates personal values.

Have you experienced this symptom?

_____ Never _____ Sometimes _____ Often

9. Unable to Discuss Problem

The alcoholic is becoming more uncomfortable with the inability to control drinking but, because of the stigma associated with the problem, feels that no one will understand. Increasing guilt increases the inability to discuss the problem.

Have you experienced this symptom?

_____ Never _____ Sometimes _____ Often

10. Memory Blackouts Increase

At this point blackouts may be a sign of neurological damage. More and more problems are caused because of memory blackouts. Alcoholics may wake to find evidence of occurrences they do not remember. It gets very frightening to find they have done things they do not know about.

Have you experienced this symptom?

_____ Never _____ Sometimes _____ Often

11. Drinking Bolstered with Excuses

The alcoholic finds reasons to continue drinking, begins creating reasons to drink, avoids the fact that drinking is a problem by finding justification.

Have you experienced this symptom?

_____ Never _____ Sometimes _____ Often

12. Decrease of Ability to Stop Drinking When Others Do

At a party the person will drink more and begin losing control more often. The inability to stop becomes more apparent to other people.

Have you experienced this symptom?

_____ Never _____ Sometimes _____ Often

13. Persistent Remorse

Behavior caused by the inability to stop produces feelings of chronic guilt, but the person does not know what to do about it.

Have you experienced this symptom?

_____ Never _____ Sometimes _____ Often

14. Grandiose and Aggressive Behavior

The persistent remorse is covered by grandiose and aggressive behavior. There is a great need and a tremendous effort to prove they are capable, that they are okay.

Have you experienced this symptom?

_____ Never _____ Sometimes _____ Often

15. Promises and Resolutions Fail

As the person loses control of life, there are more and more promises to do better, but the promises always fail.

Have you experienced this symptom?

_____ Never _____ Sometimes _____ Often

16. Efforts to Control Fail Repeatedly

There is an attempt to control by shifting brands, maintaining periods of enforced abstinence, or limiting quantity or the time when drinking takes place. All of these attempts to control fail.

Have you experienced this symptom?

_____ Never _____ Sometimes _____ Often

17. Loss of Other Interests

Drinking begins pushing everything else out of life. Drinking makes it impossible to bowl, so bowling is given up; drinking makes it impossible to dance, so the person keeps drinking and gives up dancing. The person must choose between drinking and what problems drinking is causing so will choose drinking and give up more and more interests.

Have you experienced this symptom?

_____ Never _____ Sometimes _____ Often

18. Tries Geographical Escapes

The alcoholic tries to change circumstances to try to make life better. But neither a change of job nor a change of location works.

Have you experienced this symptom?

_____ Never _____ Sometimes _____ Often

19. Work and Money Troubles

Because of the increasing inability to control behavior, problems arise with employment. It may become difficult or impossible to hold a job. Financial problems arise from unemployment or inability to handle money.

Have you experienced this symptom?

_____ Never _____ Sometimes _____ Often

20. Family and Friends Avoided

Guilt, preoccupation with drinking, loss of other interests, and feelings of failure cause the alcoholic to isolate from family and friends.

Have you experienced this symptom?

_____ Never _____ Sometimes _____ Often

21. Neglect of Food

Nutritional problems begin to develop because of the tendency to develop poor eating habits and to neglect food.

Have you experienced this symptom?

_____ Never _____ Sometimes _____ Often

22. Unreasonable Resentments

Alcoholics develop excuses for keeping others at a distance. They become overly sensitive. They believe everyone else is critical and doesn't understand.

Have you experienced this symptom?

_____ Never _____ Sometimes _____ Often

23. Tremors and Early Morning Drinks

The person needs a drink to get going in the morning, and tremors become noticeable. Alcohol intake reduces tremors and helps the person to become functional.

Have you experienced this symptom?

_____ Never _____ Sometimes _____ Often

24. Loss of Ordinary Willpower

Ability to determine direction and control of life situations decreases even in minor areas. The inability to make decisions and exercise the willpower to carry them out becomes apparent.

Have you experienced this symptom?

_____ Never _____ Sometimes _____ Often

25. Physical Deterioration

Drinking begins to take a physical toll. The person gains or loses weight, feels bad most of the time. Health problems become obvious. Obvious organ system disease develops.

Have you experienced this symptom?

_____ Never _____ Sometimes _____ Often

26. Decrease in Alcohol Tolerance

Suddenly alcohol tolerance begins to break. Small quantities of alcohol will produce drunkenness. The alcoholic can't handle alcohol as before and no longer gets relief from alcohol, yet can't quit.

Have you experienced this symptom?

_____ Never _____ Sometimes _____ Often

27. Moral Deterioration

The alcoholic can no longer maintain the values around which life has been built.

Have you experienced this symptom?

_____ Never _____ Sometimes _____ Often

28. Onset of Lengthy Intoxications

More and more frequently the alcoholic has periods of intoxication that are lengthy enough to interfere severely with maintaining an established lifestyle.

Have you experienced this symptom?

_____ Never _____ Sometimes _____ Often

29. Drinking with Inferiors

As feelings about self deteriorate, alcoholics always make sure they are in the company of someone who is worse off than they are. Then they can always say, "I'm not that bad."

Have you experienced this symptom?

_____ Never _____ Sometimes _____ Often

30. Impaired Thinking

Memory, problem-solving abilities, psychomotor skills deteriorate.

Have you experienced this symptom?

_____ Never _____ Sometimes _____ Often

31. Indefinable Fears

Impaired thinking produces free-floating anxiety. Alcoholics are afraid all the time. They don't know what they are afraid of, but they have a sense of impending doom.

Have you experienced this symptom?

_____ Never _____ Sometimes _____ Often

32. Unable to Initiate Action

The alcoholic can't get started, can only respond to the environment, is unable to take effective action.

Have you experienced this symptom?

_____ Never _____ Sometimes _____ Often

33. Obsession with Drinking

The person becomes obsessed with finding a supply, getting ready to drink, drinking, getting over the worst of it, and getting ready to drink again.

Have you experienced this symptom?

_____ Never _____ Sometimes _____ Often

34. Vague Spiritual Desires

There is frequently an awakening of spiritual feelings and an attempt to turn to God and religion.

Have you experienced this symptom?

_____ Never _____ Sometimes _____ Often

35. All Alibis Exhausted

The alcoholic can no longer rationalize that behavior is normal.

Have you experienced this symptom?

_____ Never _____ Sometimes _____ Often

Notes

1. E. M. Jellinek, *The Disease Concept of Alcoholism* (New Haven, Connecticut: Hillhouse Press, 1960).

APPENDIX E
Symptoms of Recovery
Based on the Jellinek Chart

The Jellinek Chart also describes recovery from alcoholism. This is what you can expect as you progress in recovery.

1. Honest Desire for Help

You become willing to admit that you need to get better.

2. Learns Alcoholism Is an Illness

The primary treatment for alcoholism is education. Alcoholics need to learn they are alcoholic and can recover. They must learn the relationship between alcohol and life problems.

3. Told Alcoholism Can Be Arrested

Finding out that there is a way that the illness can be arrested is what gives you hope.

4. Meets Former Alcoholics Normal and Happy

This is the beginning of the social rebuilding process. You find out it is true that there are people who recover from the illness of alcoholism.

5. Stops Taking Alcohol

Learning that alcoholism is an illness, finding out it can be arrested, and meeting others who have recovered give courage and strength to stop drinking.

6. Assists in Making Personal Stock-taking

You begin evaluating your life in terms of establishing priorities and begin taking an inventory of personal traits that can be used or modified or eliminated in the recovery process.

7. Right Thinking Begins

With the elimination of alcohol and with the help of others, you begin to make appropriate decisions about how to conduct life.

8. Physical Overhaul by Doctor

With the help of a doctor, you begin improving physically. Physical illness is identified, and appropriate treatment is initiated.

9. Onset of New Hope
As you feel better and think better, the sense of hope becomes stronger.
10. Start of Group Therapy
You get involved with a group of people discussing the issues of recovery. It may be AA or a professional group or both.
11. Regular Nourishment Taken
You start eating a balanced diet and begin feeling better physically.
12. Diminishing Fears of the Unknown Future
Fears are diminished as confidence increases because of new hope, new relationships, and improved health. Taking things "one day at a time" promotes confidence.
13. Realistic Thinking
Realistic thinking replaces wishful thinking and pipe-dreams. You begin identifying true cause/effect relationships and begin recognizing personal alibi structures.
14. Return of Self-Esteem
Because of new feelings of control over life, self-esteem is reborn. Self-esteem is directly proportional to the level of control people feel over their own lives. Paradoxically self-control comes by "turning over" unsolvable problems to a higher power and focusing on what is solvable here and now.
15. Natural Rest and Sleep
Sleep-pattern disturbances begin going away. Sleep is more natural and fears concerning sleep patterns are diminished.
16. Desire to Escape Leaves
The desire to escape decreases as reality becomes less frightening and as control, self-esteem, and self-confidence are restored.
17. Adjustment to Family Needs
The person becomes reinvolved with the family and becomes aware of and more responsible to the needs of other family members.

18. Family and Friends Appreciate Efforts

The family begins to give positive feedback as they begin to believe that this time you are going to make it.

19. New Interests Develop

Life is no longer just drinking. Until this point, life has been alcohol centered—obsession with drinking or obsession with not drinking. From this point on, ridding self of the obsession and going beyond alcohol-centered thinking becomes the issue.

20. New Circle of Stable Friends

New interests and lifestyle changes enable you to establish new relationships involving activities other than drinking.

21. Rebirth of Ideas

Original value systems are rebuilt.

22. Facts Faced with Courage

There is less need to run from reality. You can see things as they are and are capable of taking hard and serious looks at self and attitudes.

23. Increase of Emotional Control

Emotional recovery is taking place, and you become aware you can control your own responses to feeling, anxiety, and stress. Mood swings become less dramatic.

24. Appreciation of Real Values

You begin to appreciate that you can have some pride, some courage, and some dignity. You develop an awareness of people, and relationships, and a spiritual program.

25. First Steps Toward Economic Stability

You are able to initiate financial planning and to take responsibility for your own financial situation.

26. Confidence of Employer

As work performance improves, the employer sees that you have some future and places more confidence in you.

27. Care of Personal Appearance

A new sense of pride and dignity brings about a change in appearance.

28. Contentment in Sobriety

The struggle not to drink is no longer the whole focus. You are finding pleasure in nondrinking activities and having a sense of satisfaction in sobriety.

29. Rationalizations Recognized

You are able to catch yourself in denial and rationalizations before they begin to cause problems.

30. Group Therapy and Mutual Help Continue

The group-help process becomes an important part of your lifestyle. Relating to other recovering people enables you to be more accepting of yourself and more comfortable in your own situation.

31. Increasing Tolerance

You become more accepting of others, less judgmental of family, and less critical of friends. Old resentments are released and appreciation of others increases.

32. Enlightened and Interesting Ways of Life Open Up with Road Ahead to Higher Levels Than Ever Before

At this point, you enter into a new phase of recovery—a period of self-assessment followed by a reevaluation of values and birth of a new lifestyle built around new and expanding values.

APPENDIX F
Antabuse

Antabuse is a drug that makes people sick if they drink alcohol while taking it. It can help them stay sober if it is used along with a recovery program and if its use is carefully monitored. The self-regulated use of Antabuse without a recovery program and without monitoring can be harmful because it is an extension of the mistaken belief that "I can recover by myself."

When alcohol is metabolized in the liver it is changed first into acetaldehyde. The acetaldehyde is then changed into acetic acid, which leaves the liver and is changed into carbon dioxide and water. In large amounts acetaldehyde has a toxic effect on the body and causes a person to become extremely ill.

Antabuse is a drug that keeps the liver from changing acetaldehyde into acetic acid. So if you drink alcohol while taking Antabuse, acetaldehyde levels remain high and cause you to get sick. The symptoms of a high acetaldehyde level are flushing, throbbing in the neck and head, difficulty breathing, nausea, vomiting, sweating, thirst, chest pains, palpitations, headache, low blood pressure, rapid heart beat, dizziness, weakness, blurred vision, and confusion.

Antabuse is not a cure for alcoholism. It has no effect on the symptoms or causes of alcoholism. It doesn't change attitudes, thinking, behavior, or relationships. It is not a substitute for treatment, AA, or for developing a new way of life.

Antabuse builds a chemical fence between the person with alcoholism and the first drink. It forces a daily decision about sobriety. It is an excellent test of the desire to stay sober today. With Antabuse you make the decision not to drink once a day.

Antabuse buys time while healing takes place. It can help you keep from taking a drink on an impulse. It is much like a cast on a broken arm. A cast keeps you from moving your arm while healing of the bone takes place. The cast doesn't heal; it provides protection while the healing process is going on.

Antabuse provides protection while the healing process is going on. If you know that a drink is going to make you ill, you are going to think before taking it. Antabuse stays in your system seven to fourteen days. So if you take it when you are committed to sobriety, it is still there when you lose sight of that commitment. If you decide to stop taking it so you can drink again, you have a week or two to reconsider and to get back in touch with the resources that are enabling real recovery. The main job of Antabuse is to make it more difficult to drink than it is to stay sober!

The use of Antabuse is somewhat controversial. Many people with alcoholism can be successfully treated without Antabuse, and for some patients there are risks to taking it. The decision to take it or not to take it should be made carefully and in cooperation with your therapist. You must weigh the potential risks against the potential benefits.

Potential Risks:

1. Possible allergic reaction (as with any drug)

2. Possible side effects (as with any drug)

3. Seriousness of an Antabuse reaction should you drink while taking it

4. Risk of inhibiting long-term recovery if Antabuse is used longer than a year

Potential Benefits:

1. Reducing likelihood of impulse drinking

2. Forces a daily decision about sobriety

3. In case of relapse, interrupts relapse quickly and forces immediate treatment

4. Makes an intent to drink obvious to family and helping person.

There are two types of people with alcoholism who find Antabuse especially helpful. One is the person who has relapsed many times in spite of efforts to stay sober. The other is the periodic drinker, the person who stays sober for long periods and then binges. Periodic drinkers should stay on Antabuse two-and-a-half times the normal relapse cycle. For example, if they have stayed sober three months at a time, then they should stay on Antabuse eight months.

For most people, Antabuse doesn't have any effect on the body if they don't drink alcohol. It doesn't do anything but block the production of the chemical that metabolizes acetaldehyde. However, Antabuse should not be taken by people with certain conditions, especially chronic diseases like heart disease, diabetes, cirrhosis of the liver, epilepsy, nephritis. The reason for this is not that Antabuse itself has any effect on any of these diseases or symptoms of these diseases. It is because people with these diseases may not be healthy enough to survive a reaction to Antabuse should they drink. Anyone considering taking Antabuse should be thoroughly checked by a physician.

While you are taking Antabuse, it is especially important to be careful of alcohol intake from unexpected sources—certain foods, medications, mouthwashes. Always check labels, and do not use products with alcohol in them. Even aftershave with alcohol, especially if you have a cut in the skin, can cause a mild reaction. It is important, too, to be careful of what you eat. Check it out, ask questions when you go out to eat. If food contains alcohol that has not cooked for an hour or so, you shouldn't eat it. This applies even if you are not taking Antabuse because the alcohol could reactivate the urge to drink. But if you are taking Antabuse, it can make you very ill.

Don't hesitate to even check prescription medication to be sure you do not accidentally consume alcohol.

Remember that taking Antabuse is not long-term treatment. It is intended only as an aid to protect you while you are learning long-term sobriety skills.

Suggested Reading List

Alcohol and the Addictive Brain by Kenneth Blum, Ph.D. New York: The Free Press, A Division of Macmillan, Inc., 1991.

Alcoholics Anonymous. Alcoholics Anonymous World Services, Inc., 1955.

Alcohol Problems & Alcoholism: A Comprehensive Survey by James E. Royce. New York: The Free Press, A Division of Macmillan, Inc., 1989.

Another Chance by Sharon Wegscheider Cruse. Palo Alto, California: Science and Behavior Books, Inc., 1989.

The Broken Cord by Michael Dorris. Harper Perennial, A Division of Harper Collins Publishers, 1989.

Eating Right to Live Sober by Katherine Ketcham and L. Ann Mueller, M.D. Seattle, Washington: Madrona Publishers, 1983.

Family Recovery by Merlene Miller and Terence T. Gorski. Independence, Missouri: Herald House/Independence Press, 1982.

It Will Never Happen To Me by Claudia Black. Denver: M.A.C. Publishing, 1981.

Loosening the Grip by Jean Kinney and Gwen Leaton. St. Louis: Mosby-Year Book, Inc., 1991.

Maintaining Recovery: Enjoying Life Without Cocaine by Dr. Arnold M. Washton. Center City, Minnesota: Hazelden, 1990.

Narcotics Anonymous. Narcotics Anonymous World Service Office, Inc. C.A.R.E.N.A. Publishing Co., 1982.

Passages through Recovery: An Action Plan for Preventing Relapse by Terence T. Gorski. Center City, Minnesota: Hazelden, 1989.

Preventing Adolescent Relapse by Tammy Bell. Independence, Missouri: Herald House/Independence Press, 1990.

Quitting Cocaine: The First Thirty Days by Dr. Arnold M. Waston. Center City, Minnesota: Hazelden, 1990.

Staying Off Cocaine: Cravings, Other Drugs, and Slips by Dr. Arnold M. Waston. Center City, Minnesota: Hazelden, 1990.

Staying Sober: A Guide for Relapse Prevention by Terence T. Gorski and Merlene Miller. Independence, Missouri: Herald House/Independence Press, 1986.

Treating Cocaine Dependency by David E. Smith, M.D. and Donald R. Wesson, M.D. Center City, Minnesota: Hazelden, 1988.

Twelve Steps and Twelve Traditions. New York: Alcoholics Anonymous World Services, Inc., 1952.

Under the Influence by James R. Milam, Ph.D. and Katherine Ketcham. Seattle, Washington: Madrona Publishers, 1981.

Understanding the Twelve Steps by Terence T. Gorksi. New York: Prentice Hall Press, 1989.

Merlene Miller, M.A., combining her writing skills and professional knowledge, has authored numerous books on addiction and overeating and develops educational material for addiction treatment centers.

Terence T. Gorski, M.A., C.A.C., is president of The CENAPS Corporation. He is also Clinical Director of the National Relapse Prevention Certification School. He is a nationally and state certified addiction counselor. Mr. Gorski is a nationally and internationally recognized speaker and author.

David Miller, M.A., is an author and lecturer and also does private counseling specializing in food addiction, chemical dependency, and attention deficit disorder.